Slow and Sudden Violence

Slow and Sudden Violence

WHY AND WHEN UPRISINGS OCCUR

Derek Hyra

UNIVERSITY OF CALIFORNIA PRESS

University of California Press
Oakland, California

Cover Image: Jacob Lawrence (1912–2000), United States, *We have no property! We have no wives! No children! We have no city! No country!— petition of many slaves, 1773*, panel 5, 1955, from Struggle: From the History of the American People, 1954–56. Egg tempera on hardboard, 16 x 12 in. Collection of Harvey and Harvey-Ann Ross, © The Jacob and Gwendolyn Knight Lawrence Foundation, Seattle / Artists Rights Society (ARS), New York, photograph courtesy of the Peabody Essex Museum.

Library of Congress Cataloging-in-Publication Data
Names: Hyra, Derek S., author.
Title: Slow and sudden violence : why and when uprisings occur / Derek Hyra.
Description: [Oakland, California] : University of California Press, [2024] | Includes bibliographical references and index.
Identifiers: LCCN 2023049638 (print) | LCCN 2023049639 (ebook) | ISBN 9780520401464 (hardback) | ISBN 9780520401471 (paperback) | ISBN 9780520401488 (ebook)
Subjects: LCSH: Urban renewal—Social aspects—Missouri— Ferguson. | Urban renewal—Social aspects—Maryland—Baltimore. | Police shootings—Missouri—Ferguson—21st century. | Police brutality—Maryland—Baltimore—21st century. | Riots—United States—21st century.
Classification: LCC HT177.F4 H973 2024 (print) | LCC HT177.F4 (ebook) | DDC 363.3209752/6—dc23/eng/20240221
LC record available at https://lccn.loc.gov/2023049638
LC ebook record available at https://lccn.loc.gov/2023049639

32 31 30 29 28 27 26 25 24
10 9 8 7 6 5 4 3 2 1

To Allison, Avery, and Barrett

For those who dominate and oppress us benefit most when we . . . have nothing left, no "homeplace" where we can recover ourselves.

BELL HOOKS

Contents

III · Breaking the Cycle

Illustrations

Acknowledgments

This type of research cannot be successfully accomplished without a cadre of support. Numerous students, colleagues, community members, friends, and family assisted with this manuscript's completion. While the help they provided was immeasurable, I can only compensate them with words of gratitude.

I researched and wrote this manuscript over six years (2016–23) with the assistance of numerous graduate students at American University's Metropolitan Policy Center, which I direct. I thank Maya Kearney, Liz Mariapen, Kai Thompson, and James Wright II for research that laid the foundation for the Ferguson chapters. I also thank Katharine Silva for her help in scheduling and coconducting many Ferguson-related interviews. Lawrence Anderson and I collaboratively completed the Baltimore fieldwork and interviews. Grace Cerand, Kaitlin Ferguson, and Niya Garrett also assisted with the Baltimore research, gathering information on the city's Tax Increment Financing (TIF) districts, public housing redevelopments, and Low Income Housing Tax Credit (LIHTC) developments. Richard Takacs collected descriptive statistical data and Christian Wiskur compiled data as well as produced detailed city maps. Alex Campbell organized the figures and references. I also acknowledge Christopher Campbell, Sarah Edwards, and Ashley Scott for excellent manuscript editing, and Christopher Tyler Burks for his insightful input on this book. This work was a collective endeavor and I owe so much to my students for their important contributions.

Several American University (AU) colleagues read parts of the manuscript, listened to my emerging thoughts, and provided constructive feedback as this project progressed. I thank Mike Bader (now at Johns Hopkins University), Kyle Dargan, Bradley Hardy (now at Georgetown University), Michael R. Fisher Jr. (now at Ohio State University), Theo Greene (now at Bowdoin College), Cathy Schneider, and David Schwegman. I also thank Meagan Snow (now at the Library of Congress) for constructing some of the book's maps. I especially thank Vicky Wilkins, acting provost of AU, and Alison Jacknowitz, interim dean of AU's School of Public Affairs, for providing much of the financial support that undergirded this work.

I need to recognize several colleagues outside of AU as well. I cannot thank enough Howard Gillette, Blair Ruble, Larry Vale, and Bill Wilson for providing letters of recommendation for book-related fellowship applications. Awards from the American Council of Learned Societies (ACLS) and the Rockefeller Foundation allowed me to execute the research and writing. Equally important was the ongoing encouragement these intellectual heavyweights provided me, keeping my manuscript motivation high, especially during the height of the pandemic. Additionally, I thank Isabelle Anguelovski, Japonica Brown-Saracino, Maribel Campos, Angeliz Encarnación Burgos, Mindy Fullilove, Joseph Gibbons, Jackelyn Hwang, Loretta Lees, Mai Nguyen, Jeffrey Parker, Zawadi Rucks-Ahidiana, Jeffrey Timberlake, and Shannon Whittaker for conversations that contributed to this work. I also acknowledge my two anonymous reviewers whose insightful suggestions sharpened the final version.

I owe much gratitude to Willow Lung-Amam, a professor at the University of Maryland's Urban Studies and Planning Program. We spent the fall of 2021 reading and critiquing our in-progress books. Willow provided me with sound advice on how to streamline my urban renewal unrest arguments. I thank her for her friendship and extremely helpful guidance.

I also acknowledge two individuals whose unrest scholarship was inspirational. Both Janet Abu-Lughod and Michael Katz's quintessential uprising books set me on a path to undertake this manuscript. I was fortunate to meet Janet in 2007 when she asked me to serve on an American Sociological Association author-meets-critic panel in New York City. Little did I know then she was helping to position me to eventually write this manuscript. I never met Michael, but his 2012 book was the intellectual spark that drove my research. Janet and Michael have passed, and I wished I could have communicated with them about how their written words inspired me.

Several Baltimore and St. Louis academic experts deserve a special thanks. In St. Louis, Andrea Boyles, Colin Gordon, John Robinson, and Todd Swanstrom provided professional and personal information to ground this book. In Baltimore, Matthew Crenson, Stefanie DeLuca, and Lawrence Brown offered their Charm City political, housing, and racial insights that made my assessment, with much help from Lawrence Anderson, possible.

Academic information without a neighborhood perspective can be meaningless. Several community stakeholders made me see, hear, and understand the realities of life in Ferguson and Baltimore. In Ferguson, Rob Chabot, Fran Griffin, Ella Jones, and James Knowles provided their "home" perspectives, and I am grateful. In Baltimore, Raymond "Ray" Kelly and Rev. Douglas Miles, who passed in 2021, did the same.

As noted, I received two wonderful fellowships that helped me complete this book. The ACLS award released me from teaching so I could collect data. The Rockefeller Foundation Bellagio fellowship allowed me the time and space to write. My Bellagio Center cohort was extraordinary. They provided me with critical feedback that broadened the manuscript. I especially want to acknowledge Mourid Baraghouti and Vanessa Watson, two stellar intellects who took a keen interest in my work. Mourid, a poet, and Vanessa, an urban planner, worked in different ways to change the world, and both helped me better understand the interrelationships, and importance, of home, homeland, and health. They have since passed, but I fondly remember the remarkable time I had with them and my other Bellagio cohort members.

A book is only as good as its publisher; thank goodness I have a great one. Naomi Schneider at the University of California Press has been so supportive of this book's journey ever since I pitched it to her in 2017 in Montreal. Through busted deadlines and reworked outlines, she stayed incredibly committed to this manuscript. Thank you.

My unit, my team of family and friends, helps me so much in my scholarly work. Anthony Gill, Illan Goldenberg, Chad Hill, Adam Hughes, Matthew Goodman, Kabir Kamboh, David Kirk, Percival Matthews, Matthew Miller, Robert Renner, John Wedges, and Andy Young, thank you for your friendship and repeatedly listening to me talk about different parts of the book over the years. While working on this manuscript in 2019, we lost my mom, Miriam Hyra, to pancreatic cancer. She was the base, and glue, of my natal family. Her love, compassion, and commitment to social justice, and to her family, are the moral compass that guided this book. I thank her and my dad, Richard Hyra, for providing a loving foundation. I also thank the Matthieus: Jennifer, my sister, Scott, my brother-in-law, and Amanda, my niece, for their support. When my mom passed, the Deschamps family stepped up. Thank you Eldi, my father-in-law, Denise, my mom-in-law, and Christopher, my brother-in-law, for being there for me. Allison, my spouse, friend, and toughest editorial critic, helped this manuscript in so many ways. Thank you for being my partner and assisting me in my academic and personal pursuits. Allison, Avery, my son, and Barrett, my daughter, this book is dedicated to you. You three collectively provided the life force, joy, and passion embedded in these pages. I cherish the moments we are together and am so glad you are with me for life's wonderful, and wild, ride.

Preface

I developed an interest in uprisings during my formative years. On April 29, 1992, after four police officers were acquitted in the vicious beating of Rodney King, Los Angeles (LA) started to burn. The next day I drove the Sawmill River Parkway from Somers, New York, to Harlem in New York City (NYC), an hour-long trip. At the time, I was living in a relatively affluent, majority-white NYC suburb, north of the city, and had been playing basketball for two years for the Riverside Hawks, an Amateur Athletic Union team based in the basement of Riverside Church in West Harlem.

I had been making this weekly trip in the spring and summer months to practice and play throughout Harlem, but this day was different. I entered the Riverside Church gym and my coach immediately said, "Derek, you might need to leave." When I asked why, he replied, "There are reports rioting has broken out on the east side of 125th." The aftermath of the Rodney King verdict the day before had made its way across the country. Upon hearing my coach's advice, I decided it was best for me to leave. I bolted back up to the segregated NYC suburbs.

While Harlem was spared major damage, LA experienced five days of civil unrest.[1] When the smoke cleared, 52 people were dead, 2,250 injured, 9,400 arrested, and 1,120 buildings damaged at an estimated cost of $450 million.[2] To this day two scenes associated with the LA riots remain embedded in my mind: the video of two white police officers, Laurence Powell and Timothy Wind, relentlessly striking African American Rodney King, and Damian Williams, a nineteen-year-old African American man, throwing a red brick at the head of Reginald Denny, a white man lying in the street after being pulled from his truck in South Central during the upheaval. Neither of these brutal acts was justified, and both illustrated how terribly dysfunctional America could be.

For a naïve and idealistic teenager like me, the TV coverage of the LA uprising was hard to comprehend; however, race riots were nothing new to America. In East St. Louis in 1917, white mobs killed nearly five hundred African Americans and drove seven thousand others from their homes.[3] In Chicago in 1919, white and Black groups clashed after whites stoned and let drown a Black boy for swimming too close to a "whites only" South Side beach section, resulting in thirty-eight deaths.[4] In Washington, DC, in 1919, over one thousand white civilians and soldiers attacked African Americans throughout the city after a white woman claimed she was assaulted by a Black man, resulting in the deaths of four African Americans and three whites.[5] In Tulsa, Oklahoma, in 1921 white assailants burned over one thousand African American homes and many Black-owned businesses in the recently rediscovered "Tulsa Massacre."[6]

Undoubtably influenced by these violent occurrences, Robert Park, one of the founders of the "Chicago school" of sociology, declared in 1925 that urban communities were "in a chronic condition of crisis." Park, who was white and the first board president of the Chicago Urban League, speculated that the urban predicament was the product of an "unstable equilibrium" and "perpetual agitation" associated with modern urban life. Forces of technological advancement, mobility, and population density created and destroyed capital markets, putting people in a constant state of economic chaos. He

pondered, "To what extent are mob violence, strikes, and radical political movements the results of the same general conditions that pro-
voke financial panics, real estate booms, and mass movements in the
population generally?" Furthermore, he questioned whether social
uproars were "due to the extent and speed of [constant] economic
changes."[7] Interesting enough, even though he spent considerable
time in Chicago's South Side segregated Black Belt, he did not ask
whether white racism, and chronic Black oppression and trauma,
were the roots of unrest.[8]

America has a four-hundred-year history of Black enslavement,
and the United States continues to grapple with its horrible and preju-
diced past.[9] As Swedish sociologist Gunnar Myrdal explained in 1944,
the *American Dilemma* was the country's struggle to come to grips with
its history of racial violence on the one hand and ideals of freedom, democracy, and justice on the other.[10] America consistently makes incre-
mental progress toward racial justice and then retreats back to exploitation and discrimination: Reconstruction and then Jim Crow, civil
rights and then Martin Luther King Jr.'s assassination, Obama and
then Trump.[11] It is a history of racial progression and regression.

While the United States made advancements in civil rights during the 1960s, urban areas were on fire. Historian Peter Levy coined
this period *The Great Uprising*, as African Americans demanded a
more inclusive democracy and white America, for the most part, resisted.[12] This rising tension, along with the discontent stemming
from it, was illustrated in the flames that consumed inner-city America in the 1960s. Between 1963 and 1972, over 525 cities including
New Haven, Harlem, Newark, Baltimore, Washington, DC, Pittsburgh, Cleveland, Cincinnati, Chicago, Milwaukee, Wichita, San
Francisco, and LA experienced uprisings, many of which occurred
after the assassination of Martin Luther King Jr.[13]

Compared to the turmoil of the 1960s, urban America had relatively few incidents of unrest between 1970 and 2010. During that

time period, though, Black neighborhood poverty was pervasive.[14] In 2000, I headed to the South Side of Chicago, to the University of Chicago, to study dynamics of neighborhood change and better understand what creates conditions of concentrated poverty like I saw in Harlem. In Bronzeville, I conducted much of my dissertation research at the Stateway Gardens public housing project.[15] Between 2001 and 2003, I witnessed intense poverty, public housing demolition, and horrible police brutality—but at no time did the South Side erupt into unrest.

In 2012, urban historian and University of Pennsylvania professor Michael Katz wrote *Why Don't American Cities Burn?* He investigated why a limited number of violent protests originated from disadvantaged urban African American communities, like Bronzeville, since the 1970s.[16] Katz was motivated to write this book following the extensive, three-week-long 2005 French riots, sparked by police violence that resulted in the death of two teenagers of Tunisian and Malian decent.[17] During the three-week-long revolt, three hundred French cities experienced unrest and nearly nine thousand cars burned. Katz contemplated why American inner-city neighborhoods do not often revolt despite having similar or even worse conditions than their French counterparts.[18] He asked, "Why did no one light the match?"[19] Katz claimed that Black political incorporation and the rise of the Black middle class consumer had helped to prevent more uprisings from occurring across urban America, despite persistent unequal racial conditions.

However, just two years after Katz's publication, three U.S. municipalities went up in flames. In 2014, 2015, and 2016, unrest occurred in Ferguson, Missouri; Baltimore, Maryland; and Charlotte, North Carolina, respectively. In 2019, Memphis experienced an uprising after law enforcement killed an African American man as they attempted to arrest him for an outstanding warrant.[20] Then in 2020 unrest ripped throughout our nation following George Floyd's murder.[21] With such widespread conflict, public health scholar Lawrence Brown labeled the period between 2014 and 2020 "the Great Rebellion."[22] Michael Katz passed away in 2014. He did not, nor did most, see this wave of U.S. unrest coming. This book's aim is to advance understandings of key historic and contemporary dynamics that drove this modern period of revolt. While a historic analysis of the undercurrents of Black revolts might have begun during the era of enslavement, as artist Jacob Lawrence's cover artwork evokes, I strategically limit my focus to twentieth- and twenty-first-century urban policies, which are extensions of America's racist past.

Introduction

The nation ignores the rage of the rejected—until it explodes . . .

Psychologist KENNETH B. CLARK

The Revolts

On August 9, 2014, eighteen-year-old Michael Brown was murdered in Ferguson, Missouri, a majority-Black suburb of St. Louis.[1] Darren Wilson, a white police officer, killed Brown in the middle of the street near the Canfield Green Apartments, an affordable housing complex occupied almost exclusively by African Americans.[2] The shooting was gruesome.[3]

Wilson was patrolling the Canfield area after the police dispatch had conveyed a suspected nearby robbery at the Ferguson Market. He spotted Brown and his friend, also African American, walking in the street and ordered them to get on the sidewalk.[4] He thought they might have been involved in the reported robbery.

Wilson turned his vehicle almost horizontal to block Brown's path. Brown approached Wilson's car and allegedly put his hands inside and struck Wilson.[5] Wilson grabbed his gun and shot twice at close range striking Brown's right hand near the base of his thumb; Brown took off running. Wilson got out of his car and chased Brown.

At some point, Brown, also known as "Mike-Mike," turned back to face Wilson; some witnesses saw Brown raise his hands in surrender; others did not.[6] What happened next was indisputable; Wilson shot unarmed Brown multiple times.[7] One bullet pierced his upper right chest; another went through his right eye; another hit the top of Brown's head, killing him.[8] The sudden violent episode lasted ninety seconds;[9] however, Brown's body lay in the street for more than four hours before medical examiners took his body to the morgue.[10] The concrete soaked up the blood hemorrhaging from Brown's body.[11] Brown's mother, Lesley McSpadden, cried out, "You just shot all through my baby's body."[12] Mike's stepfather, Louis Head, held up a cardboard sign: "Ferguson Police Just Executed My Unarmed Son!"[13]

Anguish filled the air at the Canfield Garden Apartments. Sociologist Andrea Boyles, who was there the day Brown died, wrote, "It was indescribable, and everyone appeared deflated from seeing traces of blood still on the ground and the pain of Brown's family." Boyles expressed, "Words could not capture *this* climate change."[14] After Brown's body was removed from the street, his mother sprinkled rose petals on the spot her son had occupied to form a makeshift memorial.[15] People gathered around her to collectively support one another through songs, prayers, and hugs.[16]

During this intimate grieving moment, police cars rushed into the area with "sirens blaring and light flashing." The police drove "straight through [the street] and decimated the new memorial," emerging from their squad cars with attack dogs and raised rifles. Boyles wrote that, when the police destroyed the memorial and disrespectfully pushed their way through the funeral-like proceeding, some people "just lost it."[17]

That night, no major incident occurred between the protesters and the police. However, an uproar ensued the next evening. About a

FIGURE 1. Police on West Florissant. Reuters/photo by Mario Anzuoni.

hundred mainly Black protesters gathered at the site of Brown's death and some blocked traffic on West Florissant, East Ferguson's main business district. They chanted, "Hands up, don't shoot."[18] The protesters were met by a wall of white police officers in riot gear.[19] Behind the police was a large armored, tank-like truck with a top positioned officer who aimed his high-powered rifle at the protesters (figure 1).[20]

The tension between the police and protesters was extremely elevated. Police, armed with riot gear, used tear gas and rubber bullets to break up the protests.[21] Some individuals threw bottles at the police.[22] A nearby gas station store was burned and looted and several parked cars were damaged.[23] Duane Finnie, a childhood friend of Brown's father, exclaimed, "People are tired of being misused and mistreated, and this is an outlet for them to express their outrage and anger."[24] When the smoke cleared, Ferguson was in the national spotlight as one of the first modern Black American suburbs to revolt, igniting the national and international Black Lives Matter movement.[25]

Less than a year later, inner-city Baltimore burned. On April 19, 2015, twenty-five-year-old Freddie Gray, known as "Peppers," died following his April 12 arrest and police-induced "rough ride."[26] Gray, an African American resident of the impoverished West Baltimore Sandtown-Winchester community, was arrested after running from a police officer with whom he made eye contact.[27] Three police officers chased Gray down and detained him for allegedly carrying a pocketknife.[28]

Gray's arrest was agonizing. Two officers held him face down on the concrete. One pressed his knee into Gray's back. The other put his legs into leg irons. Gray screamed as officers carried his body into a white police van.[29] As the police dragged Gray, a woman shouted at the officers, "Hey! His leg look broke. Look at his fucking leg. . . . That boy's leg look broke. His leg is broke and you all dragging him, like that!"[30] Gray's legs were not broken but he was about to experience unimaginable pain due to antagonistic police action.

Gray experienced a forty-five-minute "rough ride." A rough ride is an illegal police tactic to transport a person in a way that tortures the suspect.[31] The police did not secure him with a seat belt, and he was violently tossed back and forth during the police transport.[32] By the time he arrived at the precinct, he was unconscious. He was rushed to the hospital and underwent surgery for three fractured vertebrae, an injured larynx, and an almost completely severed spinal cord.[33] Gray never woke up from surgery and died from spinal cord trauma on April 19.[34]

After Gray's death, the Baltimore uprising began. On Saturday, April 25, activists organized a protest march beginning in West Baltimore, where Gray was arrested, heading by downtown's City Hall and then to nearby tourist locations: the Inner Harbor and Camden Yards baseball stadium.[35] Marchers chanted: "No justice, no peace." "What do we want? Justice! When do we want it? Now!"[36] "All night, all day, we are going to fight for Freddie Gray."[37] The peaceful demonstration turned violent as marchers, drunk sports fans, and the police collided just west of downtown.[38] During the melee, store windows were shattered, fistfights broke out, and police cars were set on fire.[39]

Following Gray's funeral on Monday, April 27, civil disorder occurred again just north of Sandtown at the Mondawmin Mall.[40] City officials shut down the subway system near the mall and sent police officers to the mall as students were released from the nearby Frederick Douglass High School.[41] The city's transportation and police departments reacted to rumors on social media that some students were planning a "purge"[42] moment, packed with property destruction and violence.[43] When the students, without transportation options, encountered police in riot gear, a violent confrontation broke out.[44]

The mayhem moved south to Sandtown-Winchester's Pennsylvania (Penn) Avenue commercial corridor, close to where Gray had been arrested.[45] Near the Penn and North Avenue intersection, stores were looted, and a CVS pharmacy and police vehicles were set ablaze.[46] That afternoon a group of African American political, civic, and religious leaders, including Congressman Elijah Cummings, Councilman Nick Mosby, and Rev. Donté Hickman, held a prayer march in the Sandtown streets.[47] They prayed for the safety of their city's youth. Around midnight that night, Mosby, still wearing the suit he wore to Gray's funeral, went back to Penn and North and pleaded with young people to leave the streets. One teenager spoke with Mosby. He said, "No justice, no peace. I ain't going nowhere."[48] Between April 28 and May 3, Baltimore's inner-city streets, mainly on the city's west side, burned (figure 2).[49]

Fast forward to May 25, 2020, when police murdered George Floyd, a forty-six-year-old African American man.[50] Floyd had used a twenty-dollar bill to buy a pack of menthol cigarettes at CUP Foods at the intersection of Thirty-Eighth Street and Chicago Avenue in

FIGURE 2. Baltimore burns. Baltimore Sun/photo by Algerina Perna.

South Minneapolis. The cashier thought the bill was fake and one of the CUP employees called the cops. The police quickly responded to this racially diverse and gentrifying area, which some perceived to be a "hot spot for gang activity."[51]

The police confronted Floyd while he was sitting in the front seat of his car. Police forcefully pulled Floyd out and handcuffed him. When the police tried to push Floyd into a squad car, a scuffle ensued, and unarmed Floyd was forced to the ground. White police officer Derek Chauvin methodically pressed his knee into Floyd's neck for nine minutes and twenty-nine seconds. Though people outside of CUP Foods pleaded for the officer to stop, Floyd died of suffocation while softly repeating, "I can't breathe. I can't breathe."[52]

A video of the merciless incident surfaced on social media the next day, and massive protests erupted in over 450 American cities.[53] The majority of these protests were peaceful, but some turned violent.[54] Looting and property damage were witnessed in many major cities including Minneapolis, Boston, New York City, Chicago,

Detroit, Denver, Washington, DC, Charlotte, Columbia, Atlanta, Louisville, Houston, Dallas, San Antonio, Austin, Los Angeles, Seattle, and Portland.[55] The magnitude of the uproar following Floyd's death had not been seen in America since the 1968 assassination of Martin Luther King Jr.[56]

Just the Police?

For several scholars, the contemporary unrest narrative mainly rests on the institutionalization of excessive, aggressive, and deadly police force toward African Americans.[57] In criminologist Jennifer Cobbina's notable 2019 book *Hands Up, Don't Shoot*, she claims the Ferguson and Baltimore's uprisings centered on "the nature of police organizations and how they systematically police poor communities of color."[58] Similarly, urban politics scholar Cathy Schneider argues, "The structure of policing shaped the geography of urban unrest."[59] Sociologists Rory Kramer and Brianna Remster assert, "The impact of modern policing practices for Black and Brown Americans in everyday life is part of why civil unrest and protests have reached new heights of late."[60]

While police brutality is often an unrest trigger, uprisings are rarely driven by a single cause.[61] Many people I talked with in Ferguson and Baltimore mentioned policy brutality as a primary undercurrent of unrest; however, they also spoke about other things that greatly frustrated them. Several individuals expressed that displacement and the destruction of Black homes, and "homeland," over time were vexing and painful experiences. For instance, LaTasha Brown, a tenant leader from the area where Michael Brown was killed, declares, "You gotta identify the true problems instead of what's right there on top. Mike Brown was right there on top; however, it was a whole bunch of layers up under him."[62]

Historian Michael Katz proclaims, "In almost every instance, police actions had ignited long-standing grievances whose roots lay in racism and economic deprivation."[63] African American studies scholar Keeanga-Yamahtta Taylor pronounces, "Incidents of police brutality have typically sparked Black uprisings, but they are the tip of the iceberg, not the entirety of the problem."[64] My aim is to not to examine the "tip of the iceberg," the police, but rather to dive beneath the cold water to examine and explain the buildup of long-standing grievances across time and space. I want to understand how persistent racism, economic deprivation, and police brutality are connected to the mountain of frustrations that at certain moments erupts.

One of those eruption periods was in the 1960s when hundreds of American cities went up in flames. The 1968 Kerner Report of the presidentially appointed National Advisory Commission on Civil Disorders famously stated that our fractured society of "one [B]lack, one white–separate and unequal" was at the core of America's unrest.[65] According to the report, the civil disorders were a direct result of racist, white-led policy actions. In the 1940s, 1950s, and 1960s, housing, community development, and transportation policies destroyed Black communities and created a racially uneven metropolitan context of mainly affluent white suburbs and depleted Black urban communities.[66] It was in disadvantaged Black ghettos where frustration fumes were ignited mainly by aggressive police actions.[67]

Yet, our current national unrest discussions have largely relegated neighborhood inequality and dire ghetto conditions to the background. For many scholars, it is all about the police.[68] In contrast, this book asks: in addition to hostile police actions, what other dynamics, both historic and contemporary, undergird America's modern unrest? Moreover, how are urban development patterns and aggressive policing policies linked?

To answer these questions, I turned to the cities where the Great Rebellion began: Ferguson and Baltimore. While Cobbina conducted a remarkable assessment of aggressive policing in these cities,[69] my intuition was that certain housing and community development policies were critical components of the nation's contemporary unrest narrative. My research gaze was less on formal organization of policing and centered more on political dynamics that produced and reinforced persistent unequal community conditions. How have previous and current American housing and community development politics and policies, at national and local levels, set the contemporary context of neighborhood racial inequality?

Linking Slow and Sudden Violence

Many police-induced deaths involved sudden or fast violence.[70] Sudden violence refers to a quick episode, like the ninety-second shooting of Brown, the unbearable nine minutes of pain and suffocation that ended Floyd's life, and the approximately forty-five minute "rough ride" of unimaginable agony experienced by Gray. Several scholars focus on these sudden, unjust police spectacles, and the reactions of protesters, to explain instances of unrest.[71] While understanding and stopping aggressive police actions is crucial, the police explanation of unrest falls short as decades of unjust police killings have occurred,[72] but rarely do they evoke widespread unrest.

Rather than exclusively focusing on sudden, unjust police violence, I argue that the accumulation of *slow violence* against African Americans in the twentieth and twenty-first century sets a critical context for understanding aggressive policing and modern unrest. By slow violence, I refer to scholar Rob Nixon's conceptualization of policy violence that unfolds over years, decades, and centuries across different generations and geographies. According to Nixon, slow violence is "a violence that occurs gradually and out of sight, a violence of delayed destruction that is dispersed across time and space, an attritional violence that is typically not viewed as violence at all."[73]

I posit that repeated state-supported slow violence produces a cycle of *segregation*, *divestment*, *displacement*, and *gentrification*, setting the context for the police killing of Brown, Gray, and Floyd.[74] Black neighborhoods are consistently separated, stripped of resources, destroyed, and gentrified. Policies of slow violence advance and perpetuate *neighborhood racial inequality*, concentrating white power and affluence and Black poverty in particular places, reinforcing a racial hierarchy and the onset of aggressive policing in the *chronic ghetto*.[75] By chronic ghetto, I refer to the persistence of low-income segregated Black communities in metropolitan regions across various spaces and time.[76]

In suburban Ferguson, the uneven racial geography is represented in the stark differences between South and West Florissant. Primarily white South Florissant Road is lined with red brick municipal buildings, sidewalks, parks, and sit-down restaurants. West Florissant Avenue, the city's low-income Black section, is flanked by pawnshops, payday lenders, and liquor stores. In Baltimore, public health scholar Lawrence Brown called the city's enduring racial inequality a "Black Butterfly," with its eastern and western impoverished Black neighborhoods fanning out from a north/south line of white affluence.[77] This landscape of racial inequality is also replicated in Minneapolis and throughout metropolitan America.[78]

It is not just racially unequal neighborhoods that are unsettling for low-income Black residents. It is the linkage between repeated state-sanctioned policies of slow violence and the formation of *chronic displacement trauma*.[79] Chronic displacement trauma is the accrued, intergenerational psychological effect of community destruction and continuous displacement for particular people from their "homeplace."[80] Through a perpetual community upheaval and destruction process, people experience what Mindy Fullilove describes as "root shock," where one's entire social-support and "emotional ecosystem" is destroyed.[81] Displacement leaves people feeling a profound sense of loss, grief, depression, anxiety, and anger that corresponds to symptoms of post-traumatic stress disorder (PTSD).[82]

However, important differences exist between chronic displacement trauma and PTSD. PTSD typically relates to a specific event that is traumatic to an individual, while chronic displacement trauma affects a group repeatedly and is passed from one generation to the next.[83] The trauma and knowledge of forced displacement is transferred from generation to generation, where "the accumulation of stress, fear, insecurity, and grief makes itself felt and known over years [and decades]."[84] Ongoing racial uprooting leads to a generalized group "feeling of being out-of-place"[85] and "cut off from 'home,' broadly defined."[86]

Chronic displacement trauma is often suppressed, as people must cope and carry on in their everyday lives to survive.[87] "To protect against the pain of the recognition of what has been lost," and the humiliation and anger at feeling unable to manage their relocation, people erect "defense systems."[88] But the suppressed painful memories and anger linked with chronic displacement trauma can be surfaced by a triggering event.

The murder of Brown, Gray, Floyd, and many others, at the hands of the police, surfaced the repressed trauma of the unrelenting cycle of racial and spatial repression. Baltimore's Rev. Yeary stated, "[There is] a persistent despair that contributes a lot to the angst that simmers just beneath the surface. Folks try to live with a sense of dignity and commitment but then there's that proverbial straw that breaks the camel's back." The police killings, the sudden violence, were the "straws," the triggering events, that made some African Americans more aware of the ongoing American policy practices of systemic slow violence.[89] These deaths surfaced the deeply seated, often repressed, racial trauma frustrations that bubbled up and were channeled into actions on the streets between 2014 and 2020, the years the United States experienced "the Great Rebellion."[90] I argue that the historic and cyclical housing and community development policies of slow violence that repeatedly segregate, divest, uproot, and gentrify Black communities perpetuate chronic displacement trauma, and this helps to explain why sudden police violence in some instances ignites unrest.

Advancing the Unrest Conversation

This book advances our national conversation on the relationships among race, policy, and neighborhood inequality in several ways. Important works by Andrea Boyles, Paul Butler, Jennifer Cobbina, Marc Lamont Hill, Wesley Lowery, Anne Nassauer, Cathy Schneider, and others detail how appalling police actions stoked the flames of discontent in Ferguson, Baltimore, and beyond.[91] However, none thoroughly delves into how the urban housing and community development policies of the 1990s and 2000s, as well as the Great Recession's fallout, relate to neighborhood inequality. Nor do these works assess how past and more recent policies of slow violence build and accumulate frustrations in impoverished Black spaces. This investigation argues that racially biased housing and community development policies facilitate community destruction, neighborhood racial inequality, and police brutality.

Scholar Michelle Alexander argues in her critically acclaimed book *The New Jim Crow* that contemporary racial inequality is perpetuated through an unjust criminal justice system.[92] The police arrest African Americans at higher rates. African Americans also receive harsher sentences than whites for similar crimes and disproportionately comprise the prison population. Upon release, many African Americans with felony convictions are stigmatized and legally discriminated against in the labor and housing markets, widening racial economic inequality.

I expand Alexander's *New Jim Crow* analysis by explaining how America's housing and community development policies also contribute to and facilitate contemporary racial inequality. Just as there were old and new Jim Crow periods, there are parallel old and new urban renewal phases, linked to controlling and segregating Black lives. The old urban renewal was a set of community development, housing, and highway policies that destroyed and segregated Black communities from the rest of the urban fabric.[93] These redevelopment policies protected white-owned downtown properties from Black encroachment and made it possible for white suburbanites to easily commute from segregated suburban communities to the downtown.[94] Many African Americans displaced during the old urban renewal phase found new residences in high-rise public housing built on the periphery of downtown.[95] The old urban renewal policies, combined with discriminatory Federal Housing Administration (FHA) lending policies, known as redlining, helped to create affluent, white urban and suburban spaces, and depleted Black, inner-city neighborhoods.[96]

In the 1990s, new urban renewal policies, including the Housing Opportunities for People Everywhere (HOPE VI) program and Tax Increment Financing (TIFs) districts, advanced these preexisting racial and spatial inequalities.[97] HOPE VI funds were used to raze public housing and some of the neighborhoods where the projects once stood gentrified with TIF investments and an influx of upper-income white people. Meanwhile, low-income African Americans who were displaced ended up in impoverished ghettos slightly farther from the downtown.[98] Other African Americans were displaced to declining suburbs, like Ferguson.[99] A modern demographic metropolitan inversion, supported by new urban renewal policies, perpetuated racial inequality.[100]

As the public housing went down in the 1990s, aspects of the New Jim Crow, such as "stop and frisk" policing, began to take hold in Ferguson and Baltimore's low-income, Black communities. The public housing high-rises represented stigmatization and segregation. They were symbolic but they were also very tangible and visible. Without the signs and symbols of segregation, a new form of enforcement was created: broken windows, also known as postindustrial, policing.[101] Postindustrial policing contained ghetto residents in their new communities,[102] while their old communities received new public and private investments to support white residents, the high-wage workers of the advanced service sector economy.[103] Thus, the impact and meaning of the New Jim Crow and punitive penal state, and their connections to inequality and unrest,[104] can only be fully understood by considering their intersection with a racially unjust contemporary housing and community development system.

Gentrification is a form of slow violence connected with the chronic ghetto and unrest.[105] Old urban renewal policies as a form of violence and community destruction has been widely recognized,[106] but there is less understanding of new urban renewal process, such as gentrification, as being violent. New urban renewal policies, such as HOPE VI and TIFs, are displacing people, destroying their homeplace, and resegregating the metropolitan environment. These new and existing areas of Black poverty concentration are being heavily policed. This book aims to convince policymakers and scholars that some of our contemporary urban development is violent, causing people harm by taking away their homes, and this is connected to frustrations linked with our modern unrest.

Unlike other uprising scholarship, this book investigates how local political systems and decisions, both white- and Black-controlled, advance racial inequality. Ferguson and Baltimore have unique political histories and characteristics.[107] Baltimore historically had a higher level of Black political representation compared to St. Louis and Ferguson. Baltimore's first African American mayor was elected in 1987; St. Louis's in 1993; and Ferguson's in 2020.[108] Despite greater Black political representation, Baltimore still experienced unrest. This political difference allows for an analysis of how race and class contribute to setting the uneven conditions undergirding unrest.

While some might argue that racial political representation is insufficient to address centuries of racial discrimination and economic inequality,[109] I claim that local elite African American political leaders and their policy decisions, in some circumstances, contribute to and exacerbate racial neighborhood inequality. I posit that we must go beyond racial representation and look to *racial recognition* and *racialized policies* to confront key interconnected unrest conditions, including displacement, poverty concentration, and postindustrial policing.

Where We Are Heading

The book has three parts: Understanding Unrest, Linking Slow and Sudden Violence, and Breaking the Cycle. Part I, chapter 1, provides a theoretical structure for the book's empirical chapters by defining unrest, assessing prior uprising explanations, and building my urban renewal unrest framework. Part II, chapters 2 to 7, contains in-depth understandings of unrest in Ferguson and Baltimore. Chapter 2 explains how segregation, divestment, and serial displacement destroyed some of St. Louis's Black communities. From the redevelopment of the St. Louis waterfront to Mill Creek Valley to suburban Kinloch, mainly white-led development coalitions crushed African American communities and pushed low-income Black "refugees" to other segregated spaces.[110] Chapter 3 explicates the factors related to the modern movement of Blackness and poverty from St. Louis to suburban Ferguson. Those forces are central city public housing demolitions and gentrification, as well as ongoing Black neighborhood disinvestment. Chapter 4 demonstrates how Ferguson's white-controlled political structure implemented economic politics that exacerbated racial inequality and tensions. In 1970, Ferguson was less than one percent Black; by 2010 the African American population soared to 67 percent. Yet, the racial demographics of the city's political structure and police force did not change as rapidly as its population. This chapter focuses on Ferguson's plantation politics and how it intensified frustrations among vulnerable, low-income Black residents.

Chapters 5 to 7 take us to Baltimore. Chapter 5 centers on the city's early history of Black segregation, displacement, and poverty concentration. A white-led political coalition protected white downtown property interests by displacing African Americans and putting up walls of high-rise public housing just outside of the central business district. In the east and west side ghettos, known as the "ring of blight," unrest exploded in 1968. Chapter 5 focuses on how old urban renewal policies created the conditions associated with this uprise. Chapter 6 shifts to the new urban renewal period and the political processes and outcomes related to Charm City's inner-city gentrification and "Disneyfication."[111] In Baltimore, the local government, controlled for the most part by elite African Americans, redeveloped the city's Inner Harbor to promote tourism as well as upscale commercial and residential development.[112] The Inner Harbor and the surrounding neighborhoods, many of which contained public housing developments, were redeveloped. When the inner-city projects near the Inner Harbor were demolished by the Housing Authority of Baltimore City with federal resources, the more peripheral neighborhoods, such as West Baltimore's Sandtown-Winchester, became increasingly concentrated with impoverishment. This chapter illustrates how the successful redevelopment of the Inner Harbor relates to the displacement and the demise of certain Black neighborhoods, creating difficult and uneven economic conditions that set the context for Baltimore contemporary uprisings. Chapter 7 explains how Inner Harbor revitalization exacerbated neighborhood inequality, aggressive policing, and the weight of violence in Sandtown-Winchester and throughout the city. I explain how political fragmentation relates to street-level violence, an important condition associated with Baltimore's ethos and its modern uprisings.

Part III concludes the book. In chapter 8, I summarize the main drivers of unrest in Ferguson and Baltimore. I then revisit past theoretical perspectives and lay out their limitations and the merits of my urban renewal unrest framework. I end by offering an array of racialized national and local policy recommendations to stabilize Black communities, with a heavy emphasis on ending aggressive police practices, reducing displacement, and breaking the cycle of racial and spatial repression.

My Disposition and Research Approach

Uprisings are at times both necessary and scary, and this is my attempt to better understand their historic and contemporary drivers. Incidents of unrest are important, emotionally charged forms of political protest originating from conditions of despair.[113] In 1965, psychologist Kenneth B. Clark characterized revolts as "signals of distress, an SOS from the ghetto."[114] In 2017, scholar Mustafa Dikeç claimed, "Urban uprisings are political in that they expose patterns, dynamics and structures of exclusion and oppression that have become routine and normalized."[115] When routine racial repressions like spatial segregation, serial displacement, Black poverty concentration, and police violence are confronted, it can result in an emotional uproar.

Just as uprisings are sometimes a release and expression of emotional anger, they can elicit passionate responses from those who assess them.[116] My drive to understand the uprisings came in 2014 when my Twitter (now X) feed erupted with the news of Ferguson. Like many others, I thought something was profoundly wrong with the police shooting of Michael Brown. Then I felt the same thing in 2015 with the arrest and death of Freddie Gray in Baltimore. I watched Sandtown's CVS store burn via social media, and knew I had to commit myself to writing this book.[117] I needed to meet with people in these areas to understand why these communities were hurting and what fueled it. For me, this is a systematic academic endeavor, yet it is driven by an emotional calling to understand and alleviate unjust circumstances.[118]

The book's undertaking was demanding for several reasons. First, I am a white, middle-aged researcher attempting to gain access to, and comprehend, conditions in African American communities and cities where I had few personal contacts. While it can be difficult for white scholars to gain access to African American communities, I have experience building trust and learning from Black neighborhoods. My prior ethnographic research was about the redevelopment of Harlem in New York City, Bronzeville in Chicago, and Shaw/U Street in Washington, DC.[119] Second, while I had considerable involvement investigating neighborhood change processes in low-income Black communities, I had not previously written about unrest. It took nearly three years, between 2016 and 2018, to familiarize myself with this academic literature.[120] Third, I typically conduct my community research by living in or working in neighborhoods and partnering with local institutions over a long period of time.[121] Because of the two-city research comparison, my professional and family commitments, and the COVID pandemic, I was unable to live in Ferguson or Baltimore. Thus, I did not conduct a "standard" ethnography but instead relied heavily on in-person and virtual site visits between 2018 and 2022, forty-two interviews with key stakeholders, and archival records as data sources.[122]

To establish trust and obtain information, I relied and leaned on local experts in each city. In Baltimore, I was fortunate to have the help of Lawrence Anderson. Anderson, an African American man in his late 30s, lived in Baltimore for six years and worked closely with Baltimore politician Nick Mosby. Lawrence was a graduate student at American University in 2018 and 2019, and he had a fellowship to work at my research center. Lawrence guided my understanding of

Baltimore politics and assisted with the Baltimore interviews and fieldwork. I greatly benefited from his keen Charm City knowledge and experiences, which we discussed in depth during our weekly forty-five-minute car rides between Washington, DC, and Baltimore. Lawrence was the insider; I was the outsider. We brought our collective thoughts together to grasp and communicate the complexities of Baltimore.

In Ferguson, I was on my own but early on considerably benefited from the advice of St. Louis scholars including Andrea Boyles, Colin Gordon, and Todd Swanstrom. These scholars and others helped me gain a solid St. Louis grounding before I entered Ferguson. In Ferguson, I was guided by Ferguson Mayors Ella Jones and James Knowles, former City Council Member Fran Griffin, and Ferguson Main Street Chair Robert Chabot.

In 1965, Kenneth B. Clark stated that unrest "is the expression of the anarchy of the profoundly alienated."[123] This is so true today. We must listen to those who feel unheard and excluded across America and address occurrences of racial injustice. My hope is that this book puts forth new policy perspectives, based on the testimonies of those often disregarded, and provides concrete recommendations to help make our neighborhoods and nation more equitable, stable, and just.

I   *Understanding Unrest*

1 Riots or Revolts?

An Urban Renewal Unrest Perspective

*What is social unrest, and what are the conditions under which it
manifests itself?*

Sociologist ROBERT PARK

What's a Riot?

Riots are deeply embedded in the foundation of American democracy.[1] Our nation was formed when rioters demanded representation
and confronted unjust British taxation and imperial rule. Historian
Paul Gilje wrote, "The United States of America was born amid a
wave of rioting,"[2] including the Stamp Act riots of 1765, the Boston
Massacre of 1770, and the Boston Tea Party in 1773.[3] "Rioting is part
of the American past," insisted Gilje.[4]

Even though riots were essential to the formation of American
democracy, some scholars have been hesitant to put collective violence against racial injustice in that same category. When the term
riot is used in the context of African American uprisings, some people immediately think of rogue and senseless individuals involved in
civil disturbances. Unrest expert Malcom McLaughlin acknowledges, "Historians have sometimes backed away from the term 'riot'

precisely because it is often taken to express disapproval or imply irrationality."[5] However, when the terms *rebellion, uprising, ghetto revolt,* and *insurgency* are used to describe these same events, people assume the actors involved were politically rational and organized.[6] McLaughlin emphasizes there are "implications of the words we use to describe these events."[7]

The 1968 Kerner Report was one of the most in-depth studies of unrest in America's Black ghettos in the 1960s.[8] Lyndon B. Johnson's 1967 presidential executive order formed and tasked the National Advisory Commission on Civil Disorders to answer three questions: "What happened? Why did it happen? What can be done to prevent it from happening again?"[9] In the 1968 write-up dubbed the Kerner Report, the commissioners went for a "neutral-sounding" way to describe the events that took place during this tumultuous period.[10] The commission chose the phrase *civil disorders.*

While the Kerner Commission settled on civil disorder, other writers and scholars selected different terms. Historians Peter Levy and Elizabeth Hinton used *uprisings* and *rebellions,* rather than *riots,* to describe the incidents of turmoil and conflict that occurred throughout Black inner-city America in the 1960s and early 1970s.[11] Other scholars used the terms *collective violence,*[12] *Black insurgency,*[13] *ghetto revolts,*[14] *Black revolts,*[15] *insurrections,*[16] and *rebellions.*[17] Some scholars simultaneously used several phases. Sociologist Janet Abu-Lughod, in her 2007 book *Race, Space, and Riots in Chicago, New York, and Los Angeles,* deployed the terms *riots, insurrections, rebellions, ghetto revolts,* and *ghetto uprisings.*[18]

Before interrogating the circumstances that led up to incidents of unrest in Ferguson in 2014 and Baltimore in 2015, we need greater conceptual clarity on how to characterize and define the events that took place. Were they riots or revolts?

I learned firsthand that distinctions between these words matter. In 2018, I organized a half-day workshop in Baltimore for approximately twenty Annie E. Casey Foundation program officers on anti-displacement strategies. While the workshop's purpose was to discuss strategies to minimize displacement, I briefly recounted some of this book's aims and initial findings. I mentioned I was examining the "roots of the riots." After I finished my overview, the first comment was fired. "We did not have riots in Baltimore; they were uprisings!" snapped a program officer. Even academics fiercely questioned the use of *riots* to describe the Ferguson and Baltimore situations. At a 2018 Urban History Association conference in South Carolina, I delivered a presentation linking old and new urban renewal policies to neighborhood conditions undergirding the riots of the 1960s and 2010s. The initial audience question was why I chose *riots* to portray collective violence. It was clear some people were caught up on terminology.

The words used to identify collective dissent are associated with how people perceive the causes and meanings behind these communal acts. It is difficult to separate the words *riots* and *uprisings* from their causes and consequences. Historian Thomas Sugrue contends, "The terms that commentators chose—'civil disorder,' 'disturbance,' 'riot,' 'rebellion,' 'uprising'—signaled their position on the meaning of the events."[19] Sugrue notes that *riot* was the most common term used in the 1960s and described "a seemingly senseless, inarticulate expression of violence or rage" associated with "mobs and irrationality." He adds that the word *uprising* was the least-used term and suggests that it connotes "a spontaneous upsurge of protest or violent expression of discontent, something with political content, but short of a full-fledged revolutionary act."[20]

Some people prefer calming or neutral words; I do not. I favor accurate terms, regardless of how some people may interpret them. *Uprising*, *revolt*, and *rebellion* may reassure some people because they imply that a political motive undergirds participating in collective violence. I lay little blame on those involved in collective violence to fight injustice. In my view, they are not the "riffraff," "hoodlums," "delinquents," "thugs," or "gangbangers."[21] They are everyday citizens who express and target their frustrations on public symbols of state power oppressing them. This seems very rational. How do you fight laws that were purposely set up to hold you back? You revolt, rebel, and riot.

Whether *riot*, *uprising*, or *revolt* is used, I assume a political purpose to collective acts of violence against racial injustices. Political scientist Cathy Schneider claims, "Most riots begin as nonviolent gatherings and pleas for justice by families, friends, and neighbors of the victims [of police brutality]."[22] In Ferguson and Baltimore, there were peaceful calls for justice for the families of Michael Brown and Freddie Gray before unrest unfolded.[23] But eventually, these peaceful events turned violent. What do we call spontaneous collective violence involving looting, burning, tanks, and tear gas in the face of racial injustice? Scholar Marc Lamont Hill has advocated for the term *rebellion* because "it spotlights organized resistance by the oppressed against the systems that dominate them . . . . [where] there is a great deal of spontaneity and emotion."[24]

Riots, collective violence, rebellions, revolts, uprisings, and unrest are political acts. Historian Elizabeth Hinton suggests, "Violent rebellion offered a means for people of color to express collective solidarity in the face of exploitation, political exclusion, and criminalization."[25] Vicky Osterweil acknowledges: "Riots are violent, extreme, and femme as fuck: they rip, tear, burn, and destroy to give birth to a new world."[26] These acts give voice to the voiceless, power to the powerless. They are spontaneous, "emotionally-charged" acts that express and give meaning to the racial injustice rage built up over decades and generations.[27] They are chaotic and difficult to control. They are violent. They contain at least one element of the following behaviors: burning, looting, rock or bottle throwing, or shootings. They typically follow incidents of police brutality and peaceful protests before anger, rage, and frustrations spontaneously generate violent action. I use the words *riots*, *uprisings*, *revolts*, *rebellions*, and *unrest* interchangeably to describe collective political acts against racial repression when different forms of violence—burning, looting, rock or bottle throwing, fighting, or shooting—occur. This unrest definition coincides with what occurred in Ferguson in 2014 and Baltimore in 2015 and in several major U.S. cities following the murder of George Floyd in 2020.

What Drives Unrest?

With some conceptual clarity about unrest, I turn to what underlying conditions undergird these collective actions. Just as there are complexities to identifying unrest, explaining revolt drivers is also difficult. More than a half-century ago, the Kerner Report acknowledged this challenge: "The background of disorder is often as complex and difficult to analyze as the disorder itself."[28]

Several uprising theories exist. Some highlight racism, segregation, social isolation, and concentrated poverty as primary drivers.[29] Other theories suggest that intergroup competition and contact best explain violent racial and ethnic group conflict.[30] Another camp of scholars points to the primacy of ongoing police brutality against Black Americans.[31] Some academics argue that rising expectations and relative deprivation among the excluded are important contributing factors.[32] For others, it is not preexisting racial inequalities, but rather immediate situational circumstances at peaceful protests that explain why violence erupts.[33] And still for some, it is not immediate circumstances but rather historic and contextual factors that matter more.[34]

There is no consensus on specific drivers of unrest. However, most scholars agree that "riots are complex phenomena and their outbreak is inevitably symptomatic of deep societal problems."[35] In

America, our deep societal problem is ongoing intentional racial inequality within a democracy that prides itself on equality and justice for all.[36] We claim equality for U.S. citizens, yet racial inequality is profound, persistent, and almost everywhere.[37] The homeownership rate among African Americans is 42 percent, while it is 72 percent for whites.[38] The typical white family has ten times the wealth as the average Black household.[39] In 1984, the median net wealth difference between white and African American families was $84,400, and by 2013 it was $245,000.[40] In 2016, 31 percent of African American children lived in poverty compared to only 11 percent of white children.[41] As of 2013, there was a seven-year life expectancy gap between whites and African Americans.[42]

These systemic racial inequities and injustices can lead to rage and riots are often seen as the "expression of pent-up anger."[43] Sociologist Janet Abu-Lughod insists that riots "lay bare fissures in the taken-for-granted social structure, thus revealing agonizing conflicts and pain."[44] Moreover, scholar and unrest expert Mustafa Dikeç declares, "Urban uprisings [are the] exposure of injustices and grievances."[45] Consequently, police violence must be placed within a context of ongoing Black discrimination, segregation, and poverty concentration to better understand the pent-up anger that often undergirds unrest incidents.

Segregation and Poverty Concentration

The Kerner Report put the blame for unrest almost solely on racist white American society and its policies that separated whites from African Americans and that constructed impoverished, inner-city Black ghettos. The report stated, "Segregation and poverty have created in the racial ghetto a destructive environment totally unknown to most white Americans. What white Americans have never fully understood—but what the Negro can never forget—is that white society is deeply implicated in the ghetto. White institutions created it, white institutions maintain it, and white society condones it."[46] The Kerner Report further claimed, "White racism is essentially responsible for the explosive mixture which has been accumulating in our cities," expressed in the policy of segregation: impoverished Black ghettos in the cities and more affluent white suburbs.[47]

Several unrest scholars agreed with the Kerner Report's assessment that our deep societal problem was the interconnection among racism, segregation, and the creation of the toxic Black ghetto. Dennis Gale, author of *Understanding Urban Unrest*, argued, "Urban riots will occur as long as there are large numbers of disaffected people living in tightly concentrated enclaves of poverty."[48] Furthermore, Fred R. Harris, Kerner Commission member and former U.S. Senator, stressed, "The causes of the riots . . . grew out of racism and economic deprivation."[49] Kenneth B. Clark, psychologist and author of *The Dark Ghetto*, attested, "As long as institutionalized forms of American racism persist, violent eruptions will continue to occur in the Negro ghettos."[50] He acknowledged, "We cannot expect to maintain racial ghettos without paying a high price."[51] For these scholars and policymakers, impoverished Black ghettos could not be separated from rage and revolts.

Racial Competition, Inter-Group Contact

Gale, Harris, and Clark argue that Black poverty concentration is one of the leading unrest factors; however, others, such as sociologist Susan Olzak and her colleagues, surprisingly declare that poverty concentration is not a riot driver. Olzak, using econometric modeling, finds that Black poverty did not predict 154 riots between 1960 and 1993 in 55 cities. Olzak and her collaborators state, "The conventional wisdom that Black race riots are a function of high rates of Black poverty was not supported."[52] Rather, these scholars discover, "where residential contact between African Americans and Whites increases, the rate of race riots increases significantly."[53] Moreover, sociologist Seymour Spilerman examines city characteristics associated with unrest intensity in the 1960s. His statistical models show that "Negro disadvantage in a community failed to reveal significant associations with [riot] severity."[54] He measures city-level Black absolute and relative (to white) deprivation. He finds these indicators do not predict riot intensity.

Olzak and Spilerman's findings support the competition theory of unrest. This theory suggests that demographic change in cities and neighborhoods and increased competition among racial and ethnic groups for jobs, space, and political power undergird unrest.[55] While the competition theory was popular during the early twentieth century when cities were experiencing an influx of different racial and ethnic groups, most scholars in the 1960s tended to focus on persistent and intensifying poverty concentration as opposed to ethnic and racial urban population shifts. However, some sociologists, such as Max Herman, argue that several of the 1960s riots were "in large part a product of vast demographic and economic changes that transformed . . . cities and their respective neighborhoods."[56] He and others, including Olazk and Spilerman, claim that Black poverty is an insufficient explanation for unrest and that analyses of changing levels of intergroup contact are needed to more deeply understand the widespread unrest of the 1960s.

Olzak and Spilerman's quantitative assessments have two important limitations. Both studies measure Black poverty at the city level with point-in-time measures. Neither examines whether the city's Black poverty rate increased, nor do they examine the spatial distribution of high-poverty neighborhoods and whether conditions in particular Black ghettos deteriorated over time. Whether the Black poverty rate worsened and how the citywide Black poverty rate is related to specific conditions in particular Black neighborhoods might be critical to understanding unrest. While the quantitative studies by Olzak and Spilerman are insightful, they are limited since they do not measure these key indicators.

Concentrated Black Poverty

Contrary to Olzak and Spilerman's approach, several influential case studies point to changing poverty concentration in Black communities as a critical undercurrent of unrest. One of the best historical analyses of unrest is Thomas Sugrue's *The Origins of the Urban Crisis*, which examines the 1967 Detroit riot.[57] Sugrue comprehensively covers the social and economic transformation of Detroit from the 1940s until the 1960s. His study suggests that multiple overlapping circumstances undergird unrest, including deindustrialization, urban renewal, and white suburbanization.

Sugrue demonstrates how these complex and interrelated factors relate to the increased concentration of poverty in particular Black spaces. He shows that the number of Detroit's majority-Black census tracts increased from eight to fifty-five between 1950 and 1960. He also demonstrates that majority-Black areas, compared to more racially integrated areas, were the most impoverished places within each decade. Moreover, he details how inner-city Black ghettos near the downtown grew worse over time. He states, "The convergence of disparate forces of deindustrialization, racial transformation and political ideological conformity laid the groundwork for the urban crisis in Detroit."[58] "The problems of limited housing, racial animosity, and reduced economic opportunity for a segment of the [B]lack population in Detroit had led to embitterment," stresses Sugrue.[59] He argues that these forces over time help to explain why some Black residents ultimately erupted in anger after a late-night police raid of a local bar, the Blind Pig, located in one of Detroit's most impoverished Black ghettos.

In another in-depth investigation of unrest across three major cities, New York, Chicago, and Los Angeles, Janet Abu-Lughod insists on the importance of the spatial and temporal aspects of Black impoverishment.[60] She demonstrates that the West Side of Chicago, where a riot took place in the 1960s, experienced an increase in the concentration of poor Black residents between 1950 and 1960. Abu-Lughod discusses how racial isolation and impoverishment relate to urban renewal and the placement of public housing in and near this community.

Both Sugrue and Abu-Lughod's studies suggest unrest is not solely about a city's Black poverty rate, the size of its Black population, or the rate of contact and competition between different racial and ethnic groups. Rather, ghetto formation and the increased intensity of poverty in particular Black places across several decades is critical. While the intensity of poverty in particular Black communities has multiple sources, including racial segregation, housing and labor market discrimination, and deindustrialization, one of the major forces identified by both authors is urban renewal policies.

Urban Renewal

Urban renewal, the deployment of major U.S. federal and local funds for community, housing, and transportation infrastructure development, has been a major driver of isolation, segregation, and increased poverty concentration in Black neighborhoods since the mid-twentieth century.[61] Between 1949 and 1974, the federal government deployed over $30 billion (in 2000 dollars) in federal resources to city and suburban areas for redevelopment.[62] The urban renewal redevelopment disproportionately affected African American communities. Between 1949 and 1973, urban renewal projects razed over 2,500 neighborhoods, mostly African American communities, in 993 cities.[63] Urban renewal displaced nearly 1.6 million people around the country, primarily African Americans.[64]

Many of those displaced ended up in public housing, packed into existing and expanding Black areas.[65] Thomas Sugrue declares, "The most obvious problem with slum clearance was that it forced the households with the least resources to move at a time when . . . tight housing market[s] could not accommodate them."[66] The razing of neighborhoods and the placement of public housing "intensified the concentration of [B]lacks in some areas, thus increasing racial segregation and poverty."[67] In Chicago, 99 percent of public housing units built after 1955 are located in all-Black neighborhoods.[68] While Chicago is an extreme example of segregation through the placement of public housing in Black communities, it is not an exception. Public housing is used by cities as redevelopment replacement housing, and "Blacks as well as whites were very conscious that the African American population was being warehoused in government-sponsored reservations where they would be out of the way of more affluent Americans."[69] Historians Mark Rose and Raymond Mohl claim, "Interstate highway construction speeded up . . . second-ghetto formation, helping mold the sprawling, densely populated ghettos of the modern American city."[70] Historian Jack Tager declares, "Urban renewal increased the ghettoization of [B]lacks"[71] through what urban renewal critic Jane Jacobs described as "planned slum shifting."[72]

Root Shock

Mindy Fullilove discusses the great "emotional pain" related to urban renewal displacement and slum shifting.[73] Fullilove, a social psychiatrist and urban planning scholar, defines *root shock* as "the traumatic stress reaction to the destruction of all or part of one's emotional ecosystem," such as when social networks are destroyed through urban renewal and displacement.[74] "Root shock undermines trust, increases anxiety, about letting loved ones out of one's sight, destabilizes relationships, destroys social, emotional, and financial resources, and increases the risk for every kind of stress-related disease, from depression to heart attack."[75] Fullilove argues this traumatic experience of root shock stays with individuals and groups for decades and even generations, going beyond the people directly displaced by urban renewal efforts. For African Americans, urban renewal displacement is "a collective complex trauma inflicted on a group of people who share a specific group identify."[76] The loss of one's home through publicly supported displacement is a harmful disruption fueling intense frustrations.

Urban Renewal and Unrest

Urban renewal and unrest are directly connected. Community destruction, displacement, and public housing placement dispensed undue burdens on low-income Black populations. Sociologist Max Herman asserts, "Urban renewal had the effect of driving a wedge through the heart of [the] . . . [B]lack community. As such, urban renewal was a major contributor to the anger . . . that spilled over in the summer of 1967."[77] In line with this assessment, historian Jon Teaford links urban renewal policies with "civil disorders erupting in [B]lack neighborhoods across the nation."[78] He states, "Highway construction and renewal would entail the displacement of thousands of residents and businesses, and many of the displaced were bitter about bearing an undue burden. . . . In cities across the nation, neighborhoods slated for destruction or radical change rose in revolt."[79] Moreover, public housing scholar Lawrence Vale comments, "Slum clearance, urban renewal, and central-city highways . . . sparked lingering resentment in [Black] residential areas."[80]

Displacement causes hardship. Concentrated poverty causes hardship. But these conditions were common in mid-twentieth-century urban America. It likely takes another factor, the increased expectations among African Americans that their conditions would improve, to ignite such intense anger and the uprisings.

Rising Black Expectations

Institutional racism and Black poverty were deeply entrenched in many U.S. cities in the twentieth century; however, unrest only occurred at certain moments. Beyond racism and poverty concentration, the Kerner Report offers an additional explanation as to why riots were ever-present in the 1960s. These elements include "hope," "self-esteem," "uplift," and "rising expectations" among African Americans.[81] "The Negro revolt, like most rebellions, was a fusion of hope, frustration, and solidarity. Rebellion depends on frustrations at the status quo but a belief in the possibility of change," argued Thomas Sugrue.[82]

In the 1960s the civil rights movement was in full swing, and African Americans were achieving important, hard-fought legal and political wins against discrimination. In 1964 the Civil Rights and Economic Opportunity Acts were passed: the former prohibited racial discrimination in public spaces as well in federally funded programs, and the latter addressed individual poverty mainly with employment programs. In 1965 the Voting Rights Act was passed, outlawing racist disenfranchisement practices that had been in place in many Southern states since the end of Reconstruction. The Civil Rights, Economic Opportunity, and Voting Rights Acts were preceded by the landmark 1954 U.S. Supreme Court *Brown v. Board of Education* decision, outlawing racially separate schools, and the 1948 U.S. Supreme Court *Shelley v. Kraemer* ruling, which made racially restrictive covenants on houses unenforceable.[83] These civil rights accomplishments created momentum and raised African American expectations for subsequent policy wins to promote improved Black community conditions.

Sociologist Doug McAdam's book *Political Process and the Development of Black Insurgency* lays out the importance of Black expectations and engagement opportunity in the development of the civil rights movement. He outlines how the "structure of political opportunities" is important to understand social mobilization efforts.[84] He states, "Most fundamentally, such shifts improve the chances of successful social protest by reducing the power discrepancy between insurgent groups and their opponents."[85] Thus, some scholars and policymakers have argued political wins of the 1960s, such as the Civil Rights and Voting Rights Acts, open opportunities and expectations for continued Black success and progress.[86] The Kerner Report noted, "Self-esteem and enhanced racial pride are replacing apathy and submission to 'the system,'"[87] ideas clearly steeped in the Black Power movement.[88]

Yet the paradox is that even with these unprecedented social justice achievements, community circumstances in many Black ghettos declined and activists who arose out of these communities expected Black protests to help make these areas better. In the 1960s, psychologist Kenneth B. Clark, speaking about the general conditions of African Americans in the inner city from the perspective of the individual African American person, declared, "He has been told of great progress in civil rights during the past 10 years and proof of this progress is offered in terms of Supreme Court decisions and civil-rights legislation and firm Presidential commitments. But he sees no positive changes in his day-to-day life."[89] This discrepancy between the promise of change and the realities of worsening community conditions leads to "frustrated hopes."[90] Historian Peter Levy argues that the Great Uprising of the 1960s "was a product of the long civil rights movement, the Great Migration, and the political economy of the postwar era, which raised but left unfulfilled the expectations of [B]lack migrants."[91]

Relative Deprivation

The notion of rising political opportunities and unmet expectations among African Americans points to the relative, rather than absolute, deprivation explanation of unrest. The relative deprivation paradigm explains that unrest was not necessarily the result of extreme poverty, but rather relative economic, social, and political deprivation. Scholars in this camp claim that frustrations fueling unrest derive from the social distance between people's expectations about equality, citizenship, and fairness and their feelings about whether those expectations are being met.[92] As noted, opportunities and expectations for political success among African Americans were on the rise but conditions in many ghettos were declining. The combination of these disjointed dynamics in the face of increasing neighborhood poverty likely led to intense frustrations, especially within a context of ever-present police brutality.

The Police

Police violence is associated with almost every instance of Black unrest in America. Cathy Schneider acknowledges, "Racially targeted police violence inflicts an ugly wound: it undermines the legitimacy of the state and sends the message that the lives of some of its citizens are not valued."[93] Schneider, in *Police Power and Race Riots*, insists, "Most riots begin as nonviolent gatherings and pleas for justice by families, friends, and neighbors of the victims [of police brutality]."[94] In her comparative investigation of the Paris and New York riots, she argues, policing undergirds unrest.

Ghetto residents were agitated by aggressive and abusive police behaviors in addition to what those actions represent. The Kerner Report claims, the "police have come to symbolize white power, white racism, and white repression."[95] In 1966, acclaimed author James Baldwin attested, "Harlem is policed like occupied territory."[96] Moreover, Kenneth Clark pronounced, "When they [the riots] do happen, the oversimplified term 'police brutality' will be heard, but the relationship between the police and residents of the ghetto is more complicated than that. Unquestionably, police brutality occurs . . . And it is certainly true that a common denominator of most, if not all, the riots . . . has been some incident involving the police . . . . The police, rightly or wrongly, are viewed not only as significant agents in exploiting ghetto residents but also as symbols of the pathology which encompasses the ghetto."[97]

Undoubtably, police aggression and abuse relate to the uprisings in Ferguson and Baltimore. Officer Wilson confronted Brown for jaywalking and Gray was taken on a "rough ride," which resulted in his death, for running from the police. Ferguson and Baltimore frustrations are associated with excessive, aggressive, and unjust police behaviors.[98] Policing in underserved low-income Black communities must be part of any unrest analysis; nonetheless, we must go beyond policing to understand how policies displace people and shape the contours of the constructed and chronic Black ghettos.[99]

Situational Factors

While several scholars focus on how abusive police actions explain unrest,[100] others narrow in on specific situational factors taking place during peaceful protests. Sociologist Anne Nassauer argues most revolts can be explicated by immediate situational factors occurring during peaceful protests.[101] Nassauer completed a situational analysis of Ferguson and Baltimore after Brown and Gray's deaths. She highlights escalating signaling behaviors as unrest instigators, such as the presence of tanks and tear gas, and miscommunication between police and protesters.

Nassauer's analysis is insightful but incomplete. Her analysis provides little understanding of what brought on abusive policing in the first place. Nor does she explain why so many protesters gathered on the streets following the police-provoked killings. Furthermore, her situational analysis fails to elucidate how public policies over time shape community conditions of deprivation and inequality that often undergird tensions following police aggression.

Broader Political Economy of Unrest

To achieve a more contextualized unrest analysis, I incorporate aspects of *The Flashpoints Model of Public Disorder*.[102] David Waddington, the British scholar who developed the flashpoints unrest paradigm, recognizes "the need to go beyond the immediate dynamics of the crowd and consider the broader context within which particular disorderly events are situated."[103] His paradigm assumes riots are the product of immediate and contextual factors.[104] In their 2016 book, Matthew Moran and David Waddington argue that "any attempt to analyze such complicated . . . social phenomena in terms of 'single factor' explanations (e.g., unemployment, 'relative deprivation', or poor police-community relations) is certain to prove unsatisfactory."[105]

The flashpoint approach is a multilevel, multivariate framework to determine why some peaceful protests devolve into unrest across different localities. It includes six integrated levels of analysis moving from more macro to micro circumstances surrounding unrest incidents. Flashpoint scholars incorporate a structural approach to identify "sources of collective grievance," such as poverty, unemployment, relative deprivation, inequality, powerlessness, and limited life chances.[106] The flashpoint perspective urges a complex political assessment of how institutions, such as national and local government agencies, influence attitudes and actions that vilify disenfranchised and excluded groups. It also encourages scholars to assess how cultural differences between conflicting groups emerged over time and are legacies of historical contexts.[107] This comprehensive historical approach goes way beyond assessing immediate situational factors.

An Urban Renewal Unrest Approach

I borrow from several theories to construct my *urban renewal unrest framework*. My approach is heavily influenced by the prior unrest literature, my neighborhood research, and contemporary urban dynamics and patterns. In 2008, I wrote *The New Urban Renewal*.[108] This book investigates the multiple dynamics connected with the economic revitalization of Harlem in New York City and Bronzeville on the South Side of Chicago, two iconic African American communities that suffered from disinvestment and decline for over fifty years. I trace how, in the 1990s and 2000s, major federal community development and housing policies, such as Empowerment Zones (EZs) and Housing Opportunities for People Everywhere (HOPE VI), as well as city programs, such as Tax Increment Financing (TIF), changed the economic trajectories of these communities in the late 1990s and early and mid-2000s.

In the 2000s, the economic upswing in Harlem and Bronzeville extended to several other historic Black neighborhoods throughout the country. While only 9 percent of low-income census tracts in the fifty most populated U.S. cities gentrified in the 1990s with rising property values, income, and education levels, 20 percent gentrified in the 2000s.[109] The redevelopment of low-income, African American communities occurred in Boston, New York, Philadelphia, Baltimore, Pittsburgh, Washington, DC, Charlottesville, Richmond, Durham, Charlotte, Cincinnati, Atlanta, Nashville, Miami, New Orleans, St. Louis, Chicago, Oklahoma City, Minneapolis, Houston, Austin, Los Angeles, San Francisco, Oakland, Seattle, and Portland.[110]

I label this widespread African American redevelopment pattern the "new urban renewal phase," and compare it to African American redevelopment patterns and displacement outcomes witnessed during the old urban renewal period of the 1940s, 1950s, and 1960s.[111]

While place-based urban development policies of the 1990s, like EZ, HOPE VI, and TIF, attempted to eliminate spatial concentrations of racial disadvantage,[112] in reality these legislative acts facilitated Black displacement not seen since the old urban renewal period of the mid-twentieth century.[113] Housing scholar Edward Goetz estimates that between 1990 and 2000 nearly 250,000 people, mainly African Americans, were displaced due to public housing demolitions facilitated by the HOPE VI program. Goetz claims, "The HOPE VI program swept in for another round of clearance in many of the same neighborhoods that had experienced urban renewal a half century earlier. The numbers quite clearly indicate that the current round of demolition and the HOPE VI program in particular has been an updated version of Negro Removal."[114]

Many redeveloping African American neighborhoods also experienced an influx of subprime loans, facilitating more Black displacement when these unsustainable mortgages defaulted.[115] The Great Recession, as well as its foreclosure fallout, was associated with the removal of an estimated seven to twelve million families from their homes due to foreclosed mortgage loans.[116] A disproportionate number of these families were of color as subprime loans and the resulting forecloses were heavily concentrated in Black and Brown communities.[117] The foreclosure fallout stripped African Americans of substantial wealth gains from the prior fifty years, turning the Great Recession into "the Great Black Depression."[118] The Great Recession made precarious African American communities even more economically vulnerable.[119] Sociologist Saskia Sassen labels this extreme level of disruption the great "economic violence" of expulsion.[120]

Prior to the 2014 and 2015 uprisings, there were also increased levels of Black displacement in the rental market. Sociologist Matthew Desmond and his Eviction Lab staff estimate that in 2010 there were over 990,000 families evicted from their rental apartments nationwide, while in 2000 this figure stood at just over 518,000 families.[121] Government place-based redevelopment policies, mortgage market turmoil, and rental market chaos ripped apart African American neighborhoods and displaced people on a level not seen since the old urban renewal period.

Forced displacement associated with HOPE VI, gentrification, and the Great Recession has detrimental health effects and disproportionately affects African Americans.[122] Edward Goetz states, "The forced removal of a household from its home is one of the most intrusive exercises of state power. The disruption to families is significant and the sense of loss, loss of home, of community, of a sense of identity and belonging can be profound."[123] Historian Robert Gioielli insists, "Being forced to move and losing a home, a neighborhood, and a community can cause significant mental trauma."[124] Furthermore, Susan Saegert and her colleagues claim that the recent wave of foreclosures is another form of ongoing "displacement for African American households," which has "negative implications for the health of individuals and groups, within generations as well as across generations."[125]

Residential displacement during the old urban renewal of the 1940s and 1950s was associated with the unrest of the 1960s;[126] however, few researchers connect modern accelerated gentrification and displacement rates in the last three decades to contemporary unrest.[127] Dikeç, in his 2017 book *Urban Rage*, argues that gentrification, with the associated African American displacement, is an important trauma that "escalat[es] [racial] tension" and modern unrest in America.[128] I expand Dikeç's revolt analysis by linking past and more recent urban renewal policies and Black displacement to unrest.

Lawrence Vale's 2013 work *Purging the Poorest* was one of the first major studies to link processes and consequences associated with the old and new urban renewal periods. He assesses racial inequities and changing American values around low-income individuals and communities by examining the political processes and consequences associated with twice-cleared, low-income communities of color. Twice-cleared, low-income minority communities were affected by the construction of public housing and highways in the 1940s, 1950s, and 1960s, and then decades later by the demolition of public housing in the 1990s and 2000s. Vale argues that "design politics" are key to understanding twice-cleared, low-income communities. By design politics, Vale refers to urban redevelopment decisions that removed "sites and sights," a "cleaning out of things" and a "reimaging" of urban communities once perceived to be mired in poverty.[129] Vale posited that "twice-cleared communities" and their surrounding areas represent a "kind of double gentrification often on the very same sites."[130]

Vale's understanding of twice-cleared communities relates to *serial displacement*. Mindy Fullilove and Rodrick Wallace define serial displacement as "the repetitive, coercive upheaval of groups."[131] Fullilove and Wallace trace how African Americans have been displaced and forced to different neighborhoods throughout Pittsburgh's history. For these authors, serial displacement is a form of "structural violence," mainly brought on by federal and local policies, that has severe health consequences. The authors claim, "At present, a persistent policy of serial forced displacement of African Americans has created a persistent de facto internal refugee population that expresses characteristic behavioral and health patterns. These include raised levels of violence, family disintegration, substance abuse, sexually transmitted disease, and so on. These harms are evidently a result of the cumulative effects—including high levels of stress—of multiple displacements."[132] I assume displacement to be a historic

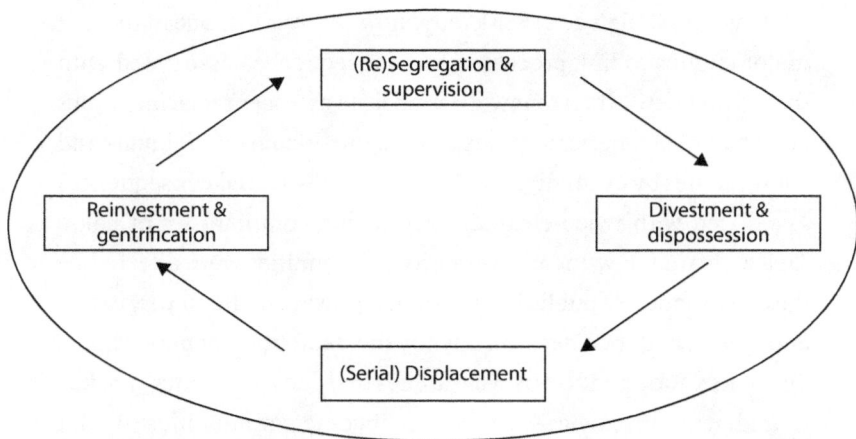

FIGURE 3. Cycle of racial and spatial repression.

and harmful process of slow violence that contributes to fueling frustrations, setting an important context for understanding contemporary unrest.[133] As public health scholar Lawrence Brown notes, "Historical trauma is not a bygone novelty. It is an ongoing reality."[134]

Building on the work of Fullilove and Vale, and coinciding with Dikeç's unrest approach, I assess public policies prior to, during, and after the Great Recession that accelerated gentrification, displacement rates, and frustrations. The rise in the churn in low-income Black neighborhoods, otherwise known as gentrification, displacement, and dispossession, partly drives the subsequent burn, the revolts. I advance Dikeç's contemporary unrest assessment by examining the relationships among neighborhood inequality, frustrations, and unrest over time and across multiple levels of analysis and geographies.[135] I link the old urban renewal to the current round of urban renewal and place our modern policing and unrest within an important historic, serial Black displacement context. I also undertake a broader Great Recession analysis to ground the Ferguson and Baltimore unrest cases within the nation's economic context. By conducting a temporal, multilevel, comparative analysis of unrest, I offer new insights on how the ongoing cycle of racial and spatial repression through segregation, divestment, displacement, and gentrification relates to our contemporary, Black-led rebellions (figure 3).[136] This cycle breeds chronic displacement trauma that gets buried until sudden violence, the police killings, brings the repressed anger to the surface on the streets.

II *Linking Slow and Sudden Violence*

2   *Segregation, Divestment, and Serial Displacement*

Ferguson must be understood in the context of that larger St. Louis geography and the history of its development.

Washington University in St. Louis Public Health
professor JASON PURNELL

Policies of *slow violence* have segregated, exploited, and expunged Black communities for over one hundred years in the St. Louis region.[1] Some African American settlements, like the Pruitt-Igoe Homes, were literally blasted into oblivion. Shockwaves reverberate from explosions and can become embedded in the people's collective family traditions, souls, and psyches.[2] The traumatic scars of serial displacement are often suppressed as people move on and struggle to maintain themselves and their families within a highly racialized and discriminatory context. But occasionally, a moment like the shooting of Michael Brown surfaces repressed feelings and frustrations.[3] Clinical psychologist Cheryle Grills and her colleagues claim: "Killings by White people of young Black men unearth deepseated, long-neglected, and often denied feelings of hurt, anger, helplessness, frustration, and injustice."[4]

The pain of Brown's death activated individual and collective memories, frustrations, and traumas across time and space from people who had been hurt for generations in the St. Louis region by slow violence and the politics of racial inequality. The pain from poverty concentration, Black community destruction, and serial displacement converged on a single municipality. This was the Ferguson uprising moment, and it was a regional revolt against institutional racism.

While there is a long history of "policing strategies aimed at controlling and monitoring the locations and behaviors of [B]lacks,"[5] one must go beyond policing to conceptualize the mounting frustrations that concentrated in Ferguson. This chapter explains the background and housing and community development policy context that led to the Ferguson uprising. Ferguson's unrest was driven by old and new urban (and suburban) renewal policies associated with Black serial displacement. Over time, economic and housing policy decisions at multiple levels drove Black poverty to different disadvantaged locations throughout the St. Louis region. These redevelopment dynamics were witnessed in other cities, but in St. Louis, segregation, divestment, and reinvestment destroyed African American communities. The culmination of systematic, state-sanctioned, slow violence, defined as racialized policies supporting segregation, divestment, and displacement, is a critical context to understand the eruption of chronic frustrations in Ferguson.

Ongoing Black Community Destruction and Serial Displacement

St. Louis has a long history of segregating its Black residents and conducting serial displacement in the name of economic progress.[6] Historian Walter Johnson laments: "Black St. Louisans have been repeatedly driven out: from East St. Louis in 1917; from the riverfront, Deep Morgan, Chestnut Valley, and Mill Creek Valley in the middle years of the century; from Pruitt-Igoe in 1972; and from whatever neighborhoods were wanted for 'economic development' down to the present day."[7] In St. Louis, Black communities were repeatedly destroyed.

In other segregated cities, iconic African American neighborhoods, like Harlem in New York City, the Hill in Pittsburgh, Bronzeville in Chicago, U Street in Washington, DC, and Sweet Auburn in Atlanta, still exist;[8] but St. Louis's historic Black communities are gone.[9] St. Louis historian John A. Wright Sr. acknowledges that several of the city's Black communities "have been forced into extinction."[10] Longtime St. Louis organizer and cofounder of the Organization for Black Struggle Jamala Rogers attests that white, elite city actors were intentional in their pursuit "to dismantle, to disrupt, dislocate the history, culture and institutions of African Americans."[11] Dr. Rev. F. Willis Johnson, who led Ferguson's Wellspring Church for over seven years, claims that the region's Black displacement and resulting community destruction was "damning, disrespectful, and dehumanizing."[12]

In St. Louis and its surrounding region, white leaders have used housing and community development policies to antagonize African Americans, chase them out of spaces, and then corral and contain them in different disadvantaged neighborhoods, only to displace them again. This systematic, state-sanctioned development process left St. Louis's Black community without a historic home. This past redevelopment context of serial displacement and chronic displacement trauma is critical for understanding the Ferguson revolt.

From the South to Segregated St. Louis

Black people have inhabited St. Louis, the "Gateway City," at least since its founding in 1764.[13] Early on, St. Louis's downtown was considered a "Creole village."[14] A Creole person descends from a mix of Spanish, French, and/or African or West Indies ancestors. Since the Mississippi River connects St. Louis to New Orleans, and the Spanish and French once controlled both territories, city inhabitants had a variety of heritages with a mélange of hues.[15] While some people of color were free in early St. Louis, many were enslaved.[16]

St. Louis, Missouri, was one of the country's border cities. Missouri entered the United States as part of the Missouri Compromise of 1820; it entered allowing the enslavement of people, and Maine denied slavery. St. Louis bordered Illinois, a free state, so it was considered a "border city" because it was an oppressive place near where many Blacks lived free from enslavement.[17]

This riverfront city in Missouri had cruel and exploitative race relations like the rest of the country and denied basic human rights to enslaved Blacks. In 1846, enslaved man Dred Scott sued his enslaver for his freedom in the St. Louis circuit court as he was forced to work across the Mississippi River in the free state of Illinois.[18] Prior to the Dred Scott case, enslaved people who could verify they were forced to work in bondage in free states were freed. In fact, the St. Louis court initially ruled in favor of Dred Scott; however, in an appeal the U.S. Supreme Court ruled that enslaved people, like Scott, "of African origin were not full human beings and had no rights of citizenship."[19] Thus, with no citizenship rights, Scott could not bring a legal case against his enslaver. This devastating federal court ruling explicitly stated that the U.S. government did not view enslaved people as humans.[20] The logic behind this ruthless decision embedded itself in St. Louis's psyche, and it eventually infected the region's racist community redevelopment policies.

From 1865 to 1900, St. Louis had an economic boom and became the fourth largest city in the United States;[21] as the city's overall population grew, it became increasingly African American.[22] Following the Civil War and emancipation, formerly enslaved people journeyed to St. Louis during the city's "Golden Age" for dignified work and to escape the racism of the Deep South.[23] Historian Charles Lumpkins notes, "Many [B]lack people left plantation districts, like the Mississippi Delta region, where they experienced grinding poverty and repressive planter rule."[24] During the 1860s St. Louis's African American population increased by 600 percent and continued to grow in the later part of the nineteenth century.[25] The once small commercial trading post along the Mississippi became an economic powerhouse with ample industrial and service labor opportunities for African Americans.

However, overt racism still loomed large over this "southern" Midwest city. In July 1877, a national railroad workers' strike became a formidable force in St. Louis as a multiracial and -ethnic industrial group of German, Irish, and African Americans formed across different city economic sectors.[26] Nearly sixty city factories shut down during the weeklong strike. African Americans also had several prominent speaking roles during two large, peaceful gatherings. African American visibility during the strike "was a challenge to the social order that paralleled and even exceeded the white workers' challenge to the economic order."[27]

The local media began fanning the fuel of racial hatred and fear by printing strike stories featuring race-baiting stereotypes of Black people. Inflammatory and racially biased language including "demons," "blood-curdling," and "dangerous-looking" described Black protesters.[28] One reporter declared Black strike organizers were planning to lead Black mobs to "strike terror" throughout the city.[29] Reacting to this racial rhetoric, the white-led St. Louis Workingmen's Party called off subsequent rallies and the labor movement's momentum was greatly diminished. With the demise of the labor strike's movement, the racial and economic hierarchy of St. Louis was restored and maintained.

One year later, a group of white elite business and civic leaders established the annual Veiled Prophet parade. The parade provided a vehicle for business leaders to "assert control over the St. Louis streets in response to the strike of 1877."[30] The parade featured a fictitious character, the Veiled Prophet, who served as the city's protector from its working-class "rabble."[31] Each year a male civic leader was selected as the Veiled Prophet.

A rendering of the Veiled Prophet features a towering figure wearing a white sheet, with a white face covering and cone hat, holding a shotgun in one hand and pistol in the another.[32] The Veiled Prophet's outfit resembles the dress of a high-ranking Ku Klux Klan member. Fittingly for a southern show of racial dominance, the first selected prophet was St. Louis Police Commissioner John G. Priest, who was recognized for his role in preserving St. Louis's racial order. The Veiled Prophet parade and ball, events steeped in appeals to white-elite racism, have been held annually since 1878.[33]

Despite St. Louis's difficult racial conditions, African Americans continued to move to the city.[34] In 1920, St. Louis had the eighth largest number of African Americans at 69,854. By 1930, African Americans were 11 percent of the city's population.[35] Near the end of World War II, over 100,000 African Americans lived in the city (13 percent of the population).[36] By 1956, there were 180,000 African Americans in St. Louis (over 20 percent of the city's population).[37]

The African American population was critical to the economy of one of the country's most important industrial, chemical, and manufacturing hubs.[38] Black men primarily worked in industrial and construction jobs and as longshoremen along the Mississippi. African American women worked in food processing and manufacturing plants and as housekeepers and wait staff.[39] While the work (and pay) was better than employment opportunities in the Deep South in some instances, African Americans were at the bottom of the city's social and economic hierarchy and experienced workplace and wage inequality. African Americans competed with Irish and German immigrants for their place in the St. Louis region.

The 1917 East St. Louis Riot

Migrating from the Deep South did not prevent Black people from experiencing overt and deadly racism in the North. When they competed with other ethnic and racial groups for employment, conflict sometimes erupted. In the industrial North, African Americans occasionally served as replacement workers when labor unions went on strike. In East St. Louis, Illinois, on May 28, 1917, a group of white Central Trades and Labor Union representatives met with the East St. Louis mayor and demanded that Black workers not be used as strikebreakers in the city. During the meeting people shouted, "East St. Louis must remain a white man's town." Over the next several days, "As many as three thousand whites took to the streets, dragging Black men off of streetcars and beating those whom they found on the street."[40] One person reported, "I saw man after man, with his hands raised pleading for his life, surrounded by groups of men . . . who knew nothing about him except that he was [B]lack—and saw them administer the historic [and horrible] sentence of intolerance, death by stoning."[41] African American women were also brutally stoned and babies were shot in the head.[42] During the 1917 riots and massacre, the official count of carnage was thirty-nine African Americans and eight whites killed and three hundred African American homes burned.[43] This is almost surely an underestimate, with some calculations placing the death of African Americans close to five hundred.[44]

The violent attack in East St. Louis forced seven thousand African Americans west across the Mississippi River to St. Louis, Missouri.[45] Black people settled in St. Louis's segregated and burgeoning African American communities, like Mill Creek Valley, and in more rural suburban areas including what would become Kinloch, one of the nation's first Black-governed municipalities on the northwestern outskirts of St. Louis.[46] This violence against African Americans was a sudden erasure of Black life in East St. Louis, but across the river the African American dispossession, displacement, and death were not so swift. For this "genteel" southern city, slow violence mostly persisted over the use of pistols.

Segregation and Redlining

Today, St. Louis is one of the nation's most segregated cities. As African Americans became an increasing proportion of the city's population, segregation increased. Between 1910 and 1940, the dissimilarity index, a measure ranging from 0 to 100 of separation between nonwhites (which in St. Louis are mostly Black people) and whites, increased from 54 to 92.[47] A score of 92 indicates almost complete residential separation between the two racial groups. Architecture scholar Catalina Freixas and urban historian Mark Abbott describe the intensity of St. Louis's hypersegregation: "Although racism and segregation plague all American cities, St. Louis is a case study in how segregation is like a cancer that eats at the soul of the metropolis."[48] In 2010, St. Louis's Black/white dissimilarity index was 70, the ninth highest in the nation (figure 4).[49] Most African Americans live in the northern part of the city and county.

St. Louis's high degree of segregation was a direct result of policy decisions.[50] In 1916, St. Louis voters approved an ordinance advocated by the local real estate industry that barred African Americans from purchasing a house or renting on blocks that were 75 percent white (and vice versa).[51] The ordinance passed with 52,220 approval votes and 17,877 in opposition.[52] In 1917, the U.S. Supreme Court's *Buchanan v. Warley* decision deemed this racialized zoning unconstitutional, but this did little to end racial segregation in St. Louis.[53] Segregation was maintained through restrictive deed covenants barring property owners from selling or renting to African Americans.[54]

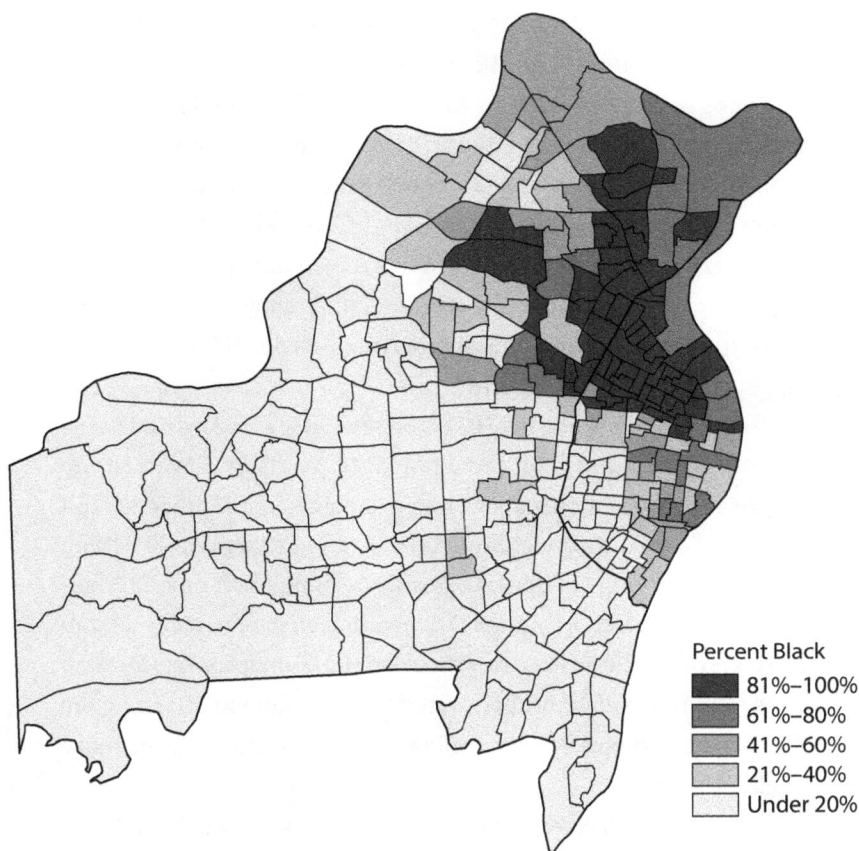

FIGURE 4. Segregation in the St. Louis region, 2010. Source: U.S. Census/designed by Meagan Snow.

As a result, most African Americans lived in the few St. Louis communities without restrictive covenants.[55] Historian Clarence Lang notes, "Although scattered in pockets across the city, most African Americans occupied the city's Central Corridor, where they crowded the northern fringes of the downtown business district and the three wards nearest the central riverfront."[56] Other African American areas included Mill Creek Valley, a working-class section of the city just west of downtown, and the Ville, a Black, middle-class community in the city's northern section.[57]

These segregated African American neighborhoods were economically underserved and divested, partly due to national housing finance policy. In 1933, the Roosevelt administration created the Home Owners Loan Corporation (HOLC) to help refinance loans and lower the monthly payments for borrowers at risk of default during the Great Depression.[58] At the time, unemployment rates were above 30 percent and millions of Americans needed this government support to prevent foreclosures.

To lend on this scale, the HOLC created new standardized home loan underwriting and appraisal practices. The HOLC worked nationwide with local home appraisers to create neighborhood default risk maps. The HOLC neighborhood risk rating system was based on housing density, age of housing stock, and population mix.[59] Neighborhoods were rated A through D depending on their perceived lending risk level.[60] The best, A, was green on HOLC maps, while D-rated areas were red. Neighborhoods rated D were redlined, meaning the HOLC would typically deny refinancing applications from those neighborhoods.

The HOLC risk categories were racially biased and aligned very closely to the racial makeup of neighborhoods. A 1937 HOLC St. Louis map illustrated the relationship between race and neighborhood rating scores.[61] The HOLC surveyors rated many white urban and suburban areas A, while communities containing African Americans were rated C or D. "All the residential sections along the Mississippi River or adjacent to the central business district [where African Americans lived] received one of the two lowest ratings. . . . Any Afro-American presence was a source of substantial concern to the HOLC."[62] Even communities with "small proportions of [B]lack inhabitants were usually rated . . . 'hazardous'" for investments.[63]

HOLC's racialized neighborhood risk assessment system institutionalized economic inequality between Black and white areas.[64] Consequently, residents of African American neighborhoods were unable to access home loans. The Federal Housing Administration (FHA), which effectively replaced the HOLC as the primary government facilitator of mortgage lending in the 1940s, 1950s, and 1960s, adopted HOLC's neighborhood risk rating system. From the 1930s until the 1960s, Black neighborhoods were redlined by the federal government and private lenders, and their residents did not receive equal credit access, compared to white neighborhoods. Nationally, "between 1945 and 1959, less than 2 percent of all federally insured home loans went to African Americans."[65]

This federal policy of redlining had huge consequences for African Americans in the St. Louis region. "Of 70,000 housing units built in the City of St. Louis and in St. Louis County between 1947 and 1952, fewer than thirty-five were available to African Americans, whether because of FHA policy, restrictive covenants, or the policy of the real estate industry," notes segregation scholar Richard Rothstein.[66] Furthermore, "Out of 400,000 FHA mortgages made in the St. Louis metro area between 1962 and 1967, only 3.3% went to [B]lack borrowers. For [B]lack borrowers in St. Louis County, that figure dropped to below 1%," documents fair housing law professor Rigel Oliveri.[67] The HOLC and FHA's underwriting practices institutionalized racial disinvestment and neighborhood inequality in the segregated St. Louis region.

African American Achievements in St. Louis

African Americans in St. Louis attained economic, cultural, and political achievements despite a caste-like racial hierarchy maintained by segregation.[68] African American education was central, and St. Louis had some of the country's earliest and best, yet segregated, public schools.[69] The city's burgeoning Black professional, middle-, and working-class populations were very politically active, and Black men and women participated in civil life, labor strikes, and affordable housing reform movements.[70] African Americans in St. Louis gained political freedoms that remained elusive in the Deep South, and their persistent advocacy against white racism "put St. Louis on the proverbial map as a site for transformative [B]lack working class struggles."[71]

Much of these Black achievements spawned from segregated communities. African American enclaves, ranked C or D by the HOLC—Deep Morgan,[72] Mill Creek Valley, and the Ville—had Black-run financial firms, hospitals, law offices, restaurants, musical venues, newspapers, civic groups, schools, religious institutions, and political organizations.[73] Some notable St. Louis African Americans from these neighborhoods included Maya Angelou, Josephine Baker, Chuck Berry, Blanche K. Bruce, Redd Foxx, Percy Green, Dick Gregory, Scott Joplin, John Berry Meachum, Hiram H. Revels, Tina Turner, and Roy Wilkins.[74] In segregated Black neighborhoods, African American contributed much to the social, economic, cultural, and political lifeblood of St. Louis and the nation.

However, almost nothing remains of these historic Black communities. St. Louis was distinct, compared to other cities, in the harshness of its urban renewal redevelopment policies that ripped apart and destroyed African American communities repeatedly throughout the twentieth century. In St. Louis, slow violence, in the form of community destruction and serial displacement, contributed to and maintained stark racial neighborhood inequality.

The "Old" Urban Renewal: Displacement, Dispossession, and Disrespect

Most historians bookend the old urban renewal period between the late 1940s and early 1970s,[75] but in St. Louis this redevelopment era began much sooner. In the 1920s, St. Louis's white political and business leaders realized the city was developing more slowly than rival municipalities such as Chicago and Cleveland.[76] Once the fourth largest U.S. city, St. Louis had dropped to sixth by 1920 and to seventh by 1930.[77] The city was experiencing some effects of early-twentieth-century deindustrialization, and local real estate boosters and planners looked for ways to stimulate industrial economic and population growth.[78] To accomplish this, they first focused on redeveloping the low-income, "blighted" neighborhoods near downtown and along the waterfront—D-rated African American neighborhoods.[79]

From the Creole Village to the Arch

St. Louis's most famous landmark is the Gateway Arch. It is the nation's tallest monument at 630 feet.[80] This impressive 886-ton stainless steel structure stands on 82 acres of parkland near the banks of the Mississippi River. The monument commemorates white settlement of the "West" (and the decimation of Indigenous populations).[81] Lewis and Clark began their legendary Corps of Discovery Expedition in 1805 from St. Louis.[82] To add insult to injury, African Americans were displaced to construct this monument.

The Arch project began St. Louis's twentieth-century process of state-financed African American serial displacement. The Arch's development displaced people of color from downtown and served as an early example of American-style urban renewal that dispossessed and dispersed African Americans from spaces considered valuable city land. "The development of the Gateway Arch reflected local leaders' efforts to reorder downtown urban space to encourage economic and social stability in St. Louis in the face of accelerating inner-city disinvestment, white flight, and ghettoization," declare scholars Joseph Heathcott and Máire Agnes Murphy.[83] Arch historian Tracy Campbell summarizes a memo written by one downtown

FIGURE 5. Cleared area for the Arch. Creative Commons/Jefferson National Expansion Memorial Archives.

engineer and planner to St. Louis's Mayor Dickmann: "Slums, and their mostly African American inhabitants, could be moved elsewhere, and in their place something beautiful could be built."[84]

Local and federal governments funded the racialized "house-cleaning" along the St. Louis waterfront (figure 5).[85] A controversial 1935 city bond referendum secured the initial funds to acquire and clear the thirty-seven-block site, which was an industrial, commercial, and Black residential area.[86] The federal government provided a three-to-one local dollar match for a $9 million commitment.[87] To complete the Arch, millions more would be needed. Alongside city leaders, St. Louis urban planner Harland Bartholomew lobbied Missouri's state capital politicians to increase the city's debt ceiling from

5 percent to 10 percent. With the city's debt ceiling raised, city voters passed a more substantial $76 million bond issuance to keep redevelopment dollars flowing into the memorial project.[88]

In 1939, the city cleared the prime waterfront site. By 1941, all of the site structures had been reduced to rubble.[89] While the residents and over 290 businesses, which employed over five thousand workers, were cleared out, the land remained undeveloped for almost twenty years due in part to the demands of World War II.[90] In 1945, the city finally returned to making what had become a large parking lot into a park and memorial. Ultimately nearly $33 million in federal funds and an additional $3.5 million in city resources were allocated for the completion of the Arch and Museum of Westward Expansion.[91]

Eero Saarinen's enormous steel arch, an architectural feat, was finished in 1965. It was a symbol of engineering innovation but also of racial and spatial inequality.[92] Historian Tracy Campbell declares, "Bankers and real estate companies profited from the condemnation of the riverfront district, while tenants and small businesses suffered."[93] One of the city's liveliest racially diverse sections along the waterfront was gone. "The site of the Creole village was . . . buried," laments historian James Primm.[94]

Millions of people visit the Arch each year.[95] They ride small tram-like cars up the Arch's legs to its apex. The Arch's top offers a magnificent downtown view. South is Busch Stadium, the home of the St. Louis Cardinals baseball team, west is the famous Old St. Louis Courthouse, where Dred Scott's case was heard, and to the north are a convention center and a giant dome stadium, the former home of the now Los Angeles Rams football team.[96]

The Arch also includes an impressive forty-two-thousand-square-foot underground museum space.[97] The museum contains huge visual displays of the city's early history and the Arch's developmental design and construction journey. It also includes some of Saarinen's initial arch sketches. However, the exhibit barely mentions the Creole village. Display pictures demonstrate the massive removal of a significant number of buildings to clear the way for the Arch. Tourists receive a sanitized story about the demolished structures without mention of the neighborhood's social features and structure. That history, just like the physical community, has been buried.

Few leaving the museum learn that the Arch's development destroyed a Black community or that the development politics of the Arch set in motion more state-sanctioned African American removal.[98] Richard Atkins, a St. Louis architect and graduate of Howard University, states, "In St. Louis we never face things head on . . . we never talk about St. Louis's racial legacy. . . . We deny it. . . . As a result, here in St. Louis, we just break out and fight."[99]

Racial Politics of Redevelopment

The progrowth coalition that ruled over St. Louis in the mid-twentieth century learned from the Arch's development process that publicly funded Black displacement was a viable redevelopment strategy. From 1949 to 1965, the white-dominated "redevelopment coalition" of elected officials included Democratic mayors Joseph Darst and Raymond Tucker, powerful bureaucrats like Harland Bartholomew and Charles Farris, and business elites, including Arthur Blumeyer of the Bank of St. Louis, August A. Busch Jr. of Anheuser-Busch, William McDonnell of McDonnell Aircraft, and Edgar M. Queeny of Monsanto Chemical. This coalition ruled over St. Louis, formalizing its power in 1953 into an organization known as Civic Progress, Inc.[100] The organization advocated for the deployment of public and private funds to redevelop St. Louis's urban core.[101] For these white economic stakeholders, actions and decisions centered on "bolstering the long-term tax and wage base of the city at any cost," which often meant eradicating "blighted" Black neighborhoods.[102] St. Louis's white real estate and corporate interests took the stance of "take it, tear it down, and bury the memory" of Black communities.[103]

St. Louis's progrowth coalition lobbied for state incentives to stimulate downtown redevelopment. Two Missouri laws, the Chapter 353 Urban Redevelopment Act of 1945 and the Chapter 99 Land Clearance Act of 1951, created the legal framework to use eminent domain to seize properties for "public" redevelopment purposes.[104] More importantly, these state laws provided a series of "tax abatement for property owners in renewal areas and an allowance for out-of-state investment . . . in [local] redevelopment corporations," like the soon-to-be-formed St. Louis Land Clearance for Redevelopment Authority (LCRA).[105] St. Louis's growth coalition led several massive redevelopment projects using 1949 and 1954 Housing Acts federal renewal funds, resulting in substantial Black displacement.[106]

Mill Creek Valley to Industrial Valley

The next major Black enclave to be razed and redeveloped after the Arch area was Mill Creek Valley, a Black community just west of downtown.[107] Many African Americans arriving in St. Louis during the first wave of the Great Migrations settled in the largely restrictive covenant–free Mill Creek Valley.[108] The community was home to important Black institutions including the Pine Street YMCA, the Wheatley YWCA, and the People's Hospital and individuals such as internationally known entertainer Josephine Baker and civil rights activist and National Association for the Advancement of Colored People (NAACP) executive director Roy Wilkins.[109] Even though this area was redlined, it contained over eight hundred businesses, institutions, and organizations, many of which were Black-led and owned.[110]

In 1959, with $7 million in local bond funding and $21 million from the federal government, the city's LCRA razed over 465 acres in Mill Creek Valley and sold the cleared and assembled parcels to real estate developers.[111] Over 5,630 units were removed, most containing African American families and businesses.[112] The city converted most of Mill Creek Valley into an industrial area, while the southern part of it became U.S. Highway 40.[113]

Like many American cities, St. Louis destroyed an important African American neighborhood for highway construction and light industrial development;[114] however, unlike other places, no traces of the former Black community remain.[115] Historian Keona Ervin declares, "The destruction of Mill Creek Valley meant that African American families lost homes, businesses, and community institutions; an area that once had been a hub for working-class life was destroyed by this forced dispersal."[116] Just like the Creole village, the entire Mill Creek African American community disappeared.

Black displacement, destruction, and disillusionment are essential elements of St. Louis's mid-twentieth-century urban redevelopment. The city became known for "ripping itself apart."[117] Between 1950 and 1970, St. Louis's urban renewal programs displaced approximately twenty thousand families or seventy-five thousand individuals, nearly 10 percent of the city's 1960 population.[118] While a small portion of those displaced were white, the African American population carried "a disproportionate burden of revitalization efforts in the 1950s and 1960s . . . [that] decimated their neighborhoods."[119] The urban renewal, in Colin Gordon's words, "was pushing people around at great public expense with little public benefit." [120] St. Louis activist Ivory Perry calls the situation "[B]lack removal with white approval."[121]

Intraracial Class Conflict and White Maneuvering for the Land Grab

While some viewed the city's redevelopment policies as "[B]lack removal with white approval," sometimes these efforts had elite African American support.[122] For instance, the *Argus*, a leading St. Louis

Black newspaper, backed the first bond issuance for the waterfront removal in 1935.[123] Elite African Americans were equivocal about redevelopment. Even though redevelopment projects often led to Black displacement, some leaders thought these deals would stimulate job creation that could eventually reduce Black unemployment. Black activists were also fighting for adequate affordable housing, and redevelopment plans were often paired with replacement public housing set aside for African Americans. Consequently, some Black leaders perceived job growth and affordable housing connected to redevelopment initiatives as ways to uplift the underserved Black community.

In the 1950s, Frankie Muse Freeman, an African American woman, Howard University graduate, and NAACP lawyer, sued the SLHA for segregating St. Louis housing project residents.[124] In 1955, a federal judge ruled in Freeman's favor and SLHA was forced to desegregate its public housing. This was a major win for the city's equal housing rights advocates.

Then in an ironic twist, SLHA hired Freeman as the general counsel of the St. Louis LCRA. At the time, the SLHA and LCRA were essentially one organization: they combined their efforts to raze and redevelop much of St. Louis's low- and moderate-income, central city African American communities.[125] In essence, Freeman joined the white power brokers' effort to displace thousands of low-income African Americans. St. Louis historian Clarence Lang states, "Relationships among St. Louis's African American population have always been deep and multiple, particularly among its political leadership. But with class stratification growing . . . the community had become more complex" and divided.[126]

Intraracial class divisions in St. Louis's African American population were evident in the 1957 debates concerning a white-led proposal to change the city's charter. The plan called for reducing the number of ward-elected city aldermen from twenty-eight to seven, a move that would greatly reduce Black political influence and remove resistance to Black neighborhood redevelopment and displacement plans. President Ernest Calloway of the NAACP St. Louis branch called the 1957 charter reform an "attempt to amputate present and potential Negro representation."[127] The plan would have reduced Black power and strengthened the "political authority of local banking and business leaders," who supported downtown development and Black displacement.[128]

The city charter reform proposal led to the "war within the war" among St. Louis's Black leaders. Some, such as Calloway, fiercely fought against the proposal; others within the NAACP governing board believed the new political structure would lead to a more efficient and effective government with limited "ward-based politics."[129] While the St. Louis NAACP membership voted down the charter reform, Board President Joseph W. B. Clark and Vice President Frankie Muse Freeman publicly supported it.[130]

The charter reform was defeated in a public referendum vote. While rich white wards supported the referendum, high voter turnout in several African American–dominated wards helped to defeat the bill. However, the situation highlighted white business attempts to limit Black political influence and the willingness of some elite African Americans to support or offer limited resistance to these white political power grab efforts.

Sociologist Andrea Boyles highlights the consistent practice of white-led attempts to wrest political power and land from African Americans throughout the St. Louis region. In the twentieth century, there were three political ward consolidation attempts to limit Black power in St. Louis; all failed.[131] Boyles labels this ongoing practice "white maneuvering" for the "landgrab."[132] She explains, "Black enclaves . . . were snatched . . . . That [was] happening over and over again . . . . It's just historic. And historic beyond Missouri even. There's a long-standing history of Black folks coming [up] . . . with property and then having systematic mechanisms . . . work to take it

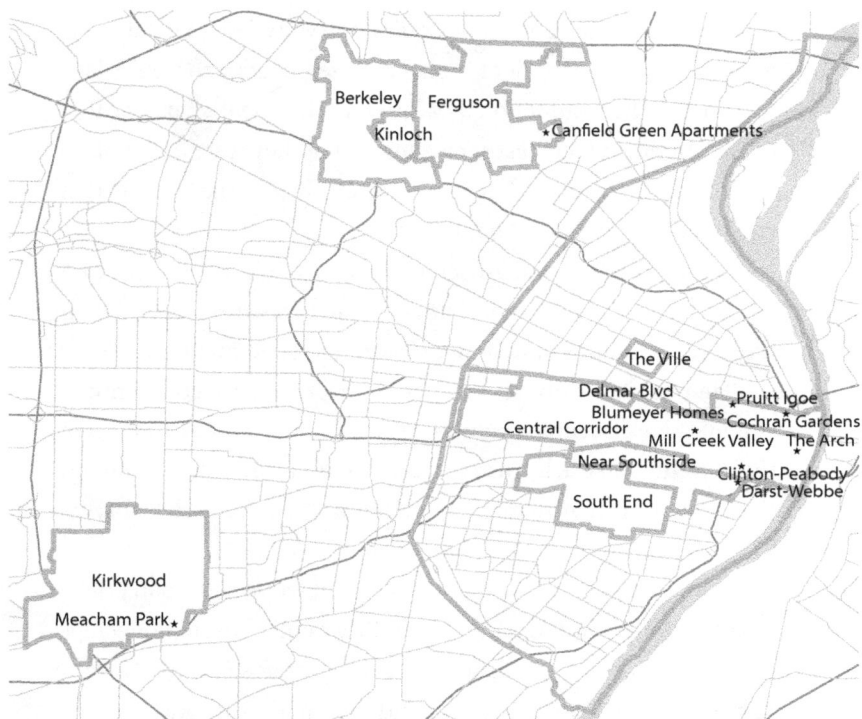

FIGURE 6. Key locations in the St. Louis region. Designed by Christian Wiskur.

from them or reclaim it . . . . It's just a consistent practice" of "white maneuvering" in St. Louis.[133] According to Boyles, white maneuvering is a long-standing tradition in urban and suburban St. Louis.

Suburban Renewal?

Mid-twentieth-century community renewal also occurred in the St. Louis suburbs. In the early twentieth century, St. Louis County had segregated Black settlements like Meacham Park and Kinloch (figure 6).[134] As whites moved in greater numbers from the city to these suburbs in the 1940s, 1950s, and 1960s, partly to remove themselves from the city's growing African American population, white-led political coalitions moved to harden the lines of suburban segregation through Black displacement. The assumption by white suburban politicians was that "African Americans were lesser citizens or that they were out of place and 'belonged' in the city."[135] Blacks were perceived as the "blight" that needed to be removed and "eradicated."

Suburban renewal and African American "removal" occurred under the guise of an economic "upgrade" to Black rural areas. Community development improvements were installed including sewer lines. Then further "improvements" were made by condemning "blighted" Black-occupied homes, razing them, and clearing them partly for industrial use in an area near single-family homes. The signal was sent. African Americans were not wanted in the suburbs; established Black enclaves were removed.[136]

In a remarkable Black displacement plan, white suburban politicians and planners intended St. Louis City public housing developments to serve as the replacement housing for those removed from the suburbs. The St. Louis County Land Clearance Authority and the SLHA established relocation procedures for African Americans to move from the suburbs to central city public housing, like the massive, soon-to-be-built Pruitt-Igoe project.[137] This was a mid-twentieth-century forced "back-to-the-city movement" steeped in racism.[138]

Black Containment and Hypersegregation

In both St. Louis and around the country, public housing was for African Americans exiled from suburban and urban renewal. Much of the country's public housing was built just beyond the perimeter of downtowns to wall off and protect the central city from African American invasion.[139] In the 1950s, the SLHA erected eight high-rise public housing projects in former low-rise "slums encircling downtown."[140] Most of these projects were constructed in the near north side of

St. Louis; a few were placed on the near south side. These high-rise projects would hypersegregate the city by placing low-income African Americans "behind ghetto walls" of subsidized housing.[141]

Pruitt-Igoe

Many African Americans displaced from the suburban and the central city redevelopment ended up relocating to Pruitt-Igoe, one of America's largest and most infamous high-rise public housing projects.[142] Pruitt-Igoe, located just north of Mill Creek Valley, was originally planned as two segregated projects: Pruitt was to be twenty eleven-story buildings for Blacks, and Igoe, thirteen high-rise structures for whites.[143] In 1954, this massive, fifty-seven-acre site of 2,762 high-rise public housing units opened for Black and white occupants.[144] However, the *Davis et al. v. St Louis Housing Authority* case, successfully argued by Frankie Muse Freeman, required the SLHA to open both projects to all races.[145] This lawsuit led to whites leaving Igoe, as well as other public housing developments, and eventually Pruitt-Igoe's twelve thousand residents were almost entirely African American.[146] The project was effectively a warehouse for ousted African Americans from other areas of the region. Some original residents came from suburban redevelopment sites, but most moved directly from the demolition of Mill Creek Valley.[147]

Pruitt-Igoe quickly decayed from disinvestment despite initially being seen as an improvement over the former low-rise neighborhoods it replaced. Frankie Mae Raglin, the project's first resident, initially claimed, "It was perfect, the nicest place I'd ever had."[148] Yet federal limits on construction costs prevented the building from being properly built. Elevators, due to funding limits, only stopped at every third floor.[149] Furthermore, "The quality of the hardware was so poor that doorknobs and locks were broken on initial use . . . . Windowpanes were blown from inadequate frames by wind pressure. In the kitchens, cabinets were made of the thinnest plywood possible."[150]

The lack of sufficient upfront investments in Pruitt-Igoe fostered financial operating challenges and tenant complains. The shoddy construction related to a higher-than-average vacancy rate; at one point 27 percent of the units were vacant.[151] The high vacancy rate led to limited overall rent collection, funds that were required to support routine maintenance and repairs. Without adequate rent revenue, conditions at the project deteriorated. In 1969, the tenants organized a nine-month rent strike to protest the dire building conditions.[152] At the time, twenty-eight of the elevators in the thirty-three high-rise Pruitt-Igoe buildings were inoperable.[153] Tenants nicknamed this poor-quality, massive development "the Monster."[154]

Beyond poor construction and fiscal management faults, Pruitt-Igoe suffered from the social devastation of isolated, concentrated poverty. Pruitt-Igoe was located in declining North City, just north of downtown, where "neither nearby shopping facilities nor health services" were available, "public transportation was inadequate," and "job opportunities were limited."[155] In 1957, the SLHA built the Vaughn Homes: four nine-story buildings of 657 units of public housing near Pruitt-Igoe.[156] The SLHA's policy decisions to place these projects next to one another in an isolated area of the city institutionalized intense Black poverty concentration.[157]

Neighborhood poverty of this magnitude correlates with several challenges including poor health, school dropout, teen pregnancy, crime, and violence.[158] Pruitt-Igoe and Vaughn Towers' residents suffered from the outcomes of monstruous policy choices that packed so many of the region's poor Black families into one place. The ill conditions created an atmosphere of intense deprivation and violence.[159]

Washington University in St. Louis sociology professor Lee Rainwater studied the difficult conditions at Pruitt-Igoe.[160] Rainwater wrote his results in *Behind Ghetto Walls*. While some scholars focused on the built environment,[161] Rainwater and his colleagues argued that the violent conditions at Pruitt-Igoe were a function of racism, concentrated poverty, and citywide inequality. He stressed these social structural issues, not the building design, led to the harsh conditions at the public housing project.[162] Historian Tracy Campbell described Pruitt-Igoe's root problem: "Impoverished African Americans were systematically removed . . . in an attempt to remake the downtown more appealing to white citizens."[163] Concentrating and containing African Americans who were not wanted elsewhere was a receipt for social disaster, and it took St. Louis policymakers eighteen years to finally realize that the Pruitt-Igoe Black isolation plan was a grave mistake.

Kill the Monster

In 1972, "the Monster" was slain (figure 7) and poor people were displaced. A couple of concrete slab high-rise buildings imploded in seconds with the strategic detonation of dynamite (we will see this in Baltimore in the 1990s).[164] Between 1972 and 1976, the remaining buildings would come down. Pruitt-Igoe tenants were dispersed across the region.[165] This was not racial redress; it simply continued serial displacement, a process that left vulnerable people, once again, without a home.

Despite Pruitt-Igoe's challenging conditions, some former residents felt a deep emotional attachment to this high-rise development. Lillian Townes, the project's last resident who lived there for eighteen years and raised ten children, said, "It's been home to a lot of people and leaving hurts some real bad."[166] Another former resident, Helen Roberson, exclaimed, "When I drive past now, I get a hurt feeling. When they blew up those buildings, I got a hurt feeling."[167]

FIGURE 7. Pruitt-Igoe's dynamite demolition, 1972. St. Louis Post-Dispatch/ Polaris/photo by Michael J. Baldridge.

The pain Ms. Townes and Ms. Roberson expressed likely stems from the experience of building a sense of community in a hostile racist environment where one is constantly contained, displaced, and forgotten by federal and local policymakers. For many, Pruitt-Igoe was home, and having your home destroyed hurts. No bulldozers this time, like with Mill Creek Valley; rather, a sudden death via dynamite was deployed.

The Ville: Death by Divestment

Some people displaced from Pruitt-Igoe moved further north to the Ville, an established Black, middle-class community. The Ville, short for Ellearsville, was originally a mixed-race St. Louis northern suburb without restrictive covenants.[168] In 1876, the Ville was annexed by St. Louis and became the home for established and affluent African Americans. Some residents chose the Ville because they did not want to live in the lower-income Black areas of Mill Creek Valley and the downtown waterfront. Between 1920 and 1950, the Ville's African American population increased from 8 percent to 95 percent.[169]

Several families displaced from earlier urban renewal developments, such as the Creole village (near the Arch) and Mill Creek Valley, also moved to the Ville.[170] The community became more economically mixed and filled with displaced Black people and institutions. For example, in 1910, Sumner High School, the first Black high school west of the Mississippi, moved for the third and last time to this community.[171] In 1937, Homer G. Phillips Hospital, a hospital for African American service and training, opened as well.[172] The community also contained Poro College, a cosmetology school founded by a successful businesswoman, African American Annie Turnbo Malone.[173]

Two important Black St. Louis political leaders, Freeman Bosley Jr. and Clarence Harmon, grew up in the Ville. In the 1990s, these men became the city's first and second elected Black mayors. Mayor Harmon, who served as the city's first Black police chief before becoming mayor, recalled the economic diversity of the Ville during his formative years: "The [B]lack community was [a] composite in the sense that everybody lived in it, whether you were wealthy or not. Certain blocks had better homes, more conveniences; a minister or an undertaker might drive a Cadillac."[174] The Ville was an economically and socially integrated Black St. Louis community, where Black entrepreneurship, education, and politics flourished. It was St. Louis's Harlem after the destruction of Mill Creek Valley.

By the time Pruitt-Igoe came down in 1972, the Ville had already started to decline economically. St. Louis's industrial economic base crumbled during the mid- and late twentieth century. "Between 1954 and 1963, the city lost one-sixth of its manufacturing activity as 260 establishments left with 26,100 jobs. From 1955 to 1967, St. Louis City lost approximately 300 major plants and 3,000 small businesses."[175] The manufacturing sector disproportionately hired African Americans, and as these middle-income jobs left, the city's Black areas declined.[176]

With a shrinking manufacturing sector, the city tried to transition to a postindustrial employment hub, which hurt the city's northern African American communities like the Ville.[177] City investments were disproportionately concentrated in the mainly white Central Corridor neighborhoods, where leading research universities, hospitals, and sports complexes were located.[178] At the same time, the Ville's Black middle class started to move to the northern suburbs.[179]

The Ville did not get razed like other St. Louis Black areas, but it suffered from the effects of deindustrialization, disinvestment, and Black middle-class flight.[180] As St. Louis architect Richard Atkins bluntly states, "The Northside was just allowed to deteriorate."[181] Colin Gordon, a historian of St. Louis's community development landscape, states, "Today, the Greater Ville claims the dubious distinction, among the City's 70 neighborhoods, of ranking first or second in vacant buildings, condemned buildings, and recent demolitions."[182] The Ville died from harmful disinvestment, another form of slow violence.[183]

In January 2022 I walked the Ville's devastated streets. The community's main business district was desolate and almost dead, and several of the commercial buildings were boarded up. The Homer G. Phillips Hospital, now a senior living building, and Sumner High School still stood. But these brick buildings were surrounded by intense poverty and deterioration, evidenced by the significant number of vacant lots and dilapidated homes. St. Louis's last remaining historic African American community was gone, a ghost of its former self.

As a newcomer to St. Louis, I was given the local advice to look for the Arch to get my locational bearings. Viewing the Arch after leaving the Ville, it dawned on me: the deterioration of this once vibrant African American community was distantly yet directedly linked to the Arch and its legacy of Black serial displacement and community destruction.[184] The Arch was more than a massive steel physical marker, it was a social signal. It represented the politics of neighborhood racial inequality and slow violence that "sent a message to . . . African American residents that the rest of the city did not care about their neighborhoods."[185] These policies of Black community removal and destruction were painful and would repeat in the 1980s, 1990s, and 2000s, creating generations of people who suffered from chronic displacement trauma.

3 Central Corridor Gentrification and Suburban Segregation

The Central Corridor is growing like gangbusters.

South St. Louis resident and researcher MOLLY METZGER

Some scholars say Skinker Boulevard, the far-west north/south street separating St. Louis City and County, is the most important dividing line in the St. Louis region; however, for me it is the "Delmar Divide," the city's east/west two-lane street.[1] Delmar Boulevard separates rich white and poor Black St. Louis.[2] One writer accurately described the Delmar Divide:

> On the south side are million-dollar mansions owned mostly by whites. On the north side, an impoverished community of almost entirely [B]lack Americans. Separated by two car lengths, yet they are as far apart as the poles.[3]

The Delmar Divide has existed for most of the twentieth century, and it continues to function as the city's twenty-first-century investment and racial fulcrum. Neighborhoods north of Delmar are Black, poor, and depleted of resources; communities south are white, more affluent, and receive investments. Many streets just south of the Delmar divide are heavily guarded by "private" road signs, metal fences, security details, and cameras signifying that these affluent spaces are off limits to residents north of Delmar Boulevard, such as low-income African Americans.

Mark and Patricia McCloskey live in one of these multi-million-dollar mansions near the Delmar Divide. On June 28, 2020, this white couple charged out of their white "palace" with guns—a hand pistol and an AR-15 semi-automatic assault rifle—as a group of Black Lives Matter protesters marched through their neighborhood.[4] The McCloskeys maintained they were protecting their home, but in a more abstract sense they were protecting St. Louis's system of neighborhood segregation.

The city's unjust economic and racial order, symbolized in the inequality at the Delmar Divide, is also evident in the surrounding suburbs. St. Louis's southern and western suburbs mainly house upper-income whites. The northern suburbs are Black and poorer compared to the white suburbs, but more prosperous than North City neighborhoods. The foundation for this regional segregation was set in motion with the HOLC neighborhood rating system, but this racial and economic division has been maintained and expanded with late-twentieth- and early-twenty-first-century housing and community development policies. While the McCloskeys outrageously "protected" their home with guns, their neighborhood and other affluent, white areas of the Central Corridor of St. Louis were "protected" by modern public policies that facilitated spatial inequality.

The U.S. cities growing during the twenty-first century, known as "superstar cities," tend to focus more on knowledge production and services, such as finance, health, and education, rather than material production.[5] Since at least the 1980s, many Midwest cities, including St. Louis, have attempted to transition from industrial to postindustrial cities.[6] To aid in this postindustrial economic turn, city leaders have typically invested resources in educational and medical institutions (eds and meds), downtown amenities including sports arenas and mixed-use luxury developments, and gentrified neighborhoods that attract high-wage service workers and their corporate employers back to the city.[7] At the same time, national and city leaders neglected support systems that traditionally assist the industrial class: public housing, public education, and working-class communities near the central city business districts.[8] As a result, superstar cities, and those striving to become one, like St. Louis, tend to be highly stratified and unequal.[9]

St. Louis's postindustrial transition was racialized and spatialized. Key federal and local housing and community development policy choices set off another round of Black displacement that "opened up" St. Louis's Central Corridor, and some south neighborhoods, to affluent whites. Some low-income African Americans were pushed north beyond the city limits as gentrification expanded the Central Corridor and divestment continued to weaken most Black North City neighborhoods. These inner-city development dynamics, in addition to the suburban airport's expansion, help to explain Black poverty concentration in North County, Ferguson.

What's Cracking?

Gentrification, the movement of upper-income people and investments to low-income communities, has swept the nation. Between 2000 and 2013, a growing percentage of low-income census tracts gentrified, compared to the prior decade, in the largest fifty U.S. cities.[10] When people think of gentrification, they often envision the movement of whites, the crackers, into low-income Black and Brown communities.[11] Historically gentrification occurs in the United States at higher rates in racially mixed neighborhoods, compared to segregated Black communities;[12] however, since 2000 there has been an increase in the likelihood that low-income African American neighborhoods will experience gentrification.[13] The influx of upper-income people and investments to low-income Black communities is sometimes associated with displacement.[14]

While certain scholars assert that gentrification, along with associated displacement, is not a major concern in "weak growth" markets like St. Louis,[15] this claim is debated. Historian Colin Gordon remarks, "It's pretty clear no one is being displaced by gentrification in St. Louis. Our vacancy is so widespread across North St. Louis and redevelopment is so scattered. . . I don't think . . . you could point to any significant gentrification."[16] St. Louis–based political scientist Todd Swanstrom concurs with Gordon and comments, "There is no gentrification in North City."[17] However, Molly Metzger, a St. Louis housing and community development expert, disagrees. She states, "It is absolutely happening. . . . Is gentrification our only problem or our defining problem? Of course not. But, is it a problem? Yes, it absolutely is."[18]

The St. Louis gentrification debate partly hinges on how individuals define and identify gentrification. Both Gordon and Swanstrom seek signs of gentrification in North City's deeply disadvantaged Black neighborhoods but find none.[19] Metzger, a resident of one of St. Louis's redeveloping southern neighborhoods, watches for gentrification in and on the fringes of the city's mainly white Central Corridor.

St. Louis's Central Corridor is an approximately five-mile stretch extending west from the central business district (and the Arch) to Forest Park (and near Washington University in St. Louis), bounded to the north by the Delmar Divide and to the south by U.S. Highway 40.[20] This area contains the city's downtown, midtown, and the far west city sections. This is the heart of St. Louis's "eds and meds" sector.[21]

Todd Swanstrom, who lives in this central area, discusses how this city section was developing:

> The Central Corridor . . . is booming . . . because there's a lot of investment, billions of dollars going in. We have Cortex, a new biotech initiative. . . . We have a light rail system, St. Louis University, Washington University, all of the amenities of the region are located in this Central Corridor . . . the zoo, the history museum,—we have this incredible Forest Park, which is one of the great urban parks in the nation, it's all free. The zoo is free. I play tennis and golf in the park. It's spectacular. You'd be amazed. But once you get north, there are very few amenities.[22]

For Swanstrom, the Central Corridor is "booming" but not gentrifying because it was already mainly white and wealthy. For him, it could not experience gentrification; for Swanstrom, and others, only low-income neighborhoods are eligible for gentrification.

However, some gentrification scholars, such as geographer Loretta Lees, view a neighborhood's upward economic trajectory as a type of gentrification, regardless of its original conditions. Lees documents how Brooklyn Heights in New York City changed from a low-income to middle-income neighborhood, and then subsequently, through "super gentrification," transitioned from middle-income to an extremely affluent place with an influx of high-income finance professionals.[23] By identifying gentrification in the Central Corridor and nearby southern neighborhoods, Metzger adheres to Lees's definition of gentrification, which states that there are different levels or stages of a community's economic ascent.

Regardless of whether it was labeled gentrification, the Central Corridor, with public investments, boomed in the 1990s and 2000s. As of 2017, over 80 percent of nearly $700 million in Tax Increment Financing (TIF) district funds had been spent south of the Delmar Divide.[24] TIFs are place-based local economic development tools and strategies to support private development with tax dollars, and are often a means to stimulate gentrification.[25] Metzger exclaims, "The Central Corridor is growing like gangbusters. The eds and meds are hot. . . . But . . . because of all these tax incentives . . . we spend all this energy on the development of the Central Corridor thinking that's going to be our savior as a city."[26] In St. Louis, business leaders "learned to leverage private-sector activity through tax incentives, tax increment financing, the pyramiding of block-grant funds, tax-exempt bond issues and private consortiums, [and] public-private partnerships," and much of this took place in the Central Corridor.[27]

Nowhere was this more apparent than with the city's investment in the Central Corridor's City Foundry STL, a large festival food market.[28] The 16.7-acre location, adjacent to the Central Corridor's Midtown Cortex Innovation District, was once the Century Electric Company's equipment manufacturing plant.[29] This large industrial property closed in 2007. Redevelopment plans called for converting the old manufacturing plant into a huge food hall with sixteen restaurants and several corporate offices. The Lawrence Group, the site's real estate development team, stacked federal, state, and local public incentives of more than $75 million, or 54 percent of the total development costs.[30] In 2021, the thirty-thousand-square-foot refurbished facility finally opened with establishments like Press Waffle Co. and Patty's Cheesecakes. It is a gentrifier's dream and an eatery for the corridor's mainly white upper-income population.[31]

While few African Americans were displaced from Central Corridor investments, like the City Foundry STL, it still demonstrates the politics of racial and spatial inequality. North City, which was almost entirely African American, had the city's highest concentration of poverty and vacant properties.[32] Yet it has received very little capital investment, compared to the Central Corridor.[33] Not only does this inequitable public investment strategy fortify the city's white Central Corridor, but it also expands it through Black displacement.

Central Corridor Expansion

In the 1990s and 2000s, the Central Corridor expanded, and its growth was linked to some public housing removal and Black displacement. Between the late 1980s and 1990s, the St. Louis Housing Authority (SLHA) was fiscally unsound and unable to properly maintain quality public housing units. This situation was the result of federal public housing cuts in the 1980s,[34] but also from local housing authority mismanagement. The U.S. Department of Housing and Urban Development (HUD) consistently rated the SLHA "troubled" for its lackluster rent collection and dubious building management practices.[35] Inconsistent rent collection led to a lack of financial ability to upkeep quality units. To reduce the number of distressed developments, the housing authority began razing its high-rise public housing in the 1990s. Between 1994 and 2009, the SLHA decreased its units by more than half, from 6,769 to 3,021 units.[36]

HUD's Housing Opportunities for People Everywhere (HOPE VI) program facilitated the destruction of St. Louis's distressed public housing just outside the Central Corridor. Between fiscal years 1993 and 2010, HUD awarded nearly $110 million HOPE VI funds to the SLHA.[37] The walls of high-rise public housing surrounding the downtown were coming down and new "walls" of gentrified neighborhoods protected and expanded the Central Corridor and maintained the city's lines of segregation.

The gentrified neighborhoods signaled to some African Americans that they were not wanted in certain South St. Louis spaces. St. Louis African American community organizer Kayla Reed, who grew up partly in North City and then in North County, states: "And even in our migration pattern, we didn't move from North City to South City, we moved North City to North County."[38] For Kayla and her family, South City might have made sense since her dad grew up in the Peabodys, a public housing project near South St. Louis. But she says the south area of the city is gentrifying and not an option.

While most of St. Louis's public housing was originally placed in North City, some was located on the near south side.[39] In 1942, the city completed the 658-unit Clinton-Peabody project, known as the Peabodys.[40] It was originally designated for whites but transitioned to African Americans after the 1955 *Davis et al. v. St. Louis Housing Authority* court case mandated the SLHA end its segregation practices. Two large high-rise public housing projects near the Peabodys, the Joseph M. Darst Apartments and Antony M. Webbe Apartments, arose in 1956 and 1961.[41] This dense public housing area, with almost 1,900 units, became known as the Peabody-Darst-Webbe neighborhood. The population of these projects was entirely African American by the 1970s and suffered from high crime rates in the 1980s and 1990s.

The SLHA dramatically transformed the Peabody-Darst-Webbe neighborhood with HOPE VI funding. In 1995, the SLHA received a $47 million federal HOPE VI grant to convert the Darst-Webbe buildings into a mixed-income development known as the King Louis Square development.[42] Of these funds, $13.2 million was used to raze and redevelop the Peabodys.[43] The number of public housing units was drastically reduced through this redevelopment. By 2006, the Peabodys only had 358 units, a 54 percent unit reduction. The Darst-Webbe development originally had 1,236 public housing units; after the execution of the HOPE VI mixed-income redevelopment plans, the number of public housing units greatly decreased to 144.[44] More than 1,300 units of public housing were reduced to rubble (figure 8).

After the public housing transformation, signs of gentrification and economic ascent appeared in this neighborhood. Part of the Darst-Webbe HOPE VI plans included the rehabilitation of a city-owned hospital into market-rate condos. Additionally, a nearby abandoned publishing building was converted into luxury lofts and

FIGURE 8. The rubble from razed Darst-Webbe high-rises. National Salvage & Service Corporation.

high-end apartments.[45] By 2020, the share of the neighborhood's Black population decreased to 80 percent and the white population increased to 15 percent.

The dismantling of public housing also facilitated the gentrification of nearby near south neighborhoods. This area, between 2000 and 2010, experienced a decrease in the proportion of African Americans and an increase in homeownership rates, property values, and the proportion of educated, young white professionals.[46] Along the southern fringes of the Central Corridor in the Tiffany neighborhood, the Gate District, and Shaw, gentrification symbols and signs were everywhere.[47] Jenny Connelly-Bowen, a white woman in her late twenties and former executive director of the Community Buildings Network of Metro St. Louis, lives in one of the city's gentrified south neighborhoods. She insists, "When we moved to the city, we were very much doing it kind of ignorant of all these other trends that were going on. We were like, 'We really like this neighborhood, and

FIGURE 9. South St. Louis's gentrification. Photo by author.

we love these amenities. And we love that we can walk to restaurants and there's this beautiful park that's like a mile wide that we can go run in.' The botanical gardens are now two blocks from our house, and we were renting at the time, but we bought our house in 2015."[48] Connelly-Bowen was not the only young, white professional to move into the popping south side neighborhoods. In the 2000s, these neighborhoods became increasingly white and were dotted with big breweries, third-wave coffeehouses, electric scooters, vibrant murals, and luxury rental units (figure 9). A 2017 St. Louis neighborhood development report issued by Swanstrom and his colleagues indicates that the highest concentration of "rebounding neighborhoods," with property value increases, was on the city's south side.[49]

The south side neighborhood redevelopment pattern was linked with Black displacement (figure 10). Swanstrom and his colleagues note, "Rebounding neighborhoods were the only neighborhood category that had a declining percentage [of] African American[s] from 2000 and 2010."[50] During this ten-year period, an average of 250

FIGURE 10. Signs of Black displacement in South St. Louis. Photo by author.

Black individuals were lost from the city's redeveloping areas.[51] Swanstrom and his colleagues assert: "It is not clear whether [B]lack households were pushed out and/or pulled by better opportunities."[52] However, in the early 2000s, lots of public housing units filled with low-income Black families were removed on the city's south side.[53] The links among neighborhood redevelopment, Black displacement, and gentrification on the city's south side were evident in the social and built environment. As high-rise public housing and Black residents were moving out, breweries, luxury apartments, and white people were coming in.

Black displacement was part of the St. Louis south side neighborhood redevelopment process. Lebet Lewis, a former Darst-Webbe resident who now resides in North County, explains:

It's a *game*. . . . I see it as a big game. If you watch it and see how they do stuff, man, just trip off it. It's a game, whether you win or lose, you see where they coming from. You *see* it, man, they doin' what they wanna do. They just doin' what they wanna do. They don't care who fall off, who starve, who don't got no home. They don't *care*. But we always knew that.[54]

Versus, another former Darst-Webbe resident, whose family relocated to the Peabodys, describes his attachment to the neighborhood.

There's no way we gonna move from here. . . . We *enjoy* the shit down here. They can't take that from us. If you right here, every day a Cardinal game go on, right on the riverfront, the VP Fair, hockey games. *We* like that type of shit, too. We *like* waking up in the morning and looking at the Arch, looking at the businesses downtown. I'm not gonna move from [near] downtown. It's a beautiful-ass sight, waking up in the morning, sun coming up over the Arch.[55]

The St. Louis "old urban renewal" redevelopment "game" was designed from the beginning to favor whites, and the "new urban renewal" development strategy was much the same. The HOPE VI policy helped to support the continuance of St. Louis's Black displacement and facilitated white-led gentrification. While Swanstrom and his colleagues document the redevelopment and rebounding neighborhoods on the city's near southside,[56] it also occurs just north of the Central Corridor and Delmar Divide.

Racial Redevelopment Reinforcements to the North

Some displacement fears, linked to the federal government's HOPE VI program, also make it to St Louis's near north side.[57] In the early 2000s, nearly all Black North St. Louis public housing projects, Arthur Blumeyer Homes and Cochran Gardens, received $55 million in HOPE VI redevelopment funding.[58] Just like on the near south side, north side public housing demolition expanded the Central Corridor and maintained the city's segregation.

The McCormack Baron Salazar firm, a St. Louis real estate company with a national reputation for revitalizing public housing into mixed-income projects, redeveloped the Arthur Blumeyer Homes.[59] The Blumeyer Homes, named after the former Bank of St. Louis CEO, were originally completed in 1968. They consisted of four high-rise buildings and forty-two smaller low-rise buildings, a total of 1,162 units, half designated for elderly-headed households.[60]

Between 2003 and 2009, the Blumeyer project was transformed into the Renaissance Place, a mixed-income housing site. The high-rises were demolished, and 789 mixed-income rental and homeownership units were constructed: 512 rental units, of which 245 were for low-income public housing residents, 116 were Low Income Housing Tax Credit (LIHTC) units for slightly higher-income low-income people, and 151 were market-rate rentals. There were also 277 homeownership opportunities, of which 30 were deemed affordable and 247 were market-rate.[61]

The revitalized project resulted in huge loss of affordable housing. Assuming all the public housing rentals, LIHTC units, and affordable homeownership opportunities were available to low-income people, the redeveloped property likely had a best-case scenario net loss of 771 affordable housing units. The mixed-income development remained largely African American:[62] however, this was state-led gentrification,[63] a publicly supported reduction in the number of low-income units and a substantial increase in the number of residences for higher-income people.

Similar to the south side, this public housing transformation stimulated revitalization of nearby neighborhoods. The Renaissance Place development helped to facilitate the emergence of the city's arts district, located just west of the new mixed-income development. A trendy coffee shop / art gallery / writing space, High Low, opened in 2019 in a redeveloped industrial brick warehouse near Renaissance Place.[64] Other older industrial buildings in this mid-Central Corridor have been converted into breweries, such as the Chestnut Midtown Brewery and Biergarten, and hip businesses like Latté Lounge + HG Eatery, a combined breakfast, coffee, and coworking space.

HOPE VI helped to usher in this "new urban renewal" phase.[65] In St. Louis, as in other cities, HOPE VI was a continuation of Black serial displacement and the "land grab" for real estate developers and white gentrifiers. Scholar Edward Goetz states, "The HOPE VI program swept in for another round of clearance in many of the same neighborhoods that had experienced urban renewal a half century earlier."[66] He claims, "In the case of public housing redevelopment, the public ownership of the land has long been an impediment to private reinvestment on-site, and the deteriorated physical asset has long impeded private investment in the surrounding community. The government-initiated [HOPE VI] demolition and redevelopment of public housing sweeps away both obstacles."[67] Housing expert Lawrence Vale labels this repeated process of urban upheaval "twice-cleared communities,"[68] and this development pattern hit the near south and north neighborhoods in St. Louis.

During the "old urban renewal" phase of the 1940s, 1950s, and 1960s, public housing was used to build a wall of protection around the central business district. In St. Louis, high-rise housing projects were mainly built just north and south of downtown.[69] This high-rise wall of public housing protected property values in the white-owned downtown as the city lost some of its white population to suburbanization. The walls signaled to African Americans to stay out of downtown. It also shielded downtown employees, shoppers, and tourists from institutionalized Black poverty tracts, maintaining stark physical and psychological lines of segregation.[70]

In the 1990s and 2000s, HOPE VI funds were used to demolish the high-rises and new mixed-income communities were built in their place. In St. Louis, the high-rise walls of public housing became "walls" of gentrified neighborhoods mainly for white residents. The walls of gentrification expanded and maintained racial inequality and segregation by building white wealth for real estate developers at the expense of low-income African Americans. "Rather than using [federal and] city money to help poor Black people maintain their homes, the city budgeted funds to drive them out" of areas just outside the Central Corridor.[71]

St. Louis's new urban renewal policies, HOPE VI and TIFs, were forms of slow violence as they supported Black displacement and racial inequality. In the 2000s, new amenities like the City Foundry Food Hall, beer gardens, and third-wave coffee shops popped up in the gentrifying Central Corridor and near north and south neighborhoods, and this neighborhood redevelopment process was associated with Black displacement. Playwright, professor, and author Sarah Schulman claims, "Gentrification is dependent on telling that things are better than they are—and this is supposed to make us feel happy. . . . Gentrified happiness is often available to us in return for collusion with injustice. We go along with it, usually, because of the privilege of dominance, which is the privilege not to notice how our way of living affects less powerful people."[72] In St. Louis, and around the country, new urban renewal policies target, displace, and gentrify Black communities for the benefit of white spaces,[73] and poverty and Blackness relocate to new places.

While Black displacement occurred in both the old and new urban renewal phases,[74] there was a key distinction. During the old urban renewal, whites were the critical redevelopment players. In the new urban renewal period, elite African American politicians played a greater role in the decisions to raze high-rise public housing projects.

Between 1993 and 2001, St. Louis was governed by its first two consecutively elected African American mayors: Freeman Bosley Jr. and Clarence Harmon. These political leaders were distinct in several ways, but both supported downtown and near-downtown developments. Mayor Bosley's major accomplishment was helping to negotiate the terms of the LA Rams football team's arrival in St. Louis in 1995. The team was enticed partly due to the state's subsidization of the $230 million multipurpose dome stadium on the city's near north side.[75] The stadium hosted the St. Louis Rams' games until they departed the city for Los Angeles in 2013.

Mayor Harmon's subsequent term also focused on downtown development. He stated: "Ours is a downtown for the region . . . and I had grown up at a time when downtown was downtown. At Christmas, you could go and look in the windows, and it was like something out of a Hollywood movie. Downtown represented to me an important statement we had to make as a city."[76] Both Black mayors supported taking down the public housing and centered their policy agendas on downtown development over investing in the declining north side of the city, where they both grew up. Just like in Atlanta and New Orleans,[77] St. Louis Black leadership focused on pro-growth development agendas that left out many low-income African Americans.

Old and New Urban Renewal, Continual and Connected Slow Violence

The city's past and contemporary redevelopment strategies were forms of slow violence. Publicly financed development supported the repeated cycle of racial and spatial repression. In St. Louis, old urban renewal initiatives, such as the Arch and Mill Creek Valley, and new urban renewal programs, such as HOPE VI and TIFs, drove Black displacement and reinforced racial segregation.[78] During the old urban renewal, whites were protected from African Americans through displacement and the strategic placement of public housing. In the new urban renewal phase, African Americans in public housing were displaced to fortify, gentrify, and expand the Central Corridor and southern neighborhoods for whites. In both periods, white neighborhoods were invested in and "protected," and Black communities were destroyed.

Serial displacement and community destruction is destabilizing. Kayla Reed, one of the St. Louis region's notable community organizers, states, "There's this deep sadness that I feel about that because there's not . . . There is nothing like brick and mortar attached to my origin story. And that in and of itself feels like erasure, that like my existence is the only thing that tells a story about where I come from."[79]

As noted, Reed's father grew up in the Peabodys. He then moved to North City, where he met Kayla's mother in a community near the Ville. Reed's parents split up when her mom developed a substance use disorder. Her father moved to North Country near Ferguson. Reed's grandmother raised her during her early years in the city, and she eventually moved in with her father in North County when she was eight. Kayla felt as if she had no St. Louis "origin story." For her, there was nothing tangible to connect her past to the city; all the city spaces where her family once lived were gone.

Reed became one of the leading Ferguson and city activists after Michael Brown was killed. When Brown was murdered, she quit her job as a pharmacy tech and joined organizers to protest police brutality in Ferguson for months. She eventually became the executive director of Action St. Louis, a leading grassroots activist organization.[80] Her Ferguson and citywide activism origin was linked to her family's serial displacement and her desire to heal from the trauma of St. Louis's history of Black community destruction. Reed worked to restore the humanity of her region, which suffered from the ongoing slow violence of serial displacement.

Other African Americans in the St. Louis region also identified the deep challenges of ongoing Black neighborhood destruction and chronic displacement trauma. Felicia Pulliam, a member of the Ferguson Commission established after the unrest, exclaims, "Every historic Black community in the St. Louis Metropolitan region was intentionally destroyed, dismantled, gone. And so those schools, those businesses gone, and how many times can one family begin again? What is that struggle? How much energy do people have?"[81]

Geographer Karen Till's understanding of "wounded cities" speaks to what Reed and Pulliam describe. Wounded cities are places where "settlement clearances have produced spaces so steeped in oppression that the geographies of displacement continue to structure urban social relations."[82] They are "densely settled locales that have been harmed and structured by particular histories of physical destruction, displacement, and individual and social trauma resulting from state-perpetuated violence . . . [where] these forms of violence often work over a period of many years—often decades—and continue to structure current social and spatial relations, and as such also structure expectations of what is considered 'normal.'" In wounded cities and regions like St. Louis, individuals, like the Reed family, suffer not simply from a one-time "root shock"[83] but from multiple "traumas of displacement."[84]

Reed and Pulliam's comments are examples of how slow violence reproduces a cycle of racial and spatial repression and Black trauma. Their displacement recollections speak to what scholar Eve Ewing coined as "institutional mourning," an "emotional experience undergone by individuals and communities facing the loss [and destruction] of a shared institution" and a historic home.[85] Their comments also connect with anthropologist Karla Slocum's arguments. Slocum states, "Gentrification, redlining, redistricting, urban renewal, and the prison industrial complex—to name some—are all instances of *spatial violence* because they spatially marginalize, contain, and displace Black people" (emphasis added).[86] The segregation, divestment, displacement, and gentrification of Black communities over time and space contribute to chronic displacement trauma and intense frustrations in areas of new Black poverty concentration, like suburban Ferguson.

Ferguson, eight miles north from St. Louis's downtown, was incorporated in 1894. The city was known as a "sundown town," meaning African Americans had to leave before nighttime to avoid serious trouble.[87] The city is located next to Kinloch, at the time a nearly all-Black suburb.[88] To protect its borders from Black invasion, Ferguson, which was all white at the time, passed zoning codes in 1932 and 1956 outlawing the construction of multifamily properties within its border.[89] Moreover, until 1968, a barrier, a fence-like structure of overgrown brush with thorns, blocked the main road that linked Black Kinloch to white Ferguson. The barrier was removed by Kinloch residents following the assassination of Martin Luther King Jr. Years later, in 1976, Ferguson residents had a yearlong debate about "building a ten-foot-high brick wall along the length of its mile-long border with Kinloch."[90] The physical wall was never built, but the debate sent a clear message: African Americans were not welcomed in Ferguson.

Despite repeated attempts to remain white, Ferguson began to experience a gradual influx of Black families. In 1970, Ferguson was 99 percent white.[91] Between 1970 and 1980, African Americans became 14 percent of the city's population. That figure would increase to 25 percent by 1990, 52 percent by 2000, and 67 percent by 2010.[92] Today, Ferguson is 80 percent African American.

Multiple factors explain the city's gradual racial transition. First, middle-class African American families left decaying North City neighborhoods. They rode the proverbial car of fair housing court cases to the suburbs.[93] Eventually lower-income African Americans followed to Ferguson, forced from the city due to razed public housing, like Pruitt-Igoe in the 1970s and the HOPE VI redevelopment sites in the 1990s and 2000s.[94] While city public housing displacement was associated with some low-income, African American influx into Ferguson, "new" suburban renewal also contributed.

Serial Suburban Displacement

The Lambert International Airport expansion greatly contributed to the movement of low-income African Americans into Ferguson by essentially destroying Kinloch, the all-Black town just west of Ferguson.[95] Kinloch was one of the earliest and largest U.S. Black, politically autonomous municipalities in the nation.[96] Some African Americans who fled East St. Louis after the 1917 riots moved to Kinloch. Kinloch was originally an unincorporated mixed-race area, but in the 1930s the white population wanted to separate. Two racially separate municipalities were formed from the unincorporated area—white Berkeley in 1937 and eventually Black Kinloch in 1948. This municipal fragmentation created separate and unequal school districts.[97] In 1967, Kinloch had over seven thousand African American residents and a Black-controlled local governing structure.[98] However, the city would become increasingly impoverished as its political leaders agreed to build public housing and received some low-income African American "refugees," displaced from old suburban renewal who did not want to move back to the city into Pruitt-Igoe.

Kinloch had three public housing projects: Dunbar Gardens, Belue-Hadnot Apartments, and the Charles Folwell Apartments.[99] In the 1960s, HUD featured Kinloch in its 1967 annual report to Congress.[100] The report quoted Homer Williams, an African American, married father of four children, who worked as a custodian and was able to purchase a Kinloch home with a rare FHA-backed Black community loan. He noted, "I pay just $78 a month for a brand new house on a 25-year loan. This place will be clear before you know it, and not only do we enjoy it now, someday it will belong to the children."[101]

Little did Williams know that the county and the airport authority would destroy almost all of his African American municipality.

In the 1980s the St. Louis Airport Authority took Kinloch's land for the airport's runway expansion plan. The airport authority purchased over thirteen hundred Kinloch properties, displacing most of the town's population.[102] In the end this destruction was for nothing. The airport expansion ultimately did not include the planned runways for the Kinloch land.[103]

I drove around devastated Kinloch in 2021 and 2022. Many vacant and deteriorating homes dotted the township. Many streets were almost completely covered with overgrown bushes and trees. Other streets were filled with garbage, used tires, and old mattresses. Sadly, parts of this once thriving Black city had become an illegal dumping ground. Kinloch looked like sections of divested North City.

When the airport authority bought up Kinloch, several displaced people made their way to Ferguson. Former public housing residents received Section 8 vouchers. The vouchers, or rent subsidies, were accepted by some multifamily apartments in certain parts of Ferguson.[104] Law professor Rigel Oliveri notes, "From 1990 to 2000, Kinloch lost over 80% of its population, and many of the residents displaced by the airport expansion [plans] ended up in Ferguson—specifically in Canfield Green, the subsidized apartment complex where Michael Brown was killed."[105] Felicia Pulliam claims, "The story of Ferguson is connected to Kinloch. You can't really understand Ferguson without understanding Kinloch. When the Lambert buyout happened, a bunch of families moved into Ferguson. . . . People were forced out of Kinloch."[106] From Mill Creek Valley to Pruitt-Igoe, to Kinloch, the state-supported Black serial displacement in the St. Louis region never stopped.

Ferguson's toxic racial tension is partly connected to the razing of Kinloch public housing and the relocation of tenants to Ferguson. Pulliam asserts: "That sense of not belonging, not having roots, not having the ability to protect yourself, your community, your schools, your institutions, your businesses, your faith houses, that at any time, a predominately white power structure can come in and target your community and take it from you and there's nothing you can do about it. What that does is, the pattern and practice of it has an emotional and social toll and with the taking of communities, your foundation and your roots, you're uprooted over and over again, and it just never gets . . . You just never get to that place where you're solid."[107]

Beyond the trauma of having your history and roots taken,[108] displacement has political consequences. Molly Metzger declares, "Displacement is politically destabilizing."[109] African Americans are now the majority in formerly white spaces, like Ferguson, yet it has taken time for political power to emerge and be maintained. African Americans in the St. Louis region have been displaced so many times it becomes hard to build solid political roots. Unrest scholar Mustafa Dikeç states, "Demolition projects create tension because they dispossess people of their resources. . . . Exclusion of inhabitants from decision-making processes adds another layer of tension."[110] The historical legacy of St. Louis's serial displacement is connected to the creation of a segregated, impoverished, and vulnerable Black enclave in Ferguson, a Black-majority city controlled politically by whites.[111]

In 2005, numerous French suburbs burned as unrest sparked by police aggression ripped through the country.[112] But the French revolts were not just about police brutality; they were also about concentrated poverty, dislocation, and dispossession in the suburbs.[113] We, in the United States, replicated the conditions in the 2010s that France faced in the 2000s.[114] Our economic development and affordable housing policies, dating back to the early twentieth century, displaced and relocated poverty to different inner city areas in the 1950s and 1960s. At that time, our transportation and lending policies brought whites out to the suburbs.[115] Now more contemporary urban policies, such as the razing of distressed high-rise public housing, set the conditions for a white "back-to-the-city movement" and displacement of low-income African Americans to certain inner suburbs.[116] We experienced what author Alan Ehrenhalt describes as the "great inversion," where affluence was moving into the central city and poverty out to the suburbs.[117] Richard Rothstein comments, "As whites in St. Louis and elsewhere find gentrifying urban neighborhoods more attractive and displaced African Americans relocate in heavy concentrations to specific suburbs, we may be replicating segregation on the European model."[118] I fully agree. But what exactly happened in the inner workings of suburban Ferguson? In the next chapter, I look closely at what occurred politically and economically in this North County suburb, and how these circumstances help to explain the Ferguson revolt.

4   Plantation Politics and Policing

When you look at a place like Ferguson and the catalyst for social unrest is that someone was shot, you have to look at the bigger picture outside of the catalyst. "Who's on the council making decisions for this city?"

Native St. Louisan and architect CHARLES BROWN

When Michael Brown was killed, all eyes turned toward the white-dominated, aggressive police tactics deployed in Ferguson.[1] Ferguson, a North St. Louis suburb of about twenty-one thousand residents, targeted African Americans for arrests and citations at unprecedented levels.[2] "After being stopped in Ferguson, Black motorists were nearly two times as likely as Whites to be searched . . . and twice as likely to be arrested."[3] According to a 2014 U.S. Department of Justice report, between 2012 and 2014, 86 percent of Ferguson drivers who were pulled over and received a citation were African American, while white drivers accounted for only 12.7 percent of all vehicle citation stops.[4] During the same period, African Americans accounted for 85 percent of vehicle stops, 90 percent of citations, and 93 percent of arrests made by the Ferguson Police Department, despite only comprising 67 percent of the city's population.

Furthermore, 88 percent of Ferguson police use of force instances involved an African American.[5]

While police aggressively targeting Black people is not unique to North County, or other cities across the country,[6] Ferguson is different. It is a suburban city that had a majority-Black population by 2010, yet in 2014 it had a Republican white mayor, a majority-white city council, an almost all-white police force, a white city manager, and white municipal court judges.[7] The white elected officials instituted a racially repressive system of law enforcement targeting African Americans that violated their constitutional rights.[8]

Many scholars, journalists, lawyers, activists, and federal government administrators have thoroughly documented Ferguson's racist policing;[9] however, police aggression was just one of the frustrating practices negatively impacting thousands of African Americans in this northern St. Louis suburb. Political scientists Barnor Hesse and Juliet Hooker acknowledge, "The police are not the only means through which the state acts on [B]lack bodies. State violence manifests itself in different ways."[10] From housing to economic development policies to police practices, Ferguson's white politicians executed slow violence to segregate and extract resources from the city's low-income African American population.[11] In the previous chapter, I explained how slow violence over time and across the St. Louis region relates to the Black poverty concentration in Ferguson, but slow violence was also furthered by Ferguson politicians, economically advantaging the city's white areas. Both local and regional slow violence at different scales set the context for the police killing of Brown and the burst of Black frustrations.

In the 1990s and 2000s, Ferguson faced increased economic pressures as low-income African Americans migrated to the city. But instead of trying to equitably grow their economic pie, the city established extractive police practices to exploit the city's increasingly poor Black population. Longtime Southeast Ferguson resident

LaTasha Brown declares that, when "the demographics in your community change, you gotta figure out how to serve this new group of people. Nobody figured out how to serve a new group of people. . . . They [white political elites] just started making a bunch of . . . ill decisions for us."[12] Sandra Moore, a seasoned St. Louis metro politics and housing expert and former CEO of Urban Strategies, insists, "As the concentration of low-income people increased, it [aggressive policing] got worse."[13] Why did Ferguson choose aggressive policing to deal with its fiscal challenges? The simple answer: Ferguson practiced *plantation politics*.[14]

Plantation Politics

Plantation politics occurs when ruling white elites dominate Black lower-income populations. Political scientist Sharon Wright Austin identified plantation politics when she assessed Mississippi Delta politics in the late nineteenth and early twentieth century.[15] In the Delta following Reconstruction, the "wealthy white elite class collaboratively promoted their racial and class interests to the detriment of the [B]lack majority."[16] The concept of plantation politics also explains some urban political exploitation outside the Deep South. Political scientist Bill Grimshaw uses the term *plantation politics* to describe how a small group of white gangsters ruled politically over a large population of African Americans on Chicago's West Side in the mid-twentieth century.[17] Ferguson's twenty-first-century political landscape represents plantation politics because it, to a certain extent, mirrors the racial hierarchy of the Mississippi Delta. In Ferguson, a small number of white elites politically dominate and economically exploit many low-income African Americans.

Katherine McKittrick, a phenomenal geographer and gender studies scholar, uses the violent hierarchy of the slave plantation, for which she coins the term *plantation futures*, to understand aspects of contemporary Black exploitation.[18] For McKittrick, the abusive, hierarchal relationships of the American slave plantation help to "uncover the interlocking workings of modernity and [B]lackness, which culminate in long-standing, uneven racial geographies while also centralizing that the idea of the plantation is migratory."[19] In McKittrick's view, the planation hierarchy still functions to affect contemporary racial inequality and Black geographies. McKittrick's plantation futures framework can be deployed as a conceptual tool for accessing circumstances in Ferguson.[20] There are no gangsters in modern Ferguson, but some Black residents perceive the actions of its white politicians, bureaucrats, and police to be a gangster-like force that deployed slow violence to maintain white power and exploit the city's low-income African American population.[21]

In Ferguson, the Black demographic majority was not proportionately represented in the city's governing machinery. In 2010, Ferguson was 67 percent Black; however, five of the six city council members, six of the seven school board members, the mayor, the city manager, the police chief (and 94 percent of the force), the director of finance, the municipal court clerk, and the municipal court judges were all white.[22] In Ferguson, there was a racial "demographic misalignment of the population and its leadership," notes geographer Jodi Rios.[23]

Ferguson's lack of Black political representation was vexing for some of the city's African American residents. LaTasha Brown asserts: "How would you want to live as a person? Would you want somebody just to dictate everything that goes on with you without your input?" She exclaims, "People was very, very very frustrated [about] not being heard," and not having racial representation.[24] For her, the city's white-dominated political leadership does not listen or respond to the growing needs of the city's increasing low-income African American population. Ms. Brown, who cofounded the Southeast Ferguson Community Association, feels the Ferguson government exploited the city's growing Black population through police fines, fees, and tickets that generated revenue for the white area of the city. Michael McMillan, president and CEO of the Urban League of Metropolitan St. Louis, further stresses, "All of these tickets and open warrants and the rest . . . built a [city] budget upon the backs of poor Black and Brown people."[25]

When I asked Dr. Rev. F. Willis Johnson, who led Ferguson's Well-spring Church from 2010 to 2018, to describe the city's political landscape and its power players, he jokingly responded, the city had "four white dudes running it. They literally met at the corner coffee [shop] every morning."[26] He then said maybe it was a few more than four but basically the city was run by "old white guys."[27] While some women and younger men also helped govern the city, Dr. Johnson's point was well taken. His perception was that Ferguson was a Black-majority city, managed for the most part by whites. McMillan described Ferguson's political landscape as an "apartheid-style government."[28] Blake Strode, who grew up in North County and is the executive director of ArchCity Defenders, says, "There's an old-guard white establishment . . . that is doing everything to maintain their power and to hold the status quo and exert social control over lower-income Black residents in that municipality." For him, much of what happens in Ferguson is "purely about racial domination and anti-Blackness."[29]

Race or Class?

Despite racially unequal political representation, prominent political scientists John Mollenkopf and Todd Swanstrom surprisingly state, "Race is not the main driver of these oppressive [police] practices [in Ferguson]."[30] These scholars claim, "To suggest . . . that Ferguson's turmoil is rooted in old-fashioned racism misses important points."[31] For them, the primary driver of Ferguson's challenges is not race per se, but rather the declining economic circumstance of a suburban region experiencing an increased concentration of poverty. For

Mollenkopf and Swanstrom, the context for Ferguson's unrest is more deeply connected to dire economic conditions than explicit racial discrimination.

Historian Colin Gordon notes the intersection of race and class concerns in Ferguson. In a discussion with me, he said, "You have a political structure in place that is fiercely attached to sustaining segregation and property values."[32] For Gordon, racial segregation and aggressive police practices are also governed by an economic rather than a racial logic, as racial tactics are used to maintain and protect property values.

For Mollenkopf, Swanstrom, and Gordon, economics are at the root of the social challenges facing Ferguson. Their economic arguments are partly backed by police evidence collected by geographer Jodi Rios. She and other scholars document aggressive police tactics to fine and extract revenue from African Americans at greater levels in nearby North County, in Black-majority population, Black–politically controlled suburbs.[33] For Rios, Mollenkopf, Swanstrom, and Gordon, the aggressive North County policing is not exclusively based on racism but rather is to capture needed municipal tax revenue. If the aggressive policing is merely race based, it should not have occurred at such high rates in Black–politically controlled municipalities, like the City of Jennings, near Ferguson.[34]

James Knowles, Ferguson's former mayor, emphasizes this point. He explains, "Everybody kept pinning [aggressive policing] on Ferguson . . . like Ferguson was . . . this outlier. Nobody in St. Louis believed that. Everyone in [the] St. Louis [region] knew that wasn't the case." Knowles felt Ferguson was unfairly targeted because nearby Black-majority municipalities were also deploying aggressive policing for revenue generation. He insists, "The great crime . . . was, everyone else got a pass."[35]

For Knowles, and some other white Ferguson residents, race was secondary. Rob Chabot, a highly engaged member of Ferguson's civic and business community, chair of the city's Main Street Association, and Mayor James Knowles's former campaign manager, states, "It's not racial." He proclaims, "When . . . we're trying to address a situation or solve a problem, race is never at the top of [the] line for me. . . . I don't really give a lot of thought to race." Chabot asserts, "People want to look at . . . race, but it is also economic."[36]

Knowles and Chabot were part of Ferguson's white political establishment and both perceived economic issues, not racism, as the city's primary problem. Following the 2014 unrest, Mayor Knowles declares, "There is *no racial divide* in the city of Ferguson—that is the perspective of all residents in our city—absolutely. This community is absolutely supportive of what we've been doing and what we're doing moving forward. . . . Black or white, we're all *middle-class citizens* who believe in the same thing" (emphasis added).[37] Mayor Knowles might have been partly in denial, but he was clearly speaking to his middle-class voting base, a much smaller segment of Ferguson's population.

While some key Ferguson leaders and prominent scholars put primacy on economic conditions, other city stakeholders claim racial discrimination was central to explaining the Ferguson uprisings. Rev. Johnson perceives the city's main issues are all about "whiteness" and a historic legacy of racial inequality.[38] Felicia Pulliam, a member of the Ferguson Commission, emphasizes the key driver of the Ferguson revolt as being "racism."[39] Fran Griffin, the former Ferguson African American city council member from Ward 3, the area where Michael Brown was killed, boils down Pulliam's uprising analysis to two words: "systemic racism."[40]

This chapter examines how both race and class help to explain Ferguson's spatial Black poverty increase and its policy choice to police it. I argue that racial exploitation is central to understanding Ferguson's politics and policies, and class considerations are secondary. To understand the poverty concentration where Brown was shot and the uproar after his killing, plantation politics and the policies of slow violence—segregation, disinvestment, and resource extraction—must be at the forefront. Brown was killed by the police; but slow violence and harmful logics and policies supporting *racialized capitalism* contribute to creating the circumstances surrounding his death. Racialized capitalism refers to a form of economic exploitation based on one's racial group identity.[41] It would not be a stretch to claim that Brown was killed by the politics of racial neighborhood inequality that proliferate in Ferguson and throughout the St. Louis region.

Waves of Black Migration to Ferguson

In the 1970s, 1980s, and 1990s, suburban Ferguson, compared to North City St. Louis, was the Black American dream. In Ferguson, "educational and employment opportunities were much better than those in the city's crumbling north-side neighborhoods."[42] Many African American families wanted to leave North City for North County. Sandra Moore notes, "The first wave of people was middle- and working-class folks who came out of the city just trying to get away from the abandonment" in North City.[43] North County provided an affordable opportunity for homeownership in what was perceived as the new promised land: "good homes, better schools, shops, and opportunities."[44]

Blake Strode, who grew up in North County and serves as the executive director of ArchCity Defenders, describes the link between perceived Black advancement and the movement to North County. "When we moved there . . . that was my parents' first home, that was very much upward mobility for our family at that moment to move into this neighborhood with a yard in the backyard in Berkeley. . . . As a kid, I remember thinking, everything feels big, it felt big, we had a yard. . . . By comparison to where we had come from it actually felt very middle-class, very stable, and it was . . . an area where middle-class Black folk were moving into during my parents' lifetime."[45] Blake's mom was a city schoolteacher, and she and her husband moved to Berkeley, close to Ferguson, to have access to a better school district for their children.

The Joneses were another Black family moving from North City to North County for an improved quality of life. Ella Jones and her husband decided to move from St. Louis to Ferguson because it offered the opportunity for their daughter to attend a better public school and was closer to her husband's job. "The main purpose for my husband and I coming to Ferguson was to give my daughter the education we wanted her to have. She was in private school long as we were living in the city, and we decided we didn't want to pay for her to be private from second grade all the way to twelfth grade, [and] then turn around and have to pay college tuition."[46]

When the Joneses moved to Ferguson in 1973, they experienced explicit racism as part of the first wave of African Americans to move to this at-the-time nearly all-white suburb. Mrs. Jones recalled, "When we first moved in, people threw eggs at our home." She knew the egging was a signal they were not welcomed by some residents in this majority-white suburb. But she and her husband, who was employed by McDonell-Douglass, a fifteen-minute drive from their new Ferguson house, were determined to make it work. She said, "We just laughed it off and kept going."[47]

Community organizer Kayla Reed, who grew up in the College Hill neighborhood in North City before moving to North County, claimed that North County was Black and "bougie."[48] For Reed's family, North County was a refuge from the violence and drugs of the city.[49] Kayla grew up in a difficult neighborhood in the 1990s at the height of the crack epidemic, where "massive drug deals" and "massive gang violence" occurred.[50] She explained that her sister witnessed a killing and her mother developed a substance use disorder and served time in prison. Her mother's substance abuse would split up her family and Kayla eventually moved in with her father in North County's Moline Acres, a small municipality next to Ferguson.

The Strodes', Joneses', and Reeds' desire for the suburbs was not isolated to North County, St. Louis; it was part of a national trend of Black suburbanization, where African Americans sought greater opportunities in the inner suburbs.[51]

The initial Black influx to Ferguson in the 1970s and 1980s were middle-class homeowners. Despite facing racism, these families, as Sandra Moore explained, had the mentality of "let me have a nice two-bedroom bungalow, and my kids go to a better school, and whatever I've got to do, I'm going to do that."[52] Moore discussed how some of the more affluent whites and African Americans moved further north to Normandy and St. Charles County as more African Americans migrated to Ferguson. She emphasized that the population replacing these departing affluent residents were lower-income African Americans. Moore acknowledged that in the 1990s and 2000s low-income families with government-issued Section 8 vouchers, also known as Housing Choice vouchers, started to move to Ferguson. She noted that voucher-holding families tended to concentrate in Southeast Ferguson, where large Low Income Housing Tax Credit (LIHTC)–supported multifamily rental apartment buildings were willing to accept voucher recipients.

In the 1990s and 2000s, Ferguson's housing market became stagnant and started to decline. Jodi Rios explains, "Initially, homes were sold to middle-class Black families at high prices due to demand and limited inventories available to Black buyers. As other areas [further out] in the county opened to middle-class Blacks, demand slowed in [inner] North County and many homes were sold 'as is' by alarmed sellers to speculators and investors looking to turn homes around quickly for a profit."[53] As this occurred, home prices declined, opening Ferguson to families with lower incomes and renters, who concentrated in the affordable apartment complexes in Southeast Ferguson.

A Suburban Ghetto?

As Southeast Ferguson became increasingly Black and impoverished, it became stereotyped as a suburban ghetto. By suburban ghetto, I mean a place where there was a perception of an association among Blackness, community disorder, and crime.[54] Jodi Rios insists, "The term 'suburban ghetto' . . . is intended to describe what happens when the suburban imaginary . . . loses its middle-class White status and becomes a container of poor non-White people, specific ethnicities, or otherwise non-conforming subjects."[55] Southeast Ferguson became part of the chronic or, as others would put it, the iconic ghetto.

Sociologist Elijah Anderson suggests that when African Americans reside in certain locations, regardless of their class status, they conjure up the "iconic ghetto" imaginary in whites.[56] The iconic ghetto is the stereotypical association between the concentration of Black people and an "impoverished, chaotic, lawless, drug-infested, and ruled by violence" place.[57] Anderson claims that African Americans, regardless of where they live, are "saddled with a provisional status" partly due to iconic ghetto stereotypes.[58] Historian Khalil Gibran Muhammad calls this racial stereotyping process the "condemnation of [B]lackness," where Blackness equates to crime and declining property values.[59]

Erica Brooks, who grew up in North County and works at a community development organization, describes the process of increased Blackness and perceptions of neighborhood decline. She states, "I think that St. Louisans . . . largely see North County as a Black community. And with that comes all sorts of mental models and feelings, and . . . St. Louis is an extremely segregated place."[60] The "mental models" Brooks refers to are the assumptions of spatial disadvantage associated with Anderson's iconic ghetto and elements of what race scholar George Lipsitz calls the "Black spatial Imaginary."[61] Lipsitz explains that Black "spatial imaginaries "honed in inner cities persist when Blacks move to the suburbs."[62] So Anderson's iconic ghetto concept of the inner city, based on the divested conditions where Kayla grew up in North City, made its way to North County.

LaTasha Brown, a resident of one of the Southeast Ferguson LIHTC apartment complexes, illuminates the idea of the isolated, iconic suburban ghetto. She says Ferguson's white policymakers tended to look at renters in the city's southeast section "as if they [are] less than nothing because they don't own where they stay. . . . We looked down on. We not . . . We not valued. . . . That's why we ain't got no parks over here in the 3rd Ward cause all the money going to January-Wabash [Park] and into that community center that can't nobody get to." She perceives that the white political leadership holds stereotypical views about the low-income renters in Southeast Ferguson. She declares that Ferguson should not be so spatially divided. She states, "Ferguson is Ferguson, regardless of what side, what corner you stay in. . . . It shouldn't be that divided like that. And people know when they're coming across the divide, they know they're coming into, "Oh these. . . . Here go these people that ain't truly wanted."[63]

With the influx of lower-income African Americans, Ferguson, compared to other parts of North County, did not completely change racially. Several of the longtime white families stayed and became very politically active. The city then became racially, spatially, and politically divided.

East and West Ferguson: Divided and Unequal

Ferguson is racially and spatially differentiated.[64] Once, "white people use[d] visual markers of difference [like high-rise public housing] to constrain Black people inside urban ghettos, spatially and relationally," but this idea of spatial containment now extends to the suburbs as well.[65] West Ferguson is well off and whiter, and East Ferguson is

Blacker and poorer.[66] West Ferguson has a downtown/Main Street, along South Florissant Road, which contains a brewery, cigar lounge, and sit-down restaurants. There is also a well-maintained park with a summer concert pavilion along South Florissant Road. This stretch of South Florissant Road also has two large red brick structures, one that contains both the Ferguson police department and municipal court. This building is located next to another large brick public building, the city's fire station, and just a few blocks north are a mainstream commercial bank, Ferguson's city hall, and the public library. Just east of these amenities are some of the largest homes in Ferguson, mostly white owned.

This quaint city section is in stark contrast to Southeast Ferguson. In Southeast Ferguson, along West Florissant Avenue, the businesses include a pawn shop, a rent-to-own furniture store, check-cash and title-loan establishments, a liquor store, a Chinese carryout, and hair and beauty shops. These small businesses serve people of a lower socioeconomic level, compared to the establishments along South Florissant Road.

LaTasha Brown describes the difference between the two Fergusons. "If you drive down West Florissant, you're not gonna see not a Christmas light, not a bow, not a holiday greeting sign, no nothing. But you go to the [South] Florissant side of Ferguson, it's lit up, [real] pretty. . . . The other side of Ferguson, it got nice restaurants, it got places for people to go and sit and mingle. They can walk down the street. On West Florissant, you really can't. All you got is the liquor store. . . . We need something more than hair weaves, cell phones, and liquor."[67] The West Florissant Avenue businesses cater to the people who live in the low-income apartment cluster in East Ferguson, the "Black ghetto," which is isolated from the rest of Ferguson.[68] There are "two Fergusons," segregated from one another by dynamics of race and class.[69] This segregation did not just happen: it was structured and shaped by public policies.

The Multilevel Politics of Racial Inequality

Michael Brown was killed in Southeast Ferguson, where over half the apartments accept voucher holders and/or are supported with LIHTCs.[70] In 2010, the Ferguson census tract where these subsidized apartments are located was nearly 87 percent African American and had a median household income of $26,758. This tract had a substantially higher Black racial composition and lower income level compared to the entirety of Ferguson, which was 65 percent Black and had a median household income of $37,517.[71] The structure of our nation's affordable housing policies has contributed to Southeast Ferguson's segregation and poverty concentration.

Lighting Up Southeast Ferguson with LIHTCs

Poverty concentration in Ferguson is connected to Missouri politics and the placement of affordable housing. The LIHTC is a federal affordable housing program primarily run through state Housing Finance Agencies.[72] Since 1986, the federal government has issued tax credits to states based on their population size.[73] State governments then specify criteria to competitively award the credits to particular development projects around their state.[74] The tax credits (i.e., tax breaks) are then sold to affordable housing investors to lower the cost of producing the units and to offset investor tax burdens.

The LIHTC program has helped to produce millions of affordable housing units throughout the country; however, LIHTC-supported affordable housing developments typically concentrate in low-income or weak housing markets, partly due to award preferences for difficult (i.e., low-income) development areas.[75] That is, LIHTC state applications for developments in low-income census tracts typically receive higher ratings and are more likely to win the competitive tax credit application process.[76] In St. Louis, almost all LIHTC units are located in segregated North City.[77] In St. Louis County, the LIHTC properties are disproportionately located in North County and in Southeast Ferguson, all Black-majority areas.[78]

Rosalind Williams, the former director of Ferguson's Department of Planning and Development, explains the relationship between LIHTCs and segregation. She states, "LIHTCs were approved by the Missouri Housing Development Commission only in areas where there was already a number of low-income African Americans. . . . Consequently, their [state-level] decisions just reinforced segregation. And as a result, you end up with this concentration of poverty."[79]

LIHTC properties accept Housing Choice Voucher (HCV) program recipients in their units.[80] The federal vouchers provide housing subsidies to low-income individuals to offset their rents.[81] While public housing was once the major provider of affordable housing, the HCV program is now the largest federal housing assistance program for low- and moderate-income people.[82] This nationwide program assists over 2.4 million low- and moderate-income households.[83] Since 1974, HUD has distributed millions of vouchers to local public housing authorities (PHAs) across the country.[84] PHAs then allocate the vouchers to families in need.

An individual typically has 120 days after the voucher issuance to find a private market property that will accept the government's payment as partial rent. Voucher recipients pay 30 percent of their income on rent and the government covers the difference between this amount and the fair market rate on units that fall under the fortieth percentile of rent for the region. Due to the fair market rate requirements and other constraints, voucher holders tend to concentrate in certain areas.[85]

The St. Louis County and St. Louis City housing authorities have issued over eleven thousand vouchers.[86] A *St. Louis-Post Dispatch* analysis of 2013 HUD voucher data indicates approximately seventy-five hundred were used in the county and forty-seven hundred in the city.[87] Virtually all (98 percent) of voucher holders in the St. Louis metropolitan region were African American, compared to 45 percent of voucher recipients nationwide. Regional voucher holders were concentrated in certain communities, like Southeast Ferguson.[88]

Sandra Moore notes the relationships among Ferguson's economic decline, the LIHTCs, and Housing Choice Vouchers. When we discuss the concentration of poverty in Southeast Ferguson, she explains how affordable private market multifamily rentals were converted to subsidized-like developments with the use of LIHTCs to rehab multifamily units and "vouchers to help pay rent."[89] Northwinds Apartments, the complex where Michael Brown's grandmother lived, received LIHTCs.[90] In 2013, the Northwinds' census tract had more voucher residents than any tract in the entire state. In this particular census tract, 20 percent of residents lived in a household that used a voucher, half of the voucher households earned $10,000 or under, and 99 percent were headed by an African American.[91] Segregation specialist Richard Rothstein claims, "When the Section 8 and tax credit programs failed to offer opportunities to settle throughout the St. Louis metropolitan area, they contributed to Ferguson's transformation from an integrated to a predominately minority and increasingly low-income community."[92] Racialized political housing decisions relate to the concentration of poverty in Ferguson, and with the Great Recession, Ferguson's financial situation became worse.

The Great Recession: Adding Fuel to the Fire

In the 1990s and early 2000s, Ferguson struggled to meet and maintain its operating budget as property values declined and low-income renters increased; however, with the onset of the Great Recession between 2007 and 2009, things became much worse. Some African

Americans who moved to Ferguson to fulfill the American Dream held subprime loans. A subprime loan is a mortgage with some predatory characteristics, such as a high interest rate, a teaser low interest rate that becomes very high after several years, or prepayment penalties, which make it difficult to refinance.[93] Subprime loans, compared to prime loans with reasonable fixed interest rates, are more susceptible to loan defaults, and these predatory loans were disproportionately offered to African Americans compared to other racial and ethnic groups.[94]

In the 2000s, North County and Ferguson filled with subprime loans.[95] In Ferguson, "more than half of the mortgages [originated] . . . from 2004 to 2007 were subprime, and these mortgages were disproportionately taken out by [B]lack borrowers. . . . By 2014, roughly one of every eleven houses in the area had gone into foreclosure."[96] Jodi Rios notes, "This area was . . . devastated by inordinate number of foreclosures during the crisis that hit in 2008."[97] In Ferguson, "mortgage investment companies (MICs) were well-placed to make high-interest loans to . . . Black buyers,"[98] particularly to "homeowners who were trying to follow the infrastructure that had been built to subsidize white flight out to the suburbs."[99]

While Ferguson was a Black destination community in the 1990s, by the late 2000s it was devastated by foreclosures.[100] Ella Jones, who was remarkably elected as Ferguson's first Black and first woman mayor in 2020, speaks about the lingering effects of the Great Recession: "We have a lot of vacant homes. If some of the neighbors will look at some of these homes, or the neighborhood will get together and do a community development cooperation and work together as a nonprofit, and buy some of these homes and restore them and sell them to people, that will be great. But buying a home in Ferguson, we're kind of upside-down. We have more renters than homeowners."[101] Jones was hoping a local nonprofit developer would buy the vacant homes, rehabilitate them, and sell them to folks keen on homeownership. She insists that by increasing homeownership the city will increase its tax base.

Eventually, many of Ferguson's foreclosed homes were bought, but not by whom Mayor Jones wanted. Real estate speculators purchased many of the foreclosed single-family homes and converted them into rental properties.[102] Raineth Housing, founded by Edward R. Renwick, was one of the firms that acquired foreclosed homes in Ferguson.[103] The firm converted some of its Ferguson housing stock into rentals for low-income Section 8 voucher holders. Resident Rob Chabot explains: "People would come in like from California and buy ten houses, flip them, put them up 'For Rental' signs. . . . It was because . . . of the number of foreclosures that we had here."[104] Scholar Allan Mallach notes, "North County [including Ferguson] became the epicenter for subprime lending in the St. Louis area."[105] Sandra Moore states, "There's . . . seething frustration and anger among middle-class and upper-middle-class Blacks about the loss of [home] value."[106] The subprime crisis, the resulting foreclosures, and the conversion of these homes to rental units made things financially difficult in Ferguson.

The subprime crisis was slow violence and an extension of serial displacement and Black exploitation. Felicia Pulliam explains the trauma of the mortgage crisis in the context of the region's history of serial displacement. "They [the banks] designed them [the subprime loans] specifically for Black folks, and then people think that finally they're owning a home, they're getting settled, life is gonna be sweet and grand, 'We're on our way. Maybe this is the time that we make significant progress as a community of people,' and the mortgage crisis happens, and Ferguson is hardest hit. The community had not recovered, and so it's just blow after blow after blow. And it's just, it's accumulating. It's the accumulative impact of injustices that just keep coming and don't stop."[107] Community development scholar Susan Saegert and her colleagues also identify "mortgage foreclosure as serial displacement by highlighting the current crisis in the context of historically repeated extraction of capital."[108] Black studies scholar Keeanga-Yamahtta Taylor notes the mortgage crisis was partly based on the financial industry's strategy of "predatory inclusion."[109]

The Great Recession erased $2.2 trillion in home equity from properties located near foreclosures. Remarkably, nearly $1.1 trillion in equity, half, was lost in homes located in segregated Black communities.[110] This is remarkable because African Americans comprise only 12 percent of the U.S. population and have much lower home-ownership rates compared to the country's white population. The Great Recession produced "the largest loss of minority wealth in US history."[111] The Black wealth loss during and after the Great Recession between 2007 and 2013 destroyed almost all of the African American economic wealth gains made, relative to whites, since the civil rights movement of the 1960s.[112] Professor Eddie Glaude deems the Great Recession "the Great Black Depression."[113]

The dynamics leading up to and the fallout from the Great Recession between 2007 and 2009 devastated Ferguson.[114] Ferguson was already becoming increasingly impoverished in the 2000s. "Poverty rates rose dramatically: between 2000 and 2013, the poor population of Ferguson doubled, by which point about one in four residents lived in poverty."[115] Due to foreclosures, Ferguson's tax revenue declined during the Great Recession period, and the city's white officials were eager to find other tax revenue sources.[116]

Plantation Politics Policing

In Ferguson, white political actors decided to make up revenue shortfalls by targeting African Americans for arrests, fines, and fees. Historian Walter Johnson explicates, "The city of Ferguson . . . was farming its poor and working-class [B]lack population for revenue."[117]

Scholar Jodi Rios claims police in Ferguson and throughout North County "view poor Black residents as 'ATM machines,' to which they return time and again through multiple forms of predatory policing."[118] The police instituted an unconstitutional "catch and release" system for revenue generation.[119]

The rap group N.W.A.'s 1988 song "Fuck Tha Police" created a lot of controversy. The lyrics discussed how the police in inner-city America abuse low-income African Americans. In Ferguson, the white police force not only targeted African Americans violently, they also exploited them economically. City officials, through the police, effectively said to its poor Black citizens: "Bitch Better Have My Money," a 2015 hip-hop song by the artist Rihanna. It was a sick and insidious move, part of Ferguson's plantation-style politics.

The white-led political leadership directed the police force to ticket the city's poor Black residents to generate revenue to mitigate the city's tax shortfalls. In Ferguson, "City officials routinely urge[d] [Police] Chief Jackson to generate more revenue through enforcement."[120] The U.S. Department of Justice's 2014 report documented emails among Ferguson's city manager, the mayor, and the police chief discussing how increased citations were needed to increase tax revenue, and it was clear "Ferguson's law enforcement practices are shaped by the City's focus on revenue rather than by public safety needs."[121] "By 2013, the Ferguson Municipal Court was processing almost twenty-five thousand warrants and more than twelve thousand court cases annually: a rate of three warrants and 1.5 cases for each household in its jurisdiction."[122] It was an alarming "taxation by citation" scheme.[123]

Michael McMillan, St. Louis Urban League president, explains the Black extraction scenario. "If you lived in St. Louis, you knew, if you drove through Ferguson, you better slow it down, you better have your tags together, you better have your blinkers together, you better have lights together, you—everything better be in order because if you don't, you will get pulled over and you'll get ticketed for all of these things at once. And you might leave, just through this small town, with $200, $300, $400, $500 worth of fines and fees."[124] People felt like the police department was preying on them. LaTasha Brown puts it more bluntly; she says people felt like they were "getting picked on" by the police.[125]

Kayla Reed describes her version of the "North County shuffle." She explains if you get pulled over and arrested and don't have the money to pay the fine you could go to jail. She says, "People are putting up their houses or taking payday loans out to fucking get you out of a municipal jail for not having [car] insurance. And [when] they get you out of jail, the case doesn't go away, it just recycles through to become another warrant. Everybody understood that . . . structure that sat over you, it was violent in the way . . . it exploited you for money." Reed proclaims, "Ferguson police harassing people, fucking with people, that's a normal day, that's like a normal day in the life of a Black person in North County."[126]

This taxation scheme is racially and spatially targeted. One of the common citations in Ferguson was nicknamed "walking while Black." Actually, the official term was "manner of walking along roadway."[127] In the area where Brown was shot, there are sidewalks in disrepair so residents frequently walk in the streets. "According to the Department of Justice, the Ferguson Police Department habitually fined and arrested [B]lack residents for violating the code and virtually never invoked it against Ferguson's white residents. . . . Effectively, the police used the rule to advance the colonialist project of occupation and exploitation through racialized containment."[128] "Policing in Ferguson . . . seems to have been . . . focused on extracting revenue from an already impoverished community."[129] "In Ferguson the policing of public order represented a rearguard action taken on behalf of a declining white population by an almost entirely white city government."[130] In 2013, court fines, totaling $2,635,400, accounted for nearly 20 percent of Ferguson's annual budget.[131]

While this situation is ridiculous, it is even more appalling that purposeful local public policy decisions could have mitigated some of Ferguson's resource woes. Instead, political decisions made by whites negatively affected low-income African Americans.

TIF'd to Death: From Kirkwood to Ferguson

The implementation of "race-based policing" can be perceived as exploitation and an extension of McKittrick's "plantation futures" when it is executed by a white-led government of a majority-Black space. In this instance, the 94 percent white Ferguson police force enforces the plantation-style politics of policing.[132] Yet this police mistreatment is just a symptom of a much deeper system of racial economic exploitation in St. Louis, St. Louis County, and Ferguson.

Not only have Tax Increment Financing (TIF) districts been used to "protect" and redevelop St. Louis's Central Corridor, but they are deployed in the St. Louis suburbs to displace and exploit African Americans. The common theme between the urban and suburban TIFs is that they benefit whites (residents and firms) and directly or indirectly hurt certain segments of the African American community. The TIF displacement pain was felt in the St. Louis region with the 1992 annexation and redevelopment of Meachum Park, an adjacent low-income Black neighborhood by the City of Kirkwood, a white, western St. Louis suburb.[133] The exploitation of African Americans by whites with the Meachum Park TIF redevelopment was so intense and agonizing, the situation eventually resulted in an awful tragedy.

The City of Kirkwood was located next to unincorporated and African American Meacham Park.[134] For decades, the two areas remained separate and unequal.[135] In the 1990s, Kirkwood and its white-dominated political structure had an idea to upgrade sections of Meacham Park with public and private resources.[136] Since Meacham Park had low-income African Americans living there, the city and real estate developers could enact a TIF district to use public re-sources to facilitate the redevelopment of the "blighted" and Black Meacham Park.[137]

Many African American Meacham Park residents were suspi-cious. Why would a white municipality that wanted to stay separate for decades now want to annex them? Was it to help or displace them? The initial redevelopment plans included the razing of one hundred Meacham Park homes and apartments, which were nearly all occu-pied by African Americans, to make way for "Kirkwood Commons," a new shopping center.[138]

One African American Meacham Park resident, Charles "Cookie" Thornton, was a big backer and supporter of the redevelopment. Thornton thought the redevelopment would bring jobs and redevel-opment contracts, particularly for him and his paving and demolition company.[139]

Despite Thornton's backing, many of Meacham Park's African American residents resisted the redevelopment. The resistance led to the original developer, Opus, pulling out of the redevelopment deal in 1995. A new local St. Louis real estate developer, The DESCO Group, took over.[140]

The DESCO Group used the city's power of eminent domain to raze much of Meacham Park, despite lawsuits to stop the develop-ment and displacement.[141] In the end, nearly half of Meacham Park was redeveloped into a $56 million shopping center, which was com-pleted with $21 million in public TIF funds.[142] Hundreds of people were displaced, and Thornton never received a single redevelop-ment contract from the city or the development team.[143]

Thornton was furious.[144] He felt humiliated and tricked by Kirk-wood city officials and the developers.[145] He received nothing, and his childhood community was torn apart; Meacham Park was "bull-dozed, uprooted and churned to make way for [a Target and] the $56 million Kirkwood Commons shopping center."[146] Thornton lost his Meacham Park, Black community standing, wife, and small business.[147]

In 2008, Thornton, a scorned fifty-two-year-old man, entered Kirkwood City Hall with a gun and fired shots, killing a police officer, the mayor, two city council members, and the Kirkwood's Public Works director.[148] Moments later a police officer killed Thornton. This was a tragic ending to a modern redevelopment nightmare, laced with racial undertones, which both communities are still grappling with.[149]

The DESCO Group made money off their Kirkwood redevelopment deal and did not want to pass on the chance to profit from a Ferguson project.[150] In 1997, The DESCO Group received $8.4 million in city authorized TIF funds to facilitate a $25.7 million, 28-acre redevelopment project known as The Crossings at Halls Ferry, located in the northeast edge of Ferguson.[151] This "underutilized" area in northeast Ferguson, not far from where Brown was shot, became a 277,000-square-foot retail shopping center, anchored by Home Depot.[152] Robert Burns, Ferguson's city manager at the time, explained, "You knew you wanted it as a city, because it could generate sale-tax revenue and create jobs." He noted, "Sale tax for municipalities at that time were real drivers of revenue for the city."[153]

TIFs are frequently used by suburban and urban municipalities throughout the United States to enhance economic activity by using public incentives to attract jobs, services, and commercial tax revenue.[154] TIFs are "particularly attractive to both cities and developers in the St. Louis region because Missouri state law allows sales taxes and property taxes to be captured by TIF."[155] However, Missouri state statues, such as Chapter 99 and 353, set the rules for utilizing local tax dollars for economic development incentives; they stipulate the need of a "blighted area," which is often code for a low-income Black area.[156] Walter Johnson claims that "politicians and developers all over St. Louis [were] trying to figure out ways to leverage small and isolated populations of poor Black people into large economic gains."[157] Ferguson had a Black population that was ripe for a rip-off.

While The Crossings at Halls Ferry development was a success for the development team, depending on your perspective it was a financial disaster for Ferguson. The property and sales tax revenue received from the city for this development was not enough to cover the interest payments and principal due on the TIF bonds. The "TIF-specific deficit" was $43,000 in 2012, so the city had to use other tax revenue generated outside of the TIF district to cover these payments.[158] When funds outside of the TIF district are needed to cover district expenses, most economic experts would deem the TIF a failure since tax revenue generated within the TIF district is supposed to pay off the TIF bonds over time. If tax dollars are needed outside of the TIF district, it means that other city services will likely need to be cut or reduced. Burns notes, "When you're looking at it from a city council / city manager perspective, you're trying to figure out, 'How do we make up for these revenue shortfalls?'"[159]

Instead of cutting services, Ferguson policymakers decided to double down with another TIF in 2002, this one on South Florissant Road, the city's main business district.[160] Moreover, two years before Brown's death, the city "built a new $8 million fire station, issued bonds to fund the portion of the $3.5 million renovation of the police station not being funded by the downtown TIF, and gave all municipal employees (almost half of whom worked for the police department) an 8 percent raise."[161] Ferguson officials went to the police for the additional tax resources generated by arresting and fining Black people for jaywalking, just like Michael Brown before he was gunned down.

In Ferguson, economic and policing policy are interrelated. Failed economic policies championed by white leaders, like the Halls Ferry Ferguson TIF, led to a revenue-generating strategy of police harassment that disproportionately targeted low-income African Americans. "In Ferguson, TIF bonds are serviced by regressive taxes and fines levied on [B]lack motorists."[162] It was a deal the "white devil" made with the economic devil, and the carnage was a young man's Black body. A police officer killed Brown, but it would not be too far off to say he was TIF'd to death.

Dance with Death

Jodi Rios articulates that, to understand Ferguson and suburban St. Louis, one must "be willing to dance with death."[163] The suburban nightmare in Ferguson did not just happen due to metro market forces, white flight, or rogue police. It was constructed through a system of racial inequality supported by public policy at multiple levels. Brown's killing is tied to the cumulative effect of slow violence, public policies, LIHTCs, Section 8 vouchers, subprime lending, and TIFs, all of which help to facilitate displacement and concentrate Black poverty. Then white municipal leaders made strategic decisions to police poverty and further extract tax revenue from the city's most vulnerable population to pay for amenities in the most affluent section of the city. Rev. Johnson exclaims, the city "used to pull everybody over and send them to court on Tuesday nights, and that's how we was able to sponsor the Christmas decorations up and down the street [on South Florissant] for a mile and a half. Okay?"[164]

Several people I spoke with noted that this racial exploitation had been occurring for years and it did not ignite unrest until Brown was killed. Kayla Reed insists, "A lot of people connected to the uprising and showed up day in day out because everybody understood being stopped by an overaggressive police officer who disrespected you, or talked to you sideways, but there were so many people who were like, 'Oh, shit that happened to me. I could have got shot.' And that was like a new reality."[165] Others thought Brown's body being on the ground for over four hours and the subsequent destruction of his makeshift memorial by the police were the sparks.[166]

For Reed and other people, Brown's death also brought to the surface the feelings of ongoing displacement that had occurred for over a century in the St. Louis region. Erica Brooks notes, "The Michael Brown shooting was tragic, it was terrible and yet it did click something."[167] The brutal killing raised the level of awareness to the slow violence and systemic racism that occurred for decades. Rev. Johnson declares that, in Ferguson, low-income "people [were] so busy trying to . . . survive and sustain that they . . . You just . . . The dysfunction was functional."[168] Reed speaks about the "dysfunction" as an inherited "caste system" of racial displacement and inequality in the St. Louis region.[169]

After Brown's death, President Obama sent Eric Holder Jr., the attorney general of the United States from 2009 to 2015, to investigate the aggressive and unconstitutional practices of the Ferguson Police Department.[170] If the administration had done its Ferguson homework, it might have also sent other attorneys, Treasury Secretary Jack Lew, and Housing and Urban Development Secretary Julián Castro. By referencing the head of the U.S. Treasury Department, I am not saying that the problems of Ferguson were economic in the way scholars Mollenkopf, Swanstrom, and Gordon have argued. The Ferguson frustrations are related to racialized displacement and economic exploitation linked with racially biased housing and community development policies, including LIHTCs, Section 8 vouchers, the subprime mess, the use of local economic policies, such as TIFs, and the revenue generation mechanism of aggressive policing. The culmination of all of these policies had tragic consequences for low-income African Americans, and partly elucidates why Black suburbanization, in certain circumstances, "did not lead to a promised land, but introduced new, underappreciated forms of racial segregation and inequality," and death.[171]

A Return to the Race/Class Debate

The politics and policy decisions in Ferguson are racialized. The twenty-first-century formation of Ferguson as a Black suburb under white control can be understood through plantation politics that infect nearly every corner of Black life in this municipality and region. Criminologist Jennifer Cobbina claims the history of race matters: "The systemic legacy of slavery and Jim Crow continues to this day to shape Black people's position in society and how they are perceived and treated by individuals and institutions, including the police." For her, it is mostly about race and "race-based policing."[172] I agree but extend and deepen this racial analysis to encompass racialized urban and suburban redevelopment policies and patterns to explain concentrated Black poverty and how it is policed. Rios notes, North County "is an extreme example of how racialized disparities are produced and policed through spatial practice and cultural politics."[173] I concur but would replace "cultural" with "plantation" to highlight Ferguson's racialized politics prior to Brown's death.

However, a racialized lens alone is short-sighted; it is important to acknowledge economic conditions and class dynamics. For instance, "municipalities with majority-Black populations are often both victim and administrator of highly racialized practices that differentiate, oppress, and exploit non-White communities."[174] Additionally, Rios writes of the "racialized means and extreme measures Black and White leaders in North St. Louis County use to extract money and resources from Black citizens."[175] Rev. Johnson states, "The magistrates in some of those places where people are getting ticketed were people of color."[176] Furthermore, Black mayors in North County have "stated things like, 'People from the projects must be taught how to act in the suburbs,' and 'People who don't know how to mow their grass have no business living in the suburbs.'"[177] In 2022, the Black–politically controlled suburban city of

Jennings separated itself from Southeast Ferguson with a concrete barrier placed in the middle of a street where the two municipalities met. In the St. Louis region, members of the Black middle class have consistently attempted to separate themselves from lower-income people of color.[178]

Even when African Americans are elected to high-level political positions, it can be difficult to change unequal economic conditions.[179] In 2020, Ferguson elected its first Black woman mayor: Mayor Ella Jones. For a city that was once considered a "sundown town," this was extraordinary, but will this political change be enough to more effectively alter the difficult economic reality facing Ferguson? Rev. Johnson states, "I'm glad Ella is the mayor. It's a historical moment for all the world and it's beautiful to be on CBS, but sister, you still don't have no revenue-generating tax base."[180] Rev. Johnson attests that several African Americans turn from a "frustrated freedom fighter" into a "fiduciary agent" once they are confronted with the city's "balance sheet."[181]

In this regard, Mayor Jones has lofted a redevelopment plan for Southeast Ferguson. The proposed development will be supported with an $18.2 million Rebuilding American Infrastructure with Sustainability and Equity (RAISE) grant from the U.S. Department of Transportation.[182] There are plans to widen the sidewalks, remove some of the liquor stores, and build mixed-income housing and mixed-use commercial spaces.[183] But some residents wonder if there will be room for the existing low-income people in these plans, such as those renting in the multifamily apartment buildings near where Brown was killed.

Furthermore, Mayor Jones must contend with the legacy of a white-controlled city. LaTasha Brown insists, "[Mayor Jones has] been having a hard time in our City Council meetings," as other members of the city council are "attacking" her and supporting the "old political guard."[184] In 2022, Fran Griffin, who represented Ward

3 and was considered part of "Mayor [Jones's] Bloc,"[185] lost her primary election to Mike Palmer, a white real estate developer with ties to the old political guard.[186] With Councilman Palmer in place, the Black voice and power in Ferguson politics is likely in decline. Mr. Palmer's election signals that whites in Ferguson are still committed to keeping low-income African Americans in "place." As Blake Strode puts it, the "white power structure [in Ferguson] has felt very entitled to maintain control and to police, both literally and figuratively, the activities and lives of Black folks who encroach into their territory."[187]

The economic situation in Ferguson and the politics of Black-led North County suggest both race and class are important in shaping the conditions that led to anger and unrest in Ferguson. Yet we must place race at the forefront since racial considerations closely relate to the politics of inequality and the interconnected slow and sudden violence that took Brown's life.

Sociologist Christopher Mele notes that both white and Black political and economic actors enact policies that negatively impact low-income African Americans through relying on "the manipulation of race,"[188] racial stereotypes of African Americans connected to Anderson's depiction of the "iconic ghetto," and Andrea Boyles's concept of "white maneuvering." Southeast Ferguson is considered by some a "ghetto," so aggressive policing and exploitation are justified. But what is important is that the exploitation was not just in policing; the policing was connected to racialized economic exploitation based on municipal revenue generation, real estate profit, and straight-up racism. This economic and policing exploitation in Ferguson and the surrounding region can be more clearly understood through a racialized lens of plantation politics.

In the subsequent chapters, I move east from Ferguson to Baltimore. As Rev. Johnson explains, Ferguson has little Black political control. He states, "It's not Baltimore, it ain't chocolate city. It ain't

Black people . . . running it."[189] What happened in a Black-majority city governed by Black people? How do we understand the undercurrents of unrest in a completely different political and geographic context—a city where African Americans have held many of the political power positions since the latter part of the twentieth century?

5 *Ghetto Walls Go Up*

I didn't expect to see it [unrest] twice in my lifetime. . . . History repeats itself when you don't sit down and look at the history and analyze it and say, "How do we keep this from happening again?"

Longtime Baltimore Sandtown-Winchester resident
DR. HELEN HICKS

Baltimore and Ferguson have some striking similarities and differences.[1] Both cities endured economic hardships, particularly during and after the Great Recession. Both have pockets of concentrated Black poverty and white affluence, and their uprisings have much to do with aggressive police actions that ended in death. However, in terms of political representation, Ferguson and Baltimore are completely different. In Ferguson, the city's Black population struggles to get a solid foothold in the political landscape; in Baltimore, African Americans have held many of the city's powerful political positions for decades. Since the 1970s, African Americans have been consistently elected to high level offices: mayor, city council member, police chief, state's attorney, and school board commissioner.

Another major difference, as Dr. Helen Hicks expressed, is that Baltimore experienced unrest twice. In April 1968, two days after

Martin Luther King Jr. was assassinated in Memphis, Baltimore's Black West and East Side neighborhoods went up in flames.[2] Over ten thousand federal guards were deployed to the city during six days of uprisings, and when the chaos ended six people had died and 5,512 had been arrested.[3] The unrest caused damage estimated at $12 million, about $87 million in today's dollars.[4]

Forty-seven years later, on April 19, 2015, Freddie Gray died at the hands of the city's police force following his April 12 arrest and "rough ride."[5] Peaceful, organized protests demanding police reforms immediately followed Gray's death; however, revolts erupted six days after his killing.[6] At least 235 people were arrested and 20 police were injured.[7] Over 250 businesses, mainly in low-income African American communities, were damaged; 144 vehicles and 15 buildings were destroyed.[8] The U.S. Small Business Administration estimated the damage to be nearly $9 million, mostly in West Baltimore.[9]

The financial damage from Baltimore's 2015 uprising was less extensive than in 1968;[10] yet, there were important parallels between the two revolts. Both events were triggered by the unfair death of African American men. Moreover, urban renewal efforts—the razing of Black neighborhoods, highway construction, and the development of high-rise public housing in the early period and the demolition of public housing, subsequent displacement, and gentrification in the latter period—were executed by the city of Baltimore prior to the uprisings.

While the contemporary connections among urban renewal policies, concentrated Black poverty, and unrest in Baltimore were similar to Ferguson, there were two important differences. First, Baltimore's 2015 uprising was concentrated in the inner city, not in an inner suburb. Second, African Americans have dominated Charm City politics since the 1990s, yet Black community disinvestment was just as intense. These unique Baltimore circumstances help unpack the complex role of race and class in the advancement of racial inequality and growing frustrations among low-income African Americans in the Sandtown neighborhood, where Gray was arrested and the uprising was most concentrated.

In the next three chapters, I elucidate how old and new urban renewal policies relate to serial displacement, gentrification, and poverty concentration in some of Baltimore's low-income, African American communities.[11] I mainly, but not exclusively, focus my analysis on changing dynamics and conditions in Baltimore's Sandtown-Winchester neighborhood, one of the city's historic African American communities where unrest occurred twice. I argue that decisions to protect and then expand Baltimore's downtown relate to a half-century of the concentration of African American poverty in Sandtown-Winchester. I also explain why and how the politics of racial inequality persisted in Baltimore in the late twentieth and early twenty-first century, despite African American representation in most of the city's high-ranking political positions. When Gray was killed, the mayor, the city council president, the police commissioner, and the state's attorney for Baltimore were African American. In Baltimore, racial inequality was not maintained by plantation politics; rather, it was a result of ongoing white racism and Black classism. I argue that racial representation is insufficient to alter historic trajectories of racial and spatial inequalities.

Black Migration to Early Baltimore

African Americans have played an important role in the city of Baltimore since it was incorporated in 1796.[12] In this principal port city, profits were made from selling grain, tobacco, and enslaved people.[13] Unlike St. Louis, early-nineteenth-century Baltimore had a common practice where enslaved people were hired out for work and allowed to retain a portion of their earnings. Sometimes these earnings were sufficient to "purchase themselves" out of bondage.[14] A significant portion of Baltimore's enslaved people were in "term slavery," meaning they were typically freed after eight to twelve years.[15] These unique city circumstances helped to clarify why Baltimore had the largest free Black population in 1860, compared to other U.S. cities.[16] By 1860, 27,898 Blacks lived in Baltimore (13 percent of the city's total population) and 25,680, 92 percent, were free.[17] At this time, Baltimore was a "mecca for free African Americans;"[18] however, "no matter how liberal Baltimore might be relative to cities in the Deep South, there existed a color line that legitimized and maintained white hegemony."[19]

The city of Baltimore is located in Maryland, a slave state until the Thirteenth Amendment, and thus subject to laws steeped in racial domination.[20] Beginning in 1807, Maryland passed a series of legislative acts, known as the "Jacobs' Laws," that attempted to bar free Blacks from entering the state.[21] In 1831, state law prohibited Black religious services unless authorized by a white clergyman.[22] In the late 1830s, "it had become customary for [B]lack Baltimoreans who wanted to hold social functions to petition the mayor for permission."[23]

Despite this explicit racism, Baltimore's Black achievements during the mid-nineteenth century were extraordinary, and this Black city strength extended into the Reconstruction period.[24] Historian Matthew Crenson states, "For its time, the free [B]lack community of Baltimore was both large and well-organized. Its population had achieved the critical mass needed to sustain a variety of independent [B]lack institutions," including prominent churches, schools, social clubs, and businesses.[25] This group of free Black individuals also owned property. In 1850, the average Black real estate owner had property holdings of $1,327, a significant amount of Black wealth at the time.[26]

After the Civil War, there was a substantial influx of Black Americans from the South who were distinct from long-term city residents. Crenson notes, "The aftermath of the Civil War brought a large population of former slaves to a city where most [B]lack people had been born free. The two groups, understandably, held different perspectives on politics and race in Baltimore. . . . Disagreements between recently freed slaves and free [B]lack Baltimoreans opened a new axis of dissension in African American politics."[27]

Following the Civil War, in 1868, state-level white political leaders in Maryland attempted to impede Black Baltimoreans' political progress. Many white state representatives refused to ratify the Fourteenth Amendment to the U.S. Constitution, which granted citizenship to African Americans, and were "emphatically opposed to the Fifteenth's mandate to grant voting rights to [B]lack men."[28] In 1870, state legislators finally approved the amendments, and the Black men of Baltimore could legally vote.[29]

Black Baltimoreans quickly made political inroads. "Between 1890 and 1931, six [B]lack Republicans held seats on the Baltimore City Council." This African American political strength garnered national attention and the Black city council members passed resolutions opening the city's public spaces for national Black organizations' annual gatherings.[30] "Blacks from all over the east coast began coming to West Baltimore for conventions of the NAACP and [B]lack fraternal societies," proclaims historian Harold McDougall.[31] Baltimore gave rise to Harry S. Cummings (first African American to hold elected office in the state of Maryland in 1890), John H. Murphy Sr., Thurgood Marshall (first African American appointed to the U.S. Supreme Court), Clarence Mitchell Jr., and Parren J. Mitchell (first African American congressional representative from Maryland), to name just some of the city's iconic Black civic leaders.[32] These social, legal, media, and political trailblazers, and many others, advocated to advance Black infrastructure such as the formation of the city's historic Black colleges and universities, Morgan State University and Coppin State University, founded in 1867 and 1901, respectively.[33] These universities provided the educational underpinnings for the city's burgeoning Black middle class.

In the late 1890s and the early twentieth century, Baltimore, like St. Louis, became an industrial manufacturing and steel-producing powerhouse.[34] With manufacturing on the rise, European immigrants and African Americans flocked to Baltimore during the first wave of the Great Migrations.[35] Between 1880 and 1910, the city's population doubled to 558,485, of whom 88,065 were African American.[36] Between 1920 and 1960, the city's African American population increased from 108,322 to 325,589.[37]

Segregated Black Baltimore

As new populations arrived, Baltimore instituted hard lines of racial segregation.[38] In 1910, Baltimore became the first U.S. city to pass an ordinance "prohibiting African Americans from moving into areas primarily occupied by whites, and vice versa."[39] In 1917, the U.S. Supreme Court ruled the Baltimore law unconstitutional, but other practices, such as street violence, blockbusting, restaurant and hotel exclusion, and urban development and displacement, enforced Baltimore's racial segregation.[40] Historian Harold McDougall declares, "By the turn of the twentieth century, [B]lacks of all classes were increasingly being made to feel unwelcome in the city's parks, hotels, theaters, and restaurants."[41] Historian Kenneth Durr writes, "In Jim Crow Baltimore the principle of white exclusivity went largely unquestioned."[42] U.S. Supreme Court Justice Thurgood Marshall referred to his hometown as "up-South Baltimore," because of its adherence to southern racial norms of separation.[43] Baltimore was highly segregated throughout the twentieth century; the segregation (nonwhite and white) index for Baltimore between 1940 and 1970 was a near constant and incredibly high 90 percent.[44] The city was "segregated from cradle to grave," from hospitals to cemeteries.[45] This hypersegregation level persists in the twenty-first century (figure 11).

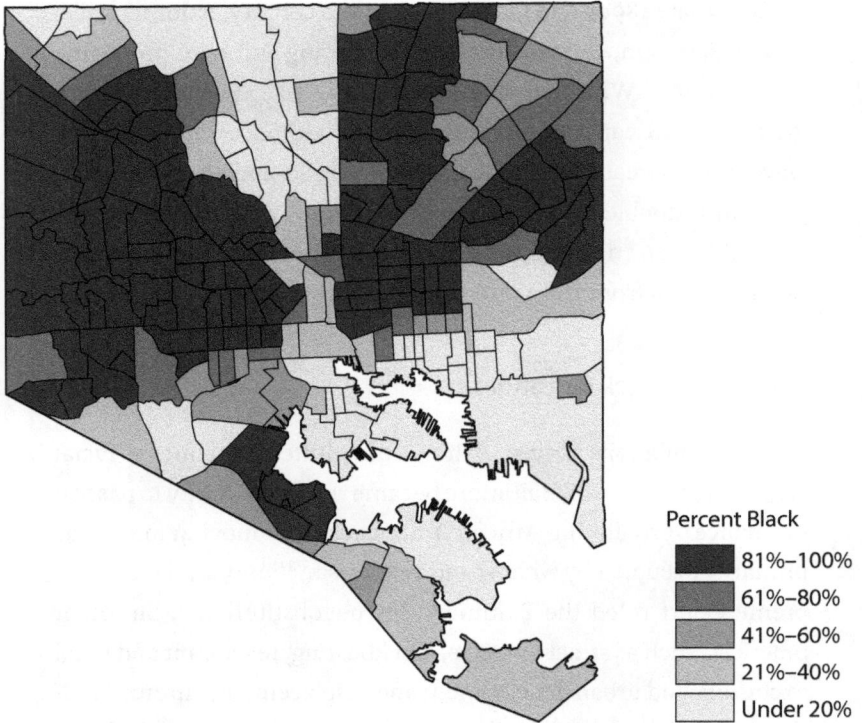

FIGURE 11. Segregation in Baltimore, 2010. Source: U.S. Census/designed by Meagan Snow.

The Start of Serial Displacement

In the 1800s, African American living quarters were scattered around the city, many in the alley homes.[46] In the late nineteenth century, African Americans were "integrated" in neighborhoods but experienced micro-level segregation.[47] Many African Americans lived in back-alley dwelling units, while whites mainly resided in homes facing the streets.[48] In 1802, 32 percent of the city's freed Blacks lived in the near east neighborhood of Fells Point, right next to the port.[49] However, Irish, German, and other white ethnics competed with African Americans for dock-related jobs and occasionally acted violently toward their Black competitors.[50] During one incident, two Fells Point alley homes were burned.[51] With the ever-present threat of white-led violence,[52] the Black population started to move west near downtown and to the city's Pigtown neighborhood, just southwest of downtown.

White-led urban development policies drove Blacks from Pigtown and downtown. Around the turn of the century, over two hundred Black Pigtown households were displaced due to the expansion of the Camden Yards Railway Station.[53] Also, alley homes occupied by working-class African Americans "were torn down to make way for industrial expansion."[54] Even elite- and middle-class African Americans, like lawyer William Ashbie Hawkins, who lived downtown, were targets of white-led urban redevelopment and removal.[55] "Black people who lived near their jobs in the center of Baltimore were displaced when financiers and commercial interests created 'downtown,' a central business district to serve industry, shipping, finance and retail sales."[56] The displaced Black population moved further west of downtown to Sandtown-Winchester.

Historic Sandtown-Winchester

The West Baltimore neighborhood of Sandtown-Winchester was once known as "Baltimore's Harlem."[57] The community became Baltimore's main African American entertainment, commercial, and residential hub in the 1930s and 1940s for several reasons.[58] African Americans first began settling in the previously white Sandtown around 1885. This movement was connected to the 1910 sale of Margaret Brewer's house, a white woman's home, to William Ashbie Hawkins, an African American lawyer who was displaced from downtown.[59] Hawkins rented his house to his African American law partner and Yale law graduate George W. F. McMechen. In a racist reaction, some white residents "threw stones through the Mc-Mechens' door and windows, dumped tar on the front steps, and smashed bricks through skylights."[60] The McMechen household was threatened, but stayed.

African Americans were pushed and drawn to Sandtown (figure 12). As displacement pushed Black Baltimore to Sandtown, many whites eventually fled to outer periphery neighborhoods, leaving a viable and beautiful housing stock.[61] Areas outside of Sandtown, at this time, had restrictive covenants, preventing home sales to African Americans. Thus, Sandtown became densely populated and segregated. By 1940, the three census tracts that made up Sandtown-Winchester were over 90 percent African American.[62] The community became a vibrant, yet overcrowded, area where African American musical and intellectual icons including Cab Calloway, Billie Holiday, and Thurgood Marshall spent much of their time.[63] The area had "a concentration of politically, spiritually, economically, and artistically developed people [who] produced a smaller-scale version of the Harlem Renaissance."[64]

Sandtown-Winchester was an African American mixed-income neighborhood for years but began to decline economically in the 1940s. First, the overcrowded conditions were taking a toll on its housing stock. Second, the area was redlined. Like in St. Louis, the HOLC drew investment risk maps of Baltimore in 1937.[65] The areas of Black settlement on the city's west side, like Sandtown-Winchester, were rated D, while white areas were disproportionately rated A.[66] In the mid- and late-1940s, other Baltimore neighborhoods started to open to African Americans due to the outlawing of restrictive covenants and the movement of middle-class whites and Blacks to the suburbs.[67] Those in Sandtown with resources left.[68]

Additionally, in 1944, Baltimore brought in Robert Moses, the infamous urban renewal planner from New York City, to consult

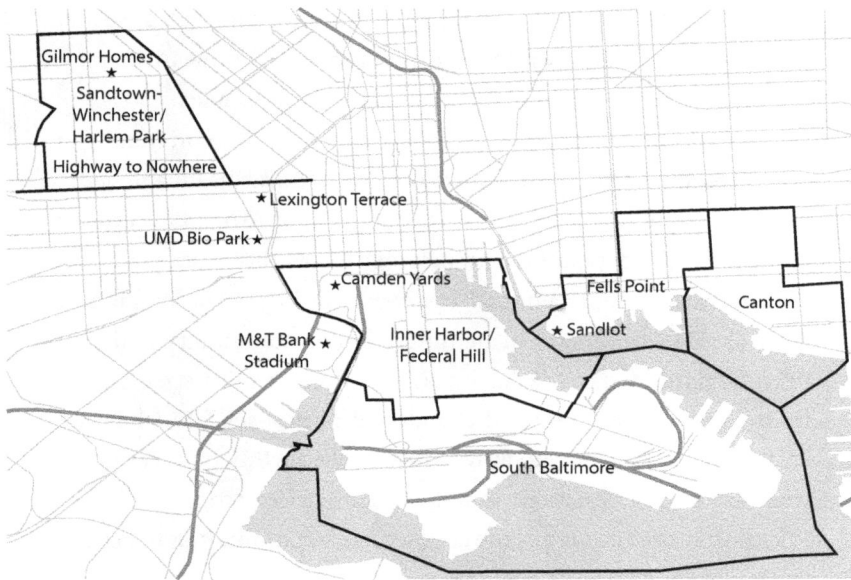

FIGURE 12. Key locations in Baltimore. Designed by Christian Wiskur.

on a massive highway plan.[69] Moses's plan would have constructed major highways through sections of the Sandtown-Winchester neighborhood, leading to massive displacement. While these plans were never fully implemented, the expectation of their execution stimulated a Black middle-class exodus, housing disinvestment, and deterioration, resulting in poverty concentration in the neighborhood.[70]

Poverty concentration brought on difficult living conditions that fueled frustrations. In 1968, two days after the assassination of Martin Luther King Jr., unrest started in East Baltimore and quickly spread to impoverished West Baltimore's Sandtown-Winchester.[71] Buildings and businesses throughout the community burned.[72] While Sandtown-Winchester was already in decline, businesses and middle-income residents continued to flee after the 1968 uprising, sending the community into a further economic downward spiral.[73] The community would remain impoverished for decades.[74]

Despite federal and local attempts to revitalize the community in the 1990s, the neighborhood stayed segregated and disadvantaged.[75] By 2010, Sandtown-Winchester was 96 percent African American; one-third of its population had incomes below the poverty line; 20 percent was unemployed; and 3 percent was in prison, the highest level of any community in Baltimore.[76] The community had also been hit hard by the foreclosure crisis and many of its streets were marred with boarded-up and abandoned rowhouses.[77] Much of the community's housing stock was filled with low-income residents who received government rental assistance.[78] In 2015, Sandtown-Winchester became one of the country's few communities to experience unrest twice.

While several scholars highlight acute police aggression as the primary contemporary uprising determinant,[79] Nick Mosby, former city council member from the Sandtown-Winchester area, 40th District State of Maryland House delegate, and current Baltimore City Council president, insists, "This is a culmination of a lot of different things. Decades old of unfair policies. Decades old of lack of development for these communities."[80] West Side Baltimoreans United in Leadership Development (BUILD) community organizer Gwen Brown reinforces Mosby's comments and maintains that the uprisings were related to "decades of not investing in the neighborhood, decades of not working diligently . . . to strategically address drug-related issues, [and] decades of the police being here."[81] As Mosby and Brown suggest, I look back at decades of policies of slow violence to better understand how segregation, divestment, displacement, and gentrification set the context for the 2015 Baltimore uprisings.

Urban Renewal

Baltimore's Old Urban Renewal: Highways and Housing

In the 1940s, 1950s, and 1960s, many leading urban planners and policymakers thought the strategic placement of highways through African American neighborhoods could spur economic development and eradicate, contain, and prevent blight.[82] Local economic development advocates believed highways would more easily bring commerce and suburbanites to the city. Strategically running highways through blighted areas could also prevent the encroachment of Blackness into the downtown.[83] Local political leaders hoped this would protect downtown property values and facilitate shopping in the central business district;[84] "Good roads would bring good people downtown."[85]

Throughout the country, the construction of the highways disproportionately impacted African American communities. Between 1957 and 1968, at least three hundred thousand urban housing units, mainly in African American communities, were razed due to the construction of the country's interstate highway system.[86] This new road system shattered African American social capital and led to the dramatic "reorganization of urban and suburban space."[87] The reorganization would result in an even more racially segregated metropolitan America.[88]

In Baltimore, something different happened: the highway planning alone devastated African American communities. While Sandtown-Winchester was not ultimately destroyed by a highway and did not experience massive displacement, the planning and discussion of highways facilitated disinvestment and Black middle-class flight. In Sandtown-Winchester, the city's highway construction plans and threat of eminent domain were enough to start the processes of disinvestment.

Part of the Franklin-Mulberry corridor, which runs through the southern border of Sandtown-Winchester/Harlem Park, was cleared and remained vacant for years before the highway construction began. The thoroughfare was only partially built, due to increasing costs and protests from city-wide interracial coalitions, and eventually became known as the "highway to nowhere."[89] During this period, area homeowners moved or gave up on maintaining their homes, expecting they would eventually be displaced when the highway plan was fully executed.[90] Thus, urban renewal plans can have a devastating effect even if they are never fully implemented. As Baltimore activist and organizer Marisela Gomez expresses, "Once an area is deemed an 'urban renewal' area, private and public investment decreases and the local residents are left on their own to stem the flow of continued decay."[91] Rev. Douglas Miles, a longtime activist and coleader of BUILD,[92] details the urban renewal devastation.[93] He professes, "That whole piece of I-70, the highway to nowhere, destroyed the heart and soul of a prosperous African American community" (figure 13).[94]

While Baltimore's highway development in the 1940s, 1950s, and early 1960s did displace some,[95] more African Americans were removed through the razing of rowhouses for the construction of public housing during this period.[96] Due to segregation, overcrowded conditions, and redlining, much of the city's dilapidated housing stock was in West and East Baltimore's African American sections just outside of the downtown, otherwise known as the "ring of blight."[97] The bulldozers did their damage in these African American city sections. Baltimore historian Sherry Olson documents, "The rate of demolition rose from six hundred households a year in the '50s to eight hundred in the early '60s, as sites were being cleared for expressways, new schools, and public housing projects all at once. The people evicted were mostly poor, often elderly, and nine out of ten were [B]lack."[98] One source estimated that between 1950 and

FIGURE 13. Highway to nowhere. Baltimore Sun/photo by Jerry Jackson.

1964, twenty-five thousand people, 85 percent of whom were Black, were displaced due to urban renewal projects that demolished more dwelling units than were eventually replaced through public housing construction.[99] By 1971, the Baltimore urban renewal displacement estimate tripled to seventy-five thousand people, the majority African American.[100]

Walls of Separation

In some cities, "invisible visible" walls separate white and Black community areas.[101] In other cities, the walls of neighborhood separation are more visible and include elevated highways, roads, and railroad tracks.[102] In Baltimore, as in St. Louis, the invisible walls were real; walls of brick and concrete, low- and high-rise public housing. The visible signs of separation between Black underclass and white and Black middle classes in Baltimore were public housing developments.

The Housing Authority of Baltimore City (HABC) erected these walls of public housing between 1940 and 1960 to secure the borders between the "ring of blight" and downtown.[103] "White Baltimoreans . . . insisted that such [public] housing should be built within the boundaries of existing [B]lack neighborhoods."[104] In these areas, low- and high-rise public projects went up and reinforced existing patterns of segregation and impoverishment. In West Baltimore, the Poe Homes, built to house the working poor, became the HABC's first project.[105] It opened in 1940 and blocked off the southern section of Sandtown from the western edges of downtown. In 1942, the Gilmor Homes were built in West Baltimore's Sandtown-Winchester neighborhood, to limit low-income African American out-migration to the city's northwest white neighborhoods.[106] Lastly, the McCulloh Homes would become part of the public housing wall on the eastern border of Sandtown.

In the late 1950s and early 1960s, the Westside ghetto wall of separation was reinforced with two large high-rise public housing projects: Lexington Terrace, which consisted of five eleven-story towers (figure 14), and Murphy Homes.[107] In East Baltimore, the public housing wall included the Lafayette Courts, one of the nation's largest high-rise housing projects, Flag House Courts, Somerset Homes, Latrobe Homes, Douglass Homes, and Perkins Homes.[108] These projects at the edge of the "ring of blight" would institutionalize poverty and Blackness just outside of Baltimore's central business district.[109] These walls of public housing would separate the downtown from census tracts where 90 percent of the population was African American.[110]

The visible walls of public housing on the west and east edges of downtown were a deliberate, white-led strategy to protect the central business district from Black encroachment.[111] Housing historian Rhonda Williams argues the West Baltimore public housing corridor was a targeted tactic by public officials "to halt [B]lack encroach-

FIGURE 14. Lexington Terrace. Getty Images/Afro-American Newspaper/ Gado.

ment" into the city's white spaces.[112] Historian Arnold Hirsch insists, "Local and federal authorities used public housing and urban renewal to contain African Americans in certain parts of the city."[113] Political scientist Marion Orr says, "Downtown . . . segregation was so bad that the majority of [B]lacks ventured there only when it was absolutely necessary."[114]

A white political coalition led the urban renewal and Black displacement process in Baltimore to keep African Americans "firmly in place."[115] Early on, this abstract coalition included people like Clarence Perkins, the city's first housing authority director, Mayor Howard Jackson, and former mayor James H. Preston.[116] Later on, white politicians, such as mayors Theodore McKeldin, Thomas D'Alesandro Jr., and William Schaefer, and white real estate investors like John Luetkemeyer, Morris Goldseker, and James Rouse, would become important city development coalition members.[117] Business and real estate interests were embedded within white-led institutions such as the city's Committee on Segregation, the Maryland

Emergency Housing and Park Commission, Housing Authority of Baltimore City, Commission on the City Plan, the Baltimore Urban Renewal and Housing Agency, the Citizens Planning and Housing Association, the Real Estate Board of Baltimore, the Greater Baltimore Committee, and the Committee for Downtown.[118] Hirsch states, "Baltimore's status as a 'hypersegregated' city was no historical 'accident,' nor were the hands involved in its creation merely the proverbial 'invisible' ones associated with an unfettered market."[119]

Mid-twentieth-century segregation in Baltimore led to tremendous hardship and fueled mounting Black frustrations, and several individuals claimed the separation between Blacks and whites was one of the primary contributors to the impoverished conditions that produced the city's unrest of 1968.[120] Theodore Cornblatt, a trial lawyer who worked in downtown Baltimore in 1960s, recalls, "Segregation was everywhere! You couldn't go to the ball game, you know. Or a movie, anywhere. It was all segregation."[121] Thomas Carney, a white elderly lifelong Baltimore resident who grew up in Pigtown, stresses that segregation was a symbol of unequal citizenship. He states, "The anger of being a second-class citizen and the anger of being pushed into a ghetto economically severed from the rest of the country is an anger that bullets don't stop, and guns don't stop, and bayonets don't stop."[122] For Carney, the segregated ghetto conditions spurred resentment and the 1968 revolt. Kurt Schmoke, Baltimore's first elected Black mayor, recounts, "Segregation is . . . a cross that we bear."[123]

The 1968 Kerner Commission Report specified that urban unrest was primarily caused by the proliferation of segregated, impoverished Black ghettos.[124] We do not know the extent to which Baltimore's old urban renewal independently contributed to concentrated Black poverty and the uprising of 1968.[125] First, the elimination of restrictive covenants and the continued movement of whites into the suburbs opened up new urban communities for middle-income

African Americans, and some moved out of places like Sandtown-Winchester.[126] Second, racist redlining lending practices promoted by the federal government as well as labor market discrimination contributed to the creation of the African American "ring of blight" in Baltimore.[127] Still, it is hard not to include deliberate highway planning and disproportionately placing public housing in African American communities as important contributing factors in concentrating poverty, rising racial animosity, and stress for African Americans—all likely critical undercurrents of the 1968 Baltimore uprising. As one author stated, "Public policy [in the old urban renewal period] declared over and over again that Baltimore's [B]lack neighborhoods were disposable" and needed to be behind ghetto walls.[128]

While the legacy of racist zoning, redlining, highway planning, displacement, downtown protection, and public housing project placement were key factors contributing to declining conditions in Sandtown-Winchester from the 1940s to the 1960s, public housing demolitions, displacement, gentrification, and downtown expansion in the 1990s and 2000s would perpetuate the community's precarious conditions.

6 *Ghetto Walls Come Down*

It's our Baltimore version of the trickle-down economic theory, which has not been successful. . . . You give all this money to folks who already have money. It's supposed to benefit poor people eventually, but it never does.

Baltimore housing activist RALPH MOORE JR.

Lawrence Anderson, chief of staff for city council president Nick Mosby, summarizes his understanding of Baltimore's racial separation and policing: "You know, East Baltimore is Black. West Baltimore is Black. The middle of the city is white. Downtown is white. You're getting roughed up [by the police] in East Baltimore or West Baltimore. You're not getting roughed up downtown."[1] Anderson's description of the city's racial landscape comes close to what scholar Lawrence Brown deems Baltimore's "Black Butterfly" and white "L" (seen in figure 11, p. 138).[2] This situation has a historic legacy of slow violence to protect downtown, but this spatial inequality has been advanced with contemporary redevelopment policies, supported by both white and African American policymakers, to expand downtown.

Baltimore's Inner Harbor redevelopment began in the 1960s,[3] but took off in the 1990s and 2000s.[4] The Inner Harbor's redevelopment

FIGURE 15. The Inner Harbor. Photograph © David Coleman.

symbolized the city's transition from a declining industrial area to a tourist-centered, entertainment-focused, postindustrial place.[5] Between 1978 and 1982, General Motors and Bethlehem Steel laid off twelve thousand workers in Baltimore and the city had to reinvent itself into a tourist and service destination.[6] Baltimore's postindustrial transformation is illustrated by one of the Inner Harbor's central sites, the 1895 Power Plant. It was redeveloped into a location for the international restaurant chain Hard Rock Café. The restaurant opened in 1997 with a huge sixty-five-foot neon guitar placed on one of the four two-hundred-foot-tall red brick smokestacks that once projected the coal-burning electrical plant's pollution clouds (figure 15).[7]

The Inner Harbor's transformation set the city's main downtown economic development strategy and growing spatial inequality in motion.[8] While over twenty-three thousand people waited for Baltimore public housing,[9] the city spent millions of its federal community development funds to undergird the Inner Harbor's development.[10] The beneficiaries of this economic development policy were white "developers, financiers, real estate speculators, suburbanites, a few affluent condo dwellers, and tourists."[11] At the same time, low-income African Americans in the "ring of blight" "sank deeper into poverty" as the private and public housing stock, within and beyond the walls of separation, fell into severe disrepair.[12] In 1970, there were seven thousand vacant housing units in Baltimore; by 1997 that figure had skyrocketed to forty thousand.[13] Deindustrialization devastated Baltimore, and downtown entertainment, "Disneyfication," was going to solve it.

White real estate developer James "Jim" Rouse masterminded the Inner Harbor's redevelopment.[14] Rouse, the Greater Baltimore Committee's first urban renewal chairman,[15] convinced local "private investors and government [actors] to work together on downtown revitalization."[16] The Rouse Company devised the redevelopment of Boston's Faneuil Hall and Quincy Marketplace and was keen on replicating this economic success in Charm City.[17] In the 1970s Rouse saw the rundown port and envisioned it as Harborplace: a "festival mall" development with shops, restaurants, a convention center, an aquarium, a science center, and hotels.[18] He believed public and private investments could turn the harbor into a tourist destination and stimulate the revitalization of nearby neighborhoods.[19]

Rouse convinced four-term mayor William Donald Schaefer (in office 1971–87) to use millions in public dollars to "create several popular Inner Harbor attractions."[20] Historian Marc Levine states, "Schaefer's audacious aim was to transform this . . . [area] into a bustling 'carnival city' of tourist attractions . . . that would lure visitors from the suburbs and beyond."[21] Undergirded with city resources, a $52 million convention center, a Hyatt Regency Hotel, an aquarium, and a Rouse-developed festival marketplace opened in and around the harbor between 1979 and 1981.[22]

Like St. Louis, Baltimore disproportionately invested in white spaces, but unlike St. Louis, Baltimore made its decision even with significant Black representation in local government. After Mayor Schaefer was elected Maryland's governor in 1986, Kurt Schmoke became Baltimore's first elected African American mayor.[23] There was hope that, with Baltimore's Black-majority population and the election of Schmoke, redevelopment priorities would be redirected to the "ring of blight" rather than downtown.[24]

Initially, Schmoke made good on his campaign promise to expand neighborhood redevelopment outside of the downtown area. Schmoke formed a partnership with the Enterprise Foundation, a community development foundation founded by Rouse, and BUILD, the progressive, congregational community organization co-led by Rev. Miles.[25] Together, these partners launched a $130 million comprehensive community initiative to tackle housing, job training, business development, education reform, policing, and community building over a ten-year period in Sandtown.[26] Rouse was committed to the Sandtown initiative, calling it "the most important work . . . in my lifetime."[27] However, the project, unlike the Inner Harbor, was woefully underfunded for the needs of the neighborhood, had management conflicts, and "failed to attract much in the way of private investment."[28]

While Schmoke created some additional neighborhood initiatives during his three mayoral terms between 1987 and 1999, his administration remained centered on downtown expansion. As one of the country's "messiah mayors," he "preached the gospel of economic growth."[29] The Schmoke administration pursued "policies of fiscal austerity, by giving generous tax breaks and a variety of subsidies, and by forming public–private relationships that privatised urban redevelopment."[30] Mayor Schmoke kept "feeding the downtown monster" created by Rouse and Schaefer.[31] Schmoke "supported property development around the Inner Harbor as vigorously as had his predecessor," with "massive public investments in tourism and entertainment facilities,"[32] which ultimately did little to improve the circumstances of low-income African Americans.[33]

In the 1990s, Mayor Schmoke also contributed to the decision to take down the city's high-rise public housing projects. Schmoke explains, "What we found was that a lot of companies—for a lot of companies—it was the safety issue [of the downtown area] that was a huge deterrent." According to Schmoke, "The high-rises had been used as agreed places for drug activity."[34] To deal with this downtown business deterrent, the perceived crime hot spots, the high-rises, had to go.

While the number of public housing projects decreased in the 1990s, the downtown development continued under the Schmoke administration with the construction of new, nearby sports stadiums.[35] In 1992 and 1998, the Oriole Park at Camden Yards baseball and M&T Bank Baltimore Ravens football stadiums opened next to each other.[36] Each was financed almost entirely with $500 million in state and city funds, and these major developments greatly advanced the downtown and Inner Harbor area expansion.[37] Baltimore continued to bet on the entertainment industry to replace its declining industrial base.[38]

These central city investments occurred during a difficult economic decline period in Baltimore. Between 1980 and 2009, manufacturing jobs decreased from 19 percent to 4.5 percent of the city's employment base. Additionally, the city continued to lose people; between 1990 and 2010, Baltimore lost nearly 16 percent of its population. The city's already high poverty rate also increased. Between 1989 and 2010, the poverty rate rose from 22 percent to 26 percent.[39] Urban policy expert Harold Wolman and his colleague deemed Baltimore the quintessential "distressed former industrial city."[40]

Despite Baltimore's doom-and-gloom economic scenario, the downtown/Inner Harbor investment gamble was perceived by some as a winning play. In the 2000s, the neighborhoods around the Inner Harbor, the city's "jewel," started to gentrify with increased income, property value, and educational levels.[41] During this period, a remarkable 23 percent of the city's lower-income census tracts, several near the Inner Harbor, gentrified.[42] These redeveloping neighborhoods included South Baltimore, Federal Hill, and Downtown. In the previous decade, a much lower percentage, only 9 percent, of Baltimore's low-income tracts gentrified.[43] The Inner Harbor redevelopment of the 1990s and nearby public housing revitalization efforts helped attract mainly white millennials to central city Baltimore in the 2000s.[44]

In the 2000s, the Inner Harbor, downtown, and Sandtown, which are relatively close to one another radiating out from the Patapsco River, had drastically different economic trajectories. Between 2010 and 2015, the citywide vacancy rate was stable at 8 percent, but this belies major within-city differences. During this period, the Inner Harbor's residential vacancy rate remained at less than one percent; downtown's decreased from 12 percent to 8 percent, while Sandtown-Winchester/Harlem Park area's rate increased from 31 percent to 35 percent.[45]

As the vacancy rate increased in Sandtown-Winchester/Harlem Park, its economic standing in relative terms to inner, whiter areas near downtown and the Inner Harbor grew worse. The median household income in Sandtown-Winchester/Harlem Park between 2010 and 2015 remained stable, increasing less than one percent from $23,974 to $24,108. During the same five-year period, the citywide median household income level improved from $38,346 to $42,241, a 10 percent increase. During this period the downtown median household income rose from $33,873 to $46,133, a 36 percent increase, and the Inner Harbor's climbed from $77,888 to $88,465, a 14 percent increase. The economic gap between nearly all-Black Sandtown and the predominately white Inner Harbor grew by 19 percentage points prior to the 2015 uprising.

Some scholars described Baltimore's central city redevelopment as "Disneyification" and "Rousification."[46] Huge amounts of public funds were deployed to the Inner Harbor to create a carnival-like atmosphere, and neighborhoods near the "carnival" began to gentrify.

FIGURE 16. The Inner Harbor's Sandlot. Photo by author.

Johns Hopkins University sociologist Stefanie DeLuca and her colleagues noted, "In the Inner Harbor, empty lots and rotting warehouses have been replaced by farm-to-table restaurants, coffee shops, galleries, and the like. Industrial areas that had been dormant for decades are now bustling with millennials and empty-nesters residing in new upscale condos and apartments."[47]

Nowhere was the central city's gentrification and postindustrial transformation more evident than at the Sandlot (figure 16). This "beach front" bar, frequented by millennials, was added to an area where a large chromium chemical plant, Mutual Chemical Company, once existed along the Inner Harbor.[48] To remediate this brownfield site, the city approved over $100 million in Tax Increment Financing (TIF) funds.[49] Developments like the Sandlot carried on the city's Inner Harbor redevelopment strategy and investment focus that catered to upper-income people.

For some, gentrification was just about neighborhood change that increased the city's tax base,[50] but others saw it as a symbol of homogenization, racism, and Black exploitation.[51] Author D. Watkins, who grew up in the "ring of blight" in East Baltimore, claims central city Baltimore was experiencing "Gentri-fuckin-cation." Watkins laments: "My city is gone, my history depleted, ruined, and undocumented. I don't know this new Baltimore, it's alien to me. Baltimore is Brooklyn and DC now. No, Baltimore is Chicago or New Orleans or any place where yuppie interests make [B]lack neighborhoods shrink like washed sweaters. A place where [B]lack history is bulldozed and replaced with Starbucks, Chipotles, and dog parks."[52] West Baltimore–born acclaimed author Ta-Nehisi Coates exclaims, "I know that 'gentrification' is but a more pleasing name for white supremacy, is the interest on enslavement, the interest on Jim Crow, the interest on redlining, compounding across the years."[53] Public health scholar Lawrence Brown adds, "Gentrification is the latest manifestation of serial forced displacement, one that ends with re-branding Black communities and erasing Black history."[54]

Some of Baltimore's gentrification relates to decades of divestment and deindustrialization,[55] but also to the demolition of the public housing projects and displacement of Black people out of "emerging market" neighborhoods near the Inner Harbor.[56] The removal of low-income African Americans made these areas targets for real estate developers seeking public funds, like TIFs, and profits.[57] While beer garden beaches, coffee shops, and luxury residences came in, public housing went down.

Public Housing High-Rise Demolition: The Ghetto Walls Come Down

The Wire, the well-known HBO series about Baltimore, was set in the fictional "Terraces." In actuality, the Terraces depicted the real-life Lexington Terrace, a high-rise public housing complex. In the show, these West Baltimore high-rises were controlled by a fictitious drug lord, Avon Barksdale. In reality, this public housing project, located just southeast of Sandtown and west of downtown, has been a place of poverty and struggle, plagued by gang and drug violence for years.[58] Former U.S. Department of Housing and Urban Development Secretary Henry Cisneros recalled that he wanted to walk through the Lexington Terrace on a 1993 city visit, but was warned by the Baltimore Housing Authority Police it was unsafe due to potential "cross-fire of a drug deal gone wrong."[59]

In the media, high-rise public housing projects are often associated with Blackness, violence, and drugs.[60] While many of the high-rises in cities like Baltimore and Chicago have elements of the drug trade in them,[61] rarely are most residents involved in these illicit activities. These places are where people live, organize, and mobilize in the face of hardship caused by intense poverty.[62] Yet public housing high-rises often carry a stigma and raise fears of violence and crime.[63] As noted by Mayor Schmoke, the projects are seen as "warehouses of poverty . . . characterized by high crime rates [and] significant unemployment."[64]

Just like the revitalization that occurred to the old warehouses and factories along the Inner Harbor, the warehouses of the poor, the projects, needed to be upgraded too. However, rather than rehabilitation, they were completely razed.[65] In the 1990s, to clear the ill "sites and sights" near downtown, Baltimore demolished most of its public housing high-rises and built mixed-income housing in their place.[66] Baltimore journalist and author Joan Jacobson details, "On its 70th anniversary, the housing authority—once on a mission to replace slums with safe homes for Baltimore's poor—is now in the demolition business; its occupied inventory has dropped by 42 percent over the last 15 years—from 16,525 units in 1992 to 9,625 in the spring of 2007."[67]

Many projects in the "ring of blight," such as the Lexington Terrace in West Baltimore and the Lafayette Courts in East Baltimore, were demolished. "In July 1996 the Housing Authority dynamited

FIGURE 17. The Lexington Terrace's dynamite demolition. AP Photo/Gary Sussman.

Lexington Terrace, nearly seven hundred dwellings, and celebrated the event with balloons and a parade" (figure 17).[68] The destruction of the wall of subsidized housing was made into a public spectacle, and hundreds of people watched from a distance as the buildings imploded. When the dynamite blasted, each high-rise building collapsed on top of itself, and a large cloud of dust rose. While some celebrated the demise of the housing projects, others felt differently. Author D. Watkins declares, "I used to hang in Lafayette Housing Projects with my big cousin Damon. . . . That place is gone."[69]

Between 1993 and 2010, the city received over $166 million from HUD through its HOPE VI program to help facilitate the razing of Baltimore's high-rise public housing wall.[70] The new rowhouse communities built in its place were mixed-income and contained both subsidized housing and market-rate units.[71] Some of the market-rate dwellings sold for over $300,000.[72] With the implementation of HOPE VI, inner areas of Baltimore's "ring of blight" became twice-cleared communities and some even gentrified.[73]

The razing of public housing removed a powerful symbol of violence and crime, signaling to investors and new residents that these areas, just beyond the traditional central business district, were now safe for redevelopment and downtown expansion.[74] While it took some time, HOPE VI neighborhoods attracted new investments. The University of Maryland at Baltimore expanded its downtown footprint and opened an $11 million BioPark located near where the Lexington Terrace project once stood.[75] Jim Hughes, director of the new technology center, notes, "We're excited that the success of the Bio-Park is spreading a little deeper into the community."[76] By "community" he meant the Black community. When asked about the impact of the public housing demolition, Mayor Schmoke acknowledges, "It aided both the [redevelopment] plans. . . . It aided the Hopkins Medical Center plans [on the east side]. And on the west side, the University of Maryland expansion was helped, because they didn't have to persuade their faculty and staff about the safety concerns, because the high-rises were gone. . . . It certainly has made the areas more attractive and inviting for families."[77]

In addition to public housing demolition, the redevelopment of the BioPark area was also aided with TIF funds. The BioPark development received $12 million in TIF funds to help build upscale high-rise housing aimed at students and staff of the University of Baltimore, with amenities including balconies with downtown views, a pool, and a dog wash station.[78] In Baltimore, like in St. Louis, TIF resources were used to undergird downtown and nearby neighborhood redevelopment. One estimate put Baltimore's TIFs at nearly $1 billion, with most of those funds concentrated in the greater downtown/Inner Harbor area.[79]

While new investments expanded the downtown footprint, the housing projects demolition led to displacement of low-income African Americans, many of whom ended up in sections of West and East Baltimore further from the central business district. A 2002 Urban

Institute study tracked the relocation of Baltimore residents from three HOPE VI sites: Lexington Terrace (on the West), Flag House (on the East), and Hollander Ridge (far East). The study demonstrated that displaced residents with rental assistance, Section 8 vouchers, went to many different neighborhoods throughout the city. A few even found housing in the Baltimore suburbs,[80] in neighborhoods that were slightly less impoverished yet similarly racially segregated. However, the study also found displaced people went to West and East low-income minority areas within or in proximity to the existing "ring of blight."[81]

The HOPE VI program in Baltimore did not alleviate concentrated poverty, but rather pushed it outward and further from the central business district. In Baltimore, public housing "displacement and disruption . . . acted to concentrate deprivation" and solidify downtown segregation.[82] Lifelong Sandtown resident Raymond "Ray" Kelly claims, "So really it's like . . . instead of finding a cure or addressing the root issues . . . you're just moving it."[83] He attests it was a "constant relocation of an impoverished people."[84] This was Baltimore's modern version of "slum shifting."[85]

Some scholars, such as Stefanie DeLuca, Susan Clampet-Lundquist, and Kathryn Edin, argued the demolition of public housing was justified because it was correlated with an overall decrease in the city's number of high-poverty census tracts from thirty-five in 1990 to twenty-five in 2008–12.[86] While fewer people lived in high-poverty tracts after the demolition of the city's high-rise projects, 52,480 in 1990 versus 31,241 in 2008–12, there was still high rates of poverty in West and East Baltimore and in the city as a whole. The percentage of those living in poverty increased from 21.9 percent in 1990 to 23.4 percent in 2008–12. Poverty just moved a little further from the downtown with the demolition of public housing; it was relocated, not alleviated.

The demolition of the projects forced many displaced people to move to West or East Baltimore, city sections already with high poverty concentration.[87] Places like Sandtown-Winchester received numerous low-income public housing refugees, while new mixed-income communities built with HOPE VI funds stimulated the revitalization of areas where the old public housing sites once stood. As one observer notes, "Displaced from other neighborhoods, criminal activity in Sandtown was on the rise" and conditions in the community became worse.[88] Others attest, during the period of public housing demolitions, "Sandtown grew increasingly poor and dysfunctional."[89]

The Subprime Mess

If the disruption of public housing removal was not enough, in the 2000s, African American communities would also be exploited by white-dominated lenders and their subprime loan departments.[90] Wells Fargo and other lenders greedy for profits targeted Black communities for the origination of unsustainable subprime loans.[91] As one of Wells Fargo's loan officers states, "We just went right after them," with "Wealth Building Strategies seminars" hosted by Black churches to peddle subprime loans to people.[92] Some Wells Fargo employees described the subprime plot as one in which they deployed "ghetto loans" to "mud people."[93] "Black [Baltimore] borrowers, [between 2000 and 2008], were systematically steered into higher cost loans, with monthly payments that were 5.3 percent higher than those of similarly qualified whites after taking into account a host of background characteristics. . . . Black borrowers were also 50 percent more likely to be channeled into high-risk loans. Because of their higher costs and risks, they were 70 percent more likely to end up in foreclosure."[94] Half of the Wells Fargo–originated mortgages in Baltimore between 2005 and 2008 went to homes that were vacant by 2009, and 71 percent of these vacant properties were in African American neighborhoods.[95] Ralph Moore Jr.,

FIGURE 18. Boarded-up buildings. AP Photo/Patrick Semansky.

who worked most of his career in Baltimore's affordable housing sector, pronounces, "People were preyed upon by this whole housing business. And people made their money on these junk deals and crappy [financial] instruments and all that kind of things. So people were ripped off."[96]

Baltimore already had one of the worst vacancy problems in the country. In 1999, the city had around 12,700 vacant units.[97] In 2010, following the Great Recession and its foreclosure fallout, the home vacancy figure rose to 16,800.[98]

The subprime crisis disproportionately impacted Baltimore's Black neighborhoods including Sandtown. In Sandtown-Winchester/ Harlem Park, the percentage of vacant housing stock increased from 31 percent in 2010 to 35 percent in 2015. A 2011 study revealed that between 2008 and 2010 the most intense concentration of foreclosures was in Black neighborhoods, like in Sandtown, where African Americans were over 70 percent of the population.[99] Comparatively, there were few foreclosures in the white areas, where African Americans were less than 10 percent of the population. The subprime mess was another form of slow violence that negatively affected Black Baltimore (figure 18).

Baltimore's public housing destruction, central city investments, and the Great Recession foreclosure fallout reinforced and perpetuated racial and spatial inequality. After the fall of the housing project, the Inner Harbor development engine "began looking for opportunities in unconquered territories farther inland, but not too far away from the waterfront."[100] "New money flowed toward the water" and Black people got pushed out further from it.[101] Urban scholar Richard Florida notes, "If Baltimore's gentrifying neighborhoods were reviving and thriving, large sections of the city were rife with poverty. Not far from the Inner Harbor, atop a hill overlooking it, stands the Sandtown-Winchester neighborhood. . . . Freddie Gray's death and the events that followed it showed how Baltimore really is two separate cities— one a thriving city of highly educated, prosperous knowledge workers, the other a sinking city of largely African Americans trapped in persistent poverty."[102] The public housing demolition, subprime mess, and unequal TIF investments were forms of slow violence that stimulated displacement and central city gentrification; maintained existing segregation; and targeted Black areas for capital extraction.

Lawrence Anderson, Nick Mosby's chief of staff, connects the new urban renewal policy of public housing demolition to the uprisings. He asserts, "When we talk about the unrest and what caused it, my initial response is a lack of humanity."[103] He continues, "You got to respect the game, and that game is rooted in the humanity of people. When you begin to view people not as persons and living things, and just a byproduct of whatever it is that you want to do, that [unrest] is going to happen. And a city like Baltimore, where things, it's a rough city, but people really do take care of each other because it's a rough city. And they don't take kindly to people who are indiscriminate in their actions."[104] He adds, "If you have a press conference and you're celebrating the explosion of a place with people cheering, that's disrespectful. Period. . . . The street corrects itself. It may not be in the most socially accepted way, but there is a rhyme and reason to it."[105]

Baltimore, even with Black representation, razed the projects. This decision had immense racial implications. Even though Schmoke infrequently spoke about race,[106] the decision to demolish the projects was a racial one. It displaced low-income African Americans and helped to stimulate white-led gentrification. Rev. Miles states, "Every major decision in Baltimore is driven by race. And anybody who denies that just has their head in the sand."[107]

The 1968 Kerner Commission report suggested that unrest primarily stemmed from the disadvantaged circumstances in isolated, impoverished, inner-city Black communities.[108] In Baltimore, old and new urban renewal policies contributed to the segregation of low-income African Americans. Serial displacement was enacted to protect and then expand the downtown. Housing historian Lawrence Vale notes in his 2013 book *Purging the Poorest*, the building and then demolition of public housing represent to some policymakers a reclaiming of space "from unruly behavior."[109] At the same time, social psychiatrist and urban planner Dr. Mindy Fullilove states that the reclaiming process through displacement is a form of state-sponsored violence.[110] "African Americans have always been displaced in this town to make way for whatever project it is that corporate Baltimore wants to do," declares longtime Baltimore activist Rev. Miles.[111] The displacement process and the impoverished conditions it facilitated might have led to other unruly acts—aggressive policing and the ensuing uprisings following Gray's death. Baltimore built the ghetto walls and tore them down, but nothing changed. Baltimore's affluent white "L" and impoverished Black butterfly remained intact; the butterfly wings just moved a little further back from the white downtown and nearby waterfront.[112] Historian Marc Levine claims, "There was very little 'trickle down' redevelopment from the rejuvenated Inner Harbor to Baltimore's most distressed neighborhoods."[113] The removal of the projects consequently facilitated racial inequality. There was not going to be trickle-down economics when the projects went down, only a beat down. Public housing went down and stop-and-frisk went up; then it all blew up.

7 *Watch Out for Broken Windows!*

I walk the streets of Baltimore and am even more appalled . . . at the lack of justice, unity and friendliness. I say 'more appalled' because now the inequalities are so striking, so blatantly unnecessary, so against any kind of reason, and so accepted as part of some immutable 'natural order of things,' that I can scarcely contain my outrage and frustration.

Geography professor DAVID HARVEY

Broken Windows and Hearts

David Harvey, the acclaimed urban theorist and longtime Johns Hopkins University professor,[1] wrote the above passage in 2000; over 20 years later it is even more apt. I had the same impression when I visited Baltimore between 2018 and 2022. The city is incredible—great people, sports, food, music, and quaint neighborhoods—but there is a tremendous amount of heavily policed poverty and pain. Rather than [B]lack and orange, the colors of the Baltimore Orioles baseball team, the city can leave you feeling "Black and Blue."[2]

In the early 1980s, two social scientists, George L. Kelling and James Q. Wilson, coined and popularized the broken windows theory of policing.[3] According to their theory, if police stop petty crimes such as loitering, graffiti, jaywalking, and broken windows, it will send a signal to criminals that people care about the community, and larger infractions, such as drug dealing, robbery, and murder, will not occur.[4] These scholars assume that once you extinguish or diminish minor infractions of the social code, major crime will occur with far less frequency.

Broken windows, also known as zero tolerance, policing was supposed to lower crime rates; instead, it fueled intense frustrations in low-income Black communities. Law and policing scholar Bernard Harcourt asserts, "I find that there is no good evidence to support the broken windows theory. In fact, the social science data reveal no statistically significant relationship between disorder and crime."[5] In the 1990s and 2000s, violent crime rates decreased nationwide, both in cities that implemented zero tolerance policing like New York and Baltimore and in cities that did not.[6]

Whether broken windows policing reduces overall crime is controversial; what is not debated is the significant harm this type of policing has caused Black and Brown people.[7] Harcourt claims broken windows policing has "significant costs, including increased complaints of police misconduct, racial bias in stop and frisks, and further stereotyping of [B]lack criminality."[8] Broken widows policing expert Jan Haldipur insists, "This approach to policing . . . led to a substantial erosion of faith in local and state institutions."[9]

In the 1990s urban public housing complexes, often sites associated with crime and disorder,[10] were razed throughout the country.[11] As discussed, over $6 billion in federal HOPE VI funds were distributed between 1993 and 2010 to local housing authorities to knock down distressed public housing developments and construct mixed-income housing in their stead.[12] These efforts contributed to Black displacement and gentrification throughout urban America, including in St. Louis and Baltimore.[13]

Much scholarly and public attention has been paid to the negative effects of broken windows policing[14] and the destruction of public housing;[15] however, few link these two policies to conditions associated with unrest.[16] The rise of broken windows policing is tied to the razing and destruction of public housing developments and the movement of the poor to other low-income Black neighborhoods. When the brick and concrete walls of separation, the projects, came down, new walls of police surveillance were "built" to monitor and contain ghetto residents.[17] Zero tolerance police practices were instituted to keep low-income African Americans in their "place."[18]

Baltimore's broken windows police practices deeply affected the city's Black population. The U.S. Department of Justice wrote a report, based on a fourteen-month investigation of the Baltimore Police Department (BPD) following the 2015 death of Freddie Gray. The report found that between 2010 and 2015, African Americans represented 84 percent of police pedestrian stops and 82 percent of traffic violation stops, despite African Americans only comprising 64 percent of the city's population.[19] Moreover, between January 2010 and May 2014, the BPD recorded over 301,000 pedestrian stops, primarily in African American neighborhoods.[20] Baltimore activist Kwame Rose proclaims, "To be Black in the city . . . is to be constantly patrolled."[21]

Baltimore police stops are not just racial; they are spatial. A disproportionate number of stops occurred in the "ring of blight" of West and East Baltimore. Forty-four percent of the total pedestrian stops between 2010 and 2014 occurred in the Western and Central districts, effectively West and East Baltimore.[22] These are the impoverished Black communities directly behind where the public housing walls once stood. With the demolition of public housing and implementation of stop-and-frisk policing, Baltimore's murder rate went down but intense pain was caused and frustrations bubbled up.

Baltimore's unrest story is different from Ferguson's. Ferguson is a Black-majority city run by a small white power structure, and where the police force is 94 percent white. Baltimore is a much larger Black-majority city, where the political structure is fragmented, has had much more racial political representation, and the police force is nearly half African American.[23] When Gray was killed, the Baltimore mayor, most of the city council members, the police commissioner, much of the police force, and the school's chief executive were African American. While it is important to examine the role of white society and the history of racial discrimination to understand the conditions associated with unrest, it is also important to examine the behavior of African American politicians.

Second, Baltimore's abusive policing did not bring in sufficient city revenue. Baltimore's punitive policing cost the city millions. Between 2010 and 2019, Baltimore paid $36.5 million to settle police misconduct cases.[24] In contrast, Ferguson paid $1.5 million to settle police misconduct cases.[25] The combined total police payout for misconduct in St. Louis and Ferguson during about the same period was only $5.2 million.[26] In Baltimore, abusive policing is not a tax revenue generator; rather, is it a surveillance and containment strategy to maintain segregation.[27]

In this chapter, I focus on how neighborhood conditions and the city's broader political structure relate to street violence. I argue that Black and white elected officials in Baltimore made housing and police decisions that replicate and advance the city's neighborhood racial inequality. It was a one-two punch to the city's poor African Americans. In the 1990s, Black mayor Kurt Schmoke made the first blow with his decisions to knock down the city's high-rise public housing. In the 2000s, white mayor Martin O'Malley threw the next punch with stop-and-frisk policing. When police violence layered on top of, and mixed with, other forms of state-led slow violence including public housing demolition, displacement, gentrification, and subprime lending, it became a toxic combination. Slow violence facilitated intolerable racial and spatial inequalities and police agony, setting the stage for another form of violence—the uprisings.

Beyond linking public housing policy, policing, and unrest, this chapter makes two other important and related contributions. I reinforce an important but often overlooked assertion: "The selective enforcement of petty crime and public disorder has become a policy tool in larger, urban projects of revitalization, gentrification, and postindustrial growth."[28] Additionally, I argue that fractured political landscapes can engender violence. Baltimore's highly fragmented political structure relates to its police and street violence,[29] and helps to explain why so many Baltimoreans carry the "weight" of violence, especially in the Black neighborhoods that went up in flames.

Unequal Neighborhoods, Unjust Policing

Baltimore's gentrification, like that of St. Louis, functions as the fulcrum of the city's racial segregation. Public housing and community development policies push low-income African Americans back from the gentrifying Inner Harbor neighborhoods. Central city investments and associated gentrification attract whites to certain neighborhoods while public housing policies both displace lower-income African Americans and prevent them from being close to these redeveloping neighborhoods. Housing and community development policies perpetuated segregation, and it is in these segregated Black Baltimore communities where aggressive policing was concentrated.

Raymond "Ray" Kelly, leader of Baltimore's No Boundaries Coalition, argues that housing policies trigger abusive police actions. After Gray was killed, Kelly helped to convene over a hundred people to document the abusive policing that took place mainly in Sandtown. Kelly grew up in the community and experienced its street life firsthand. As a recovering substance user, Kelly turned his challenging experiences into a powerful story of transformation. Kelly now mobilizes individuals to improve the conditions of his community.

Kelly's organization, No Boundaries, helped to elucidate Baltimore's abusive policing and connected it to the politics of uneven urban development and state-led slow violence. According to a 2016 No Boundaries report, "The more enduring legacy of redevelopment has been the reconfiguration of policing strategies enacted to contain poor city residents to the 'ghetto.' The fragmentation of urban space into zones within which citizens would be policed and treated differentially based upon their class, race, and residency has become a fixture of post-industrial Baltimore."[30] Housing policies, such as the demolition of public housing, are critical to the rise of Baltimore's aggressive police practices in its segregated low-income Black communities.

When the walls of public housing came down, new "walls" of police supervision went up. Between 2010 and 2014, police made 111,500 pedestrian stops in the low-income, African American West and East Baltimore areas, which contained 12 percent of Baltimore's population. Police made nearly 55,000 pedestrian stops in the smallest police district—the Western district (effectively the Greater Sandtown area), with a population of a little more than 37,000 people, 97 percent of whom are African American. In comparison, the police made only 21,000 stops in the white Northern district, an area with a population of approximately 91,000. The Baltimore Police Department made 146 stops for every 100 residents in the predominantly African American and low-income Western district, while making only 22.5 stops per 100 residents in the predominantly white Northern district—a more than 6 to 1 disparity.[31] Criminologist, sociologist, and former Baltimore police officer Peter Moskos acknowledges, "People in high-crime neighborhoods, usually young [B]lack men, are stopped and frisked far more often than people in other neighborhoods."[32]

Policing the "Ring of Blight"

Broken windows police tactics, such as stop-and-frisk, are used as a form of social control in Baltimore's "ring of blight." Moskos proclaims, "In high-drug areas, minor arrests are very common, but rarely prosecuted. Loitering arrests usually do not articulate the legally required 'obstruction of passage.' But the point of loitering arrests is not to convict people of the misdemeanor. . . . These lockups are used by police to assert authority."[33] Baltimore author D. Watkins describes the city's police practices: "Cops don't ask questions. They jump out with cocked guns and wave them at crowds of people. It doesn't really matter if you are guilty or not, that's a tax for being poor."[34] One Baltimore patrol officer bluntly blurts his version of zero tolerance policing. "You've got to be the baddest motherfucker out there," which requires one to "own the block."[35] To own the block, Baltimore police officers offend, disrespect, and abuse many low-income African Americans.

The Baltimore Police Department exhibits a "culture of police brutality" that has deeply impacted Sandtown residents. An elderly African American pastor tells a story about a time when he asked the police to move their cars, which were blocking his vehicle. He says they responded, "We do what the fuck we want."[36] A West Baltimore Black resident recalls his awful interaction with the police: "The officer picked me up and slammed me on my face, took my backpack off, and threw all my books out, and when they didn't find anything kicked me in my stomach."[37] Kelly claims Baltimore policing would "clear corners, [with] head busters," a term used to describe violent police officers.[38] There is a perception that "police officers will murder you and not feel bad because they are trained to think you are not a person."[39] Taylor, a nineteen-year-old African American and West Baltimore resident, pronounces, "Yeah people are tired, they're tired of the same thing keep happening. They're tired of the cops killing . . . young men and women, and getting away with it. So yeah, now they reached a breaking point."[40] According to criminologist Patrick Sharkey, zero tolerance policing takes "a heavy toll,"[41] and strains an already tenuous relationship between poor African American communities and the state.[42]

Police violence and disrespect breed greater violence. Kelly claims Baltimore policing was designed "to intimidate . . . and that created this situation . . . where you have violence from drug dealers combating violence from the police department."[43] Aggressive policing leads to police-induced violence. Erricka Bridgeford, founder of Baltimore Ceasefire, says: "You mentioned violence, right, and murder, I mean some people look at it as crews going after crews right, over drug territory and that's what's related to the murders. But also . . . the police [are] going after people. And that's their own crew, right, and they're murdering people."[44]

In 2017, seven Baltimore officers, part of a strategic tactical team known as the Gun Trace Task Force (GTTF), were indicted for stealing drugs and money from street dealers.[45] This "police crew" was also suspected of killing one of their own. In 2017, a Baltimore detective, Sean Suiter, was shot the day before he was scheduled to testify against his fellow GTTF officers.[46] While not convicted of the detective's murder, several members of the GTTF team went to prison for federal conspiracy, gun, and narcotics charges.[47] When some police officers disrespect, intimidate, and steal from people struggling to survive in a deindustrialized city, it is only a matter of time before those living with the burden of violence snap.

The Politics of Housing and Policing: The One-Two Punch

The Schmoke Years

In the 1960s and 1970s, there was considerable discussion about when Baltimore would elect an African American mayor as the city's

Black population percentage increased.[48] In the mid-1970s, Baltimore became a Black-majority city.[49] Other cities with large Black population shares elected Black mayors in the 1970s. In Cleveland, Carol Stokes became mayor in 1967, in Detroit, Coleman Young was elected mayor in 1973, and in Washington, DC, Walter Washington was elected in 1974.[50] Baltimore took considerably longer to elect an African American mayor. Baltimore elected its first African American mayor, Kurt Schmoke, in 1987.

Schmoke was born and raised in West Baltimore to college-educated parents.[51] He was a public high school superstar: head of his class academically and an excellent athlete. As quarterback he led his football team to the city championship in his senior year. In 1967, he matriculated at Yale University and was a Rhodes Scholar at Oxford. He subsequently earned a law degree from Harvard University in 1976.[52]

After law school, Schmoke returned to Charm City and began his political career. In 1982, he was elected the state's attorney for Baltimore, defeating a white incumbent.[53] In 1986, Schmoke ran for mayor against Clarence "Du" Burns, the African American mayor appointed by Maryland governor William Donald Shaefer.[54] Schmoke defeated Du Burns and served three consecutive mayoral terms between 1987 and 1999. During his time as mayor, he advocated for education reform, downtown growth, the elimination of high-rise public housing, and community policing.[55]

In the mid-1980s and 1990s, Baltimore's violent crime was a constant political issue.[56] This was the height of the crack epidemic which brought violence to inner-city areas across America.[57] In 1987, Baltimore had 226 murders, and by 1998 it had risen to 315.[58] This was during a period when the overall city population declined.

Mayor Schmoke insisted on downtown development and the demolition of public housing close to the city's central business district. While Schmoke's community policing strategy might have been perceived as an attempt to build trust with low-income residents,[59] his economic and housing strategy helped to advance Black displacement and inequality between the downtown and Sandtown. In 2018, I interviewed Mayor Schmoke about his decision to raze public housing in the 1990s. I ask, "In looking back . . . do you have any reservations for how the knocking down of [public] housing went?" Mayor Schmoke responds, "Not at all. See, HOPE VI became a curse word, in some cities, but I thought we did it right. I still do."[60] Mayor Schmoke thought the removal of the projects helped to stimulate the development near the razed sites. For him, the projects were deterrents to downtown economic development.

During Schmoke's last term, an up-and-coming white city council member, Martin O'Malley, consistently called for "zero tolerance" policing.[61] O'Malley, who grew up in the Maryland suburbs, thought this type of policing could address the city's rising violent crime rate.[62] With such a high murder rate,[63] Schmoke decided not to run for a fourth term. In his stead, O'Malley ran for mayor with a campaign platform to reduce the city's violence.

The O'Malley Years

In 1999, crime reduction was the central Baltimore mayoral campaign topic. While serving as a city council member, O'Malley visited New York City to learn about zero tolerance police practices instituted under New York's mayor Rudy Giuliani.[64] New York was one of the first cities to fully implement the broken windows theory of policing.[65] Mayor Giuliani hired William Bratton as the city's police commissioner, and he began to execute broken windows policing tactics with gusto.[66] Under Commissioner Bratton, those involved with petty street crimes, including jumping subway entrance turnstiles, painting graffiti, smoking marijuana, panhandling, and selling single cigarettes, were targeted.[67] Subsequently, New York City crime rates dipped, and broken windows policing was adopted across metropolitan America and became "one of the most influential police concepts of our era."[68] O'Malley assumed that tougher policing could lower Baltimore's rising crime rate.[69] He kicked off his mayoral campaign from one of Baltimore's known drug locations.[70]

During the primary race, O'Malley earned endorsements from some of the city's respected African American elected officials. Howard P. Rawlings, an African American State General Assembly delegate, supported O'Malley. Rawlings declared, "It's not a question of being the best [B]lack candidate or the best white candidate, O'Malley's the best candidate for Baltimore."[71] Rawlings bucked racial representation expectations and supported O'Malley over Lawrence A. Bell, the sitting African American city council president.

In September 1999, Martin O'Malley unexpectedly won the Democratic primary for mayor. With a 63 percent African American city population, many thought an African American would succeed Schmoke's twelve-year reign. Bell had been expected to win the Democratic mayoral primary.[72] However, in an extremely crowded primary field of over twenty-seven candidates, O'Malley stood out because of his tough-on-crime campaign and key endorsements.

Starting in 2000, O'Malley brought New York–style zero tolerance policing to Baltimore.[73] O'Malley instantly fired Schmoke's community-oriented police chief and appointed New York Police Department (NYPD) veteran Ed Norris as Baltimore's police commissioner. Norris had worked at the NYPD since 1980 and had served as its deputy inspector under Bratton.

With Norris in place, the Baltimore policing strategy shifted from talking with folks on the corners to clearing corners. "BPD supervisors encouraged officers to issue citations and make arrests for low-level 'quality of life' offenses, including loitering, trespassing, disorderly conduct, failure to obey, and disturbing the peace."[74] According to a U.S. Department of Justice report, "Throughout the 1990s and

2000s, arresting large numbers of people for minor offenses was central to BPD's enforcement paradigm; in 2005, BPD made more than 108,000 arrests, most for nonviolent offenses."[75]

During O'Malley's tenure from 1999 to 2007, Baltimore's murder numbers slightly declined, which helped to facilitate his political rise. The 305 murders in 1999 declined by 7.5 percent to 282 in 2007.[76] In part because of the perception of his crime-fighting success, O'Malley received the "America's Best Young Mayor" award from *Esquire* in 2002.[77] O'Malley used his tough-on-crime image to launch a winning campaign for Maryland's governor.

Yet there was a huge price to pay for O'Malley's aggressive policing policy, and some people argued that zero tolerance policing was wrong. Kelly states what zero tolerance policing meant for Sandtown: "People feared for the children because of the militarized actions of the police. . . . We were all seen as suspects. And, in the O'Malley era, we had these what they called street sweeping with zero tolerance, where literally people were walking down the streets in these communities and being arrested for nuisance crimes; loitering or not having an ID or whatever the case may be."[78] Rev. Miles professes, "The murder rate did go down under O'Malley but people were criminalized. . . . [Zero tolerance policing] strapped a whole lot of people with records that never should have had records. . . . The police were given free reign."[79] D. Watkins sums up his Baltimore police experiences: "Murder, extortion, harassment, brutality, and disrespect on every level."[80] This type of aggressive policing led to high levels of frustration in the city's low-income Black neighborhoods.

While some scholars and activists focus on O'Malley's zero tolerance policing in association with the uprisings, we must not dismiss how Schmoke's prior decision to knock down the projects also played a part in creating the conditions for unrest. Displacement is a violent process that destabilizes individuals, families, and communities.[81] Displacement followed by brutal policing was a painful one-two punch to the city's low-income African Americans. It was a double disrespect in West Baltimore from decisions that spawned from consecutive Black and white city administrations. Nonetheless, there is still more to understanding the city's uprise narrative and the frustrations in Baltimore's Black neighborhoods. Frustrations built among those who carried the "Baltimore weight."

The Weight

A unique aspect of Baltimore's Sandtown life, not found to the same extent in other Black communities like Harlem in NYC, Bronzeville in Chicago, and Shaw/U Street in Washington, DC, is "the weight." *The weight* refers to living with the psychological trauma of witnessing violence, experiencing the loss of a friend or loved one, and expecting violence to occur at any moment. The weight is more than fear of crime, it is the "emotional response to the possibility of victimization."[82] Scholar Patrick Sharkey claims, "Violence doesn't just affect the physical body, it gets into the mind."[83]

In Baltimore, the weight is ever-present. In 1993, Baltimore had 343 murders. While the number of murders dipped between 1994 and 2014, it increased to 342 in 2015 and averaged around 332 between 2016 and 2021.[84] Violence creates a sense of chaos and the expectation that gunfire might pop off at any time, and this contributes to the weight.[85] As one public housing resident put it, "You never know when somebody [is going to] start shooting."[86]

Baltimoreans describe the weight in different ways. No one knows the weight better than Errricka Bridgeford.[87] Bridgeford, an African American woman raised in the West Baltimore Normount Court public housing project, lost her brother to a 2007 shooting. It was not just her brother's death that affected her; she recalls, "When I was 12, I was going to funerals, and I was watching my friends die over jackets."[88] Early exposure to violence can have a dramatic and negative effect on youth.[89] It can make it difficult for them to achieve academic success and maintain emotional stability. It can also impact their earning potential. For Bridgeford, violence was a motivator.

In 2017, Bridgeford started Baltimore Ceasefire to combat the city's violence. She visited Black neighborhood street corners and talked with crews, the gangs, asking them to commit to ending the violence for at least one weekend. Bridgeford describes her Ceasefire objective: "Our goal was just to try to have three days where everybody in the city knew to do two things, be peaceful and celebrate life."[90] Her message to everyone was simple: "Nobody kill anybody."[91]

Baltimore's high murder rate did not inhibit Bridgeford's optimism for transformation; however, the weight is always with her. She states, "I understand we spitting in an ocean right now but if we keep spitting, we gonna get the ocean we want to see one day." "So no matter how much of the peace work I'm doing, I'm still losing people," she asserts. She then pauses, lowers her head, breaking eye contact, and softly repeats, "I'm still losing people." While losing people, close people, motivated Bridgeford, she acknowledges many Black Baltimoreans "are paralyzed because of so much trauma."[92]

Baltimore author D. Watkins, who turned from the drug trade to teaching college, carries the weight, and writes about it with an unfiltered honesty.[93] He states, "Many of my friends and I carry bullet fragments that click around in our joints when we walk. . . . Drugs have impacted everyone around my life, whether it was selling them, coping with addiction to them, or losing a family member or friend because of them."[94] Watkins claims there is a "false narrative that [B]lack people from [B]lack areas are desensitized by murder and that's not true," he insists. "It hurts."[95]

Sharonda Rhodes, an African American mother, understands the pain related to Baltimore's violence and the weight. She lost her nineteen-year-old son, Markel "Kel" Scott, to a shooting.[96] Her son had dropped out of school but reenrolled in Excel Academy, a West

Baltimore alternative school, and was determined to graduate. In 2017, just two months before Kel was to graduate, he was brutally murdered. Rhodes sadly states, "I grew up here and I've never seen crime like this. These are not normal times. The guns are everywhere. My son only weighed 125 pounds, but someone shot him six times, twice in the face."[97] Several students attending Excel Academy understand the weight. One of Kel's classmates, sixteen-year-old Arron Fleming, reveals, "I feel like this whole city [is] a war zone, for real."[98]

Lawrence Anderson acknowledges the Baltimore weight. He explains, "Just the perception of violence, so not even the actual violence, but boxes on the corners with flashing blue lights that take pictures of the block. You need a picture for something, and so if you're in a place that is lit up at nighttime with flashing blue lights, you know what goes down. And so there is this air of at any point something can happen."[99] One local reporter succinctly states: "More than anything else, violence is the centerpiece of Baltimore life, and its toll instills a daily sense of wariness that permeates the city."[100]

Charm City Complexities

Partly due to the weight, Baltimore residents have an edge but also a sense of humor. One day, I was driving on Martin Luther King Jr. Boulevard, a main physical and social divider between downtown and West Baltimore, and saw a white construction van with a rubber chicken hanging from the back. I watched the yellow chicken bounce up and down and move side to side on a swaying elastic string. I smiled and thought to myself, "only in Baltimore," as I watched the little plastic chicken dance while slowly moving in traffic.

The city is quirky, bizarre, and violent; things happen, which makes it both feared and loved.[101] The city is "tolerant" and "hostile" at the same time.[102] In 2021, I waited at a stop light in my car one morning near Sandtown with the windows down and had a conversation with an individual seeking change. I refused to give him any money. He was not angry and asked why I was in Baltimore. He likely noticed my Virginia state plates, or maybe it was the way I spoke. I told him I was studying Sandtown, and he said, in a caring and consoling, not intimidating, manner, "Stay safe."

Contrast this sincere scenario to a brutal 2022 event. A white man in his car at a downtown traffic light had a verbal argument with a group of Black teenagers, the "squeegee boys." In Baltimore, young Black teenagers often clean people's car windshields for change while they wait at downtown traffic lights. After the altercation, the man parked his car, got out, and approached the boys with a baseball bat. One of the teenagers shot and killed the forty-eight-year-old man.[103]

Baltimore has an edgy energy driven by its tragic violence, intense poverty, and inequality.[104] These city circumstances relate to feelings of creativity and depression. African American city council member John Bullock describes two types of Baltimoreans: those who are "hopeful" and those who are "demoralized."[105] D. Watkins says: "I couldn't avoid the violence because it was in my apartment, or across the hall, or on my block. Every road was paved with roses and thorns. You could have great experiences with amazing people, but you could also get your head cracked along the way, and that's how it is."[106] In Baltimore, there is opportunity, beauty, and violence. Matthew Crenson suggests, "The extremes of Baltimore is why people like it."[107]

Even though violence is high, and some cities might hide this fact or deny it, Baltimore shares its complex relationship with violence with outsiders. One store sold goofy t-shirts to tourists stating, "Baltimore, Maryland: There's more than murder here." One of its Inner Harbor gentrified neighborhoods coffee shops is named Order & Chaos Coffee.[108] The coffee shop's name satirizes and commoditizes the perceptions of "order" in Baltimore's white "L" and "chaos" in its Black butterfly neighborhoods.[109]

Violence and the Weight

Baltimore's intense violence and the weight are a chicken-and-egg conundrum. Did the inter-crew violence or police brutality bring it on? Did deindustrialization, disinvestment, poverty concentration, and public housing demolitions undergird this intense crew violence and police brutality? Or are these factors all interrelated? Public housing and policing practices during the Schmoke and O'Malley administrations contribute to the weight, but its formation goes way beyond mayoral politics. Baltimore's weight stems from at least four long-standing interrelated dynamics: political fragmentation, police violence, disinvestment, and crew corner community violence.[110]

How Did the Weight Originate?
Political Fragmentation

Baltimore has an extremely fragmented political system. In 2018, Lawrence Anderson and I spoke with Matthew Crenson, Johns Hopkins University professor and Baltimore political expert.[111] As we talked over crab cakes and burgers at the Hopkins University Club, he noted that Baltimore is a place where no single political leader, neighborhood, political district, or interest group controls the electoral power.

Baltimore is a Democratic city that provides numerous opportunities to enter the political arena. Unlike other Democratic cities, like Chicago and New York City, where heavy-handed Democratic clubs slate candidates and deter others from running,[112] Baltimore has many candidates in both primary and general elections. For example, the Democratic mayoral primary race, after Schmoke's retirement, had twenty-seven candidates. The Democratic mayoral primary race after the death of Freddie Gray had thirteen candidates, still a large number.[113] The sizable number of people running illustrates the unstructured nature of Baltimore politics. Crenson asserts, "What distinguished Baltimore, [compared to other big cities], was the disjointed . . . Democratic Party."[114] He declares that, with a fragmented Democratic party, "Baltimore seemed politically disabled—unable to gather itself together."[115]

Baltimore is not like other "chocolate city" political machines. In some Black-majority cities, such as Newark and Washington, DC, Black political leaders, like Sharpe James and Marion Barry, formed powerful machines in the 1980s.[116] In Baltimore, "No political leader controlled sufficient political capital to build a unified political machine," notes Crenson.[117] Other key Baltimore political actors confirm Crenson's assessment. Robert "Bob" Embry, president of the Abell Foundation and former Baltimore City Council member and housing commissioner, claims, "There is no machine in Baltimore."[118]

Some associate political machines with corruption;[119] and Baltimore has plenty of political corruption. In 2019, Baltimore's Mayor Catherine Pugh stepped down after it was revealed she accepted over $800,000 in unethical purchases of her self-published children book series, "Healthy Holly."[120] Pugh's children's books were purchased by the University of Maryland Medical System and other entities that had large city and state business contracts.[121] It was a typical pay-to-play political scheme and Mayor Pugh was caught up in it. In February 2020, Pugh was sentenced to three years in federal prison for "conspiracy to commit wire fraud, conspiracy to defraud the United States, and two counts of tax evasion."[122]

Robert "Bob" Embry was not referring to the corruption elements associated with political machines, but rather the lack of centralized power in Baltimore politics. When I asked Lawrence Anderson during one of our car rides up to Baltimore who sat on top of Baltimore's political hierarchy, he emphatically responded, "No one!" Crenson proclaims, "Baltimore . . . had no Mayor Daley, Robert Moses, Tammany, or Boss Tweed; no Rockefellers, Wanamakers, Wrigleys, Mellons, or Marshall Fields; no Bill Gates."[123]

Yet Baltimore ironically has a strong mayoral system.[124] Baltimore political expert Madeleine Pill notes, "Getting the mayor's buy-in was critical, especially given the power vested in the city's particularly strong mayoral system of government. The office is subject to a city-wide election separate from that for its 14 district council members. The mayor has ultimate decision-making power and controls the Board of Estimates. This is backed up by a mayoral veto that can only be overridden by a three-quarters City Council vote, which members are wary of using."[125]

While the formal structure of the city's mayoral office and the top-heavy budget process make it appear as though the mayor was strong, the reality was Baltimore mayors had less political power than in other cities. Fiscal limitation, due to deindustrialization and population loss, is one of the primary reasons why Baltimore mayors do not have more governing control.[126] Without a strong tax base, Baltimore mayors rely on resources from corporations, private foundations, and the state government to run the city.[127]

Mayor Kurt Schmoke recalls: "We clearly needed partners. I remember . . . one of the first times I met with the leaders of our business community, and I told them that the one thing I learned in just my few months in office was that I could win elections without the business community, but I can't govern without them. And that basically is the same message that I sent to the foundations. We really needed partners."[128] While Mayor Schmoke served three consecutive terms, he did not have a centralized political machine.

Baltimore has no defined growth machine, political machine, or political regime.[129] The city is what Yale University political scientist Robert Dahl would likely have described as "pluralism" gone wild.[130] There were lots of competing and divided interests: neighborhood interests, corporate and community interests, local and multinational corporate interests, city and state interests, Democrat and Republican (most in the suburbs) interests, Black and white interests, elite and working-class white interests, and elite and working-class Black interests.[131]

While contemporary Baltimore lacks a robust, centralized political machine, the city was once perceived as a political machine hotbed. "With few exceptions, city elections and political offices were the dominion of a citywide Democratic machine that ruled from the late 1860s into the early years of the twentieth century."[132] Later on, under Mayor William Donald Schaefer, the "imperial mayor" between 1971 and 1987, there was a machine-like structure.[133] Mayor Schaefer grew up in white, West Baltimore, on Edgewood Street, just off Edmondson Avenue. Schaefer deeply admired Richard J. Daley, the famous Chicago political machine boss.[134]

Shaefer dominated political real estate deal making. He developed a control mechanism by creating a set of twenty-five quasi-public "corporations" with strategic political appointments.[135] One of these corporate-like entities was the Loan and Guarantee Fund, headed by the city's director of finance, Charles Benton, and treasurer, Larry Daley.[136] Some critics referred to this system of private/public partnerships as Shaefer's "shadow government."[137] Shaefer used these organizations to maintain political control and "to lure developers to Baltimore by offering attractive financing, quickly and confidentially."[138] Baltimore historian C. Fraser Smith claimed that Shaefer established "a corporate machine," where "patronage in the form of low-interest loans" was distributed to Schaefer supporters.[139]

Shaefer was also masterful at co-opting his white and Black opponents. Schaefer appointed his white mayoral opponent, Robert "Bob" Embry, to state-level commissions, and African American mayoral challenger George Russell to a prestigious city-level position. Russell became Baltimore's first African American city solicitor.[140] Schaefer eventually leveraged his power in Baltimore for the highest office in the state, becoming Maryland's governor in 1986.[141]

Without Schaefer, Crenson did not think there was a Baltimore political machine anymore; other scholars disagreed. Political scientist Marion Orr argued that the legacy of white-dominated, machine-style politics continued to influence the relationships and types of negotiations that occurred between white and Black Baltimore. Orr insisted, "Black club politicians were often viewed as pawns of white political operatives and criticized for forsaking the goals of equality and equal representation for personal and economic gain."[142] Additionally, "The machine and patronage traditions often overwhelmed well-meaning African American leaders," like Schmoke.[143]

The discrepancy between Crenson and Orr's Baltimore political landscape analysis can be partly explained by the different reference points of these scholars. Crenson was more interested in the competing factions within and across racial divides, that is, political fights among downtown business interests, party interests, neighborhood interests, and the city and state governments, while Orr was more interested in the city's white and Black divides. These perspectives influenced how these scholars assessed the city's political structure and its core conflicts. Crenson underplayed the Black/white political divide, but he deeply assessed the factions within both Black and white Baltimore. Orr focused on the city's racial split, but overestimated the machine's strength and underplayed divides within both the white and Black political factions in the city's Democratic party.

Baltimore has a highly fractured political landscape. Baltimore has several influential factions: the business community, private foundation leaders, universities, elected officials, grassroots advocates, the party officials, and the church leaders. These groups are represented by organizations including the Baltimore City Chamber of Commerce, Downtown Partnership of Baltimore, Greater Baltimore Committee, Citizens' Planning and Housing Association, the

Baltimore chapter of the National Association for the Advancement of Colored People, American Civil Liberties Union of Maryland, Baltimoreans United Leadership Development, and the Greater Baltimore Board of Realtors.[144] Each of these interest groups plays a role in Baltimore politics, but none dominates.

In May 2019, D. Watkins tweeted: "West and East Baltimore need two mayors." His tweet referred to the deep historical and contemporary division between East and West Black Baltimore. After the 1968 uprising, there was nearly a city-wide consensus that African Americans needed to gain more political representation to prevent unrest.[145] While Baltimore was a racially segregated place, it was also segregated by class. East and West Black Baltimore represent this intraracial class division.[146]

Gwen Brown, a lifelong Baltimorean and BUILD community organizer, explains the East/West class divide:

> So people who may not have had the ability to go far in school kind of settled in East Baltimore. People who tended to . . . have a little more education . . . tended to end up primarily in West Baltimore . . . People who were more socially mobile tended to live in West Baltimore. Sandtown-Winchester, I mean, they were on the borderline. People, particularly Black people, who had the means moved a little further north of Sandtown-Winchester. So Ashburton, that area . . . had some really well-to-do Black people there, [the] upper-middle-class. . . . So Westside always kind of looked down at East Baltimore. . . . And so there was always this rivalry.[147]

Brown's husband was from West Baltimore's Sandtown, while she grew up in the Oliver community in East Baltimore. Despite the East/West rivalry, they developed a deep love for each other. She recounts, "I came from 21213, he came from 21217, which are considered two of the worst zip codes in Baltimore."[148] Brown and her husband married and moved out of the city's most challenging neighborhoods and raised three successful daughters. While the Browns magnificently bridged the city's East/West Black divide, that did not happen for African American leaders in the city's competitive and fragmented political landscape.

Clarence "Du" Burns was the most prominent East Side African American leader.[149] He had an incredible political career. Du Burns started as one of only two African American members of the Democratic Bohemian Club, a club of mainly Italians and Greeks. Du Burns's job was to garner the Black vote for the white Democratic party candidates on the East Side.[150] Du Burns was awarded a patronage position as locker room attendee at Dunbar High School, a position he held for over twenty years.[151] Eventually, Du Burns began his own Democratic club and was successful in turning out the Black vote for white mayors Thomas D'Alesandro Jr. and Donald Shaefer. In 1971, Du Burns was elected to a city council seat. He was elected city council president in 1983, and in 1986 he was appointed mayor by Schaefer, who had resigned to become Maryland's governor.[152] Shaefer said, "Du [Burns] was a man who got his degree on the street."[153]

Rhodes scholar Kurt Schmoke rose out of the Black elite, West Side Black political ranks, and in 1986 he would challenge and defeat Du Burns. It was a critical Baltimore moment. Du Burns and Schmoke represented distinct class interests, and each had different educational pedigrees and political visions. Du Burns paid his political dues and earned his street degree in the white-dominated machine politics of East Baltimore. Schmoke was a very polished West Baltimore politician with Ivy League degrees and support from the city's middle-class African Americans, as well as some white and Black elites.

Some viewed this election as a divide-and-conquer strategy of the city's white business elites.[154] By dividing the city's Black East and West political power bases, white business elites prevented a solid

African American–led coalition from governing the city. No matter who won, the city's African American base would remain fragmented and split.

Without Black political consolidation, the mainly white business and foundations community had disproportionate agenda-setting power. Downtown business development organizations included the Greater Baltimore Committee, Baltimore Development Corporation, Baltimore City Trustees Loan and Guarantee Program, and Downtown Partnership of Baltimore.[155] Foundation representatives, including those at the Abell Foundation, the Annie E. Casey Foundation, the Goldseker Foundation, and the Harry and Jeanette Weinberg Foundation, had a lot of power too.[156] These organizations derived their power in part because Baltimore elected officials needed outside resources from corporations and foundations to help run the city.

Municipal need for private dollars opens a space for someone to leverage political power from eliciting resources for city initiatives.[157] This helped Robert "Bob" Embry Jr. become "the gray eminence of the nonprofit sector who pulled strings behind the scenes."[158] Embry attended public high school in Baltimore, graduated from Williams College, and then earned a law degree from Harvard University. He was a political rival of Schaefer when he served on the city council.[159] He had high hopes of becoming mayor, but instead worked on national housing issues for President Carter's administration.[160] He returned to Baltimore politics through his role as the president of the Abell Foundation, a position he has held for over three decades.[161] From his powerful foundation position, he was able to set the agenda for the city by providing needed capital for city initiatives.[162]

Other foundations, such as the Annie E. Casey Foundation, provided city funds as well. Casey program officers provided relocation funds to move low-income people out of East Baltimore as Johns Hopkins Hospital expanded its eastside footprint.[163] Urban planning scholar Madeleine Pill explicates, "In Baltimore, the strictures placed upon city government given declining federal resources and a stretched local tax base, combined with rising needs, have strained its policy capacity and heightened the imperative to partner with non-governmental organizations [private foundations, corporations, and universities] in developing and implementing policy."[164] Pill identifies some of these private interests and government partners: "Johns Hopkins University and Johns Hopkins Medicine, as well as private local, or locally based, philanthropic foundations."[165]

Mayor Schmoke explains how he would not always know what was going on in his city's fragmented bureaucratic structure. He states, "The Abell Foundation was always very good on issues that were of concern to their [mainly white] board. Bob [Embry] . . . from time to time, would set—basically, they would have an agenda, which he would want the city to work with, as opposed to him waiting for me to propose something. So, often, I would find out, after the fact, that he and our housing commissioner were out doing something."[166]

The influence of the white-dominated corporate and philanthropic sectors makes it difficult for African American elected officials to solely govern and control the city. Dr. Rev. Todd Yeary of Douglass Memorial Community Church notes, "There's a difference between Black racial political representation and Black political power."[167] He insists that, with a shrinking industrial sector and tax base, Black Baltimore mayors have had to cater to the interests of white-dominated local institutions to govern the city. Pill concurs, "As the city's corporate presence continued to shrink in the 1980s and 1990s, its philanthropic sector began to play an expanded role in the city's governance regime."[168] Rev. Yeary states, "It doesn't matter what color the mayor is, the color of the political game across the country is green," and in Baltimore white-led private foundations have a lot of green power.[169]

Administrative and Street Chaos

Baltimore's bureaucratic structure, that is, its city administrative offices, is also highly fragmented, and certain city offices are highly autonomous from the city council and the mayor. The heads of the police and school system, while appointed by the mayor, do not necessarily work for the mayor since parts of their office budgets are determined by the state government.[170] Rev. Yeary indicates, "The police department historically . . . has been state controlled not city control. The transit system, state controlled not city control."[171] Thus, street-level bureaucrats such as the police, transit, and school employees have more autonomy in Baltimore compared to other cities.[172] Rev. Yeary stresses, "When your key components are quasi yours, not really yours, you really don't have Black political agency. You have Black political surrogacy."[173]

The fragmented political landscape in Baltimore is mirrored on its streets. Baltimore does not have one leading crew or gang. Unlike in *The Wire*, there is no kingpin. Baltimore's drug markets are highly fragmented and competitive, and lack of hierarchy and structure is related to the street violence.

D. Watkins's Baltimore drug dealing memoir, *The Cook Up*, is an extraordinary story of his journey from drug dealer to college professor.[174] He grew up in East Baltimore and his older brother, Bip, was a dealer. Watkins stayed clear of the drug trade as a youth and focused on grades and getting into college. After Bip's death, he dropped out of Baltimore's Loyola University and entered the drug trade. Watkins inherited his brother's stash: drugs, cocaine, and heroin; money, about $70,000; and two guns. With these items and a few friends, he started pushing and peddling drugs. After being in the drug game for some time, Watkins left the streets and went back to school.

An important part of Watkins's drug dealing strategy was that he instantly pulled together a crew of his friends and set up shop. The ability to easily enter the competitive drug market was Baltimore specific and spoke to street crew fragmentation. This dynamic was also illustrated in the nonfiction book *Pill City* about Brick and Wax, two eighteen-year-olds from Sandtown's Gilmor Homes public housing project. For a brief period following Gray's death and the uprisings, these young men took over some of the city's drug markets almost overnight with the use of the dark web, precise GPS technology, and Black Guerilla Family gang muscle.[175] In cities where gangs and drug dealing are typically more organized, such as Chicago,[176] it might have been more difficult for Watkins, Brick, and Wax to enter the drug game. The ease of entry into the drug trade suggests that not only was Baltimore's political landscape fragmented, so too were its street-level drug markets.[177]

With the fragmentation comes chaos. Both the city's political environment and its drug markets are turbulent. In Baltimore, unorganized street dealers fight over street corners, and these conflicts can escalate into murder. Rev. Miles speaks about Baltimore's violent drug markets. He explains that the intense violence is related to two dynamics: kingpin takeout and the disappearing mediating institutions. Miles proclaims: "The game in Baltimore changed when they got rid of the kingpins. And it's sad that when there were kingpins in Baltimore, there were rules in the drug culture. One, you didn't sell drugs on a Sunday. You didn't sell drugs to women. And you didn't sell drugs to children."[178] He notes that kingpin removal created havoc and the violent "gang culture."[179] He also feels that the movement of Black churches to the suburbs removed important mediating institutions that could have worked to settle some of the street beefs and violence.[180]

Baltimore's fragmented political structure relates to its fragmented drug markets and violence.[181] Crenson clarifies, "'True Baltimore' is complicated. The city of 300 residential enclaves is also reported to have approximately 300 drug gangs, most with territories embracing only a few square blocks. Hostilities across this intricate cobweb of contested boundaries have helped to give the city of intimate urban villages one of the highest homicide rates in the country."[182] David Kennedy, director of the National Network for Safe Communities, who was instrumental in organizing the nationally recognized Operation Ceasefire in Boston, explains that he could not replicate this violence reduction program successfully in Baltimore.[183] He notes that the city's "dysfunctional political culture" prevented the necessary cooperation and coordination among city agencies, including the police department.[184] He claims, "Baltimore had the worst law enforcement politics I've ever seen," and that the gangs and government officials acted similarly: "Everybody was beefing with everybody."[185] Lawrence Brown insists, "Baltimore has been a city warring with itself."[186] Since everyone was fighting over limited resources and territory, there was little political or economic slack to forge a collaborative ruling regime.[187]

Hard to Solve City Challenges

Baltimore's fragmented government structure makes it hard to tackle complex urban challenges such as community economic decline, the fallout of a nationwide subprime loan debacle, and street-level crew and police violence, all of which disproportionately impact low-income Black Baltimoreans.[188] The double trouble of deindustrialization and divestment means that people struggling to make ends meet sometimes turn to drugs to make money. Instead of creating jobs, the city's answer to the drug trade was supervision, arrests, and abuse of the street-level dealers. The harsh policing made everything worse and low-income people knew it, but the fractured political landscape made it difficult to pull back the stop-and-frisk policing after O'Malley. As Kelly notes, the police were their "own ethnicity."[189] The streets became and remain chaotic and violent.

Lack of Vision

Political and street power are dispersed in Baltimore, making it difficult to sustain a unified city vision and collective action to resolve large challenges like vacancies and violence.[190] Rev. Miles says Baltimore suffered from a "lack of vision" through several city administrations in the 1990s and 2000s.[191] I ask Mayor Schmoke about his strategy to address concentrated poverty and racial segregation during his administration. He explains he tried to tackle concentrated poverty in Sandtown with a local, place-based initiative and with the Empowerment Zone funding,[192] as well as by razing the city's public housing high-rises.[193] But he also says, "We tried to provide opportunities for everybody. . . . We didn't have a specific strategy on integrating neighborhoods. We were just trying to lift all boats, but I could not think of a specific plan that was going to overcome the history that we had."[194] Rev. Miles underscores that history and states, "Baltimore's legacy right now [is] that it's struggling under the burden of two Baltimores. . . . It's those who have and those who don't. And in Baltimore that means white and Black."[195]

Rev. Miles notes there was once a vision—the redevelopment of the Inner Harbor. He says, "Because they [corporate and political elites] lived off of the initial Inner Harbor vision for thirty years. And like I said, since that time there has been no concerted effort for the corporate community in partnership [with] . . . the city to sit down and craft a new vision for the city for the twenty-first century. So after you've redeveloped [the] Inner Harbor . . . what do you do next?"[196]

The solution for Miles is a holistic equitable development vision for Baltimore. "There is no superman or superwoman. It's going to take a community effort. . . . [But right now] it's a city without a vision. And to get biblical, where there's no vision the people perish, and that's what's happening in Baltimore. We need a vision that the majority of the city buys into and works toward. And it can't be just jumping from one development project to another. It has to be a holistic vision of the city."[197]

But in politically fragmented Baltimore, there is no centralized leadership, just chaos and "an awful mess," as stressed David Harvey.[198] Brown, the West Side BUILD organizer who worked with Rev. Miles for years, claims, "There has to be real systemic investment for change in Baltimore. One thing that we have to address is years of trauma that people have dealt with."[199] A lot of this trauma is related to a legacy of white racism, serial displacement, political fragmentation, and street violence.

The killing of Freddie Gray was the breaking point for more than two decades of government-supported violence: public housing displacement, gentrification, subprime lending, and aggressive police practices, within a context of industrial decline and political and street level fragmentation. Some might see the lack of bureaucratic coordination as "dysfunctional" and linked with street violence, but it is important to note this street dysfunction is connected to the city's long-standing culture of political fragmentation. Not only is the political structure related to the chaotic drug markets, but it also relates to why coordinated governmental efforts in Baltimore were, and continue to be, difficult. It is challenging to get city leaders to collectively act to address deindustrialization, poverty concentration, and abusive police.[200]

D. Watkins declares, "People weren't smashing police cars and ripping apart some of these buildings just for attention. There's a reason for that. This goes back from years and years and years of police brutality that not only children went through but their parents and their grandparents and their great grandparents. There's generations of this stuff. A huge disconnect has been going on for all of these years and it finally reached a tipping point and exploded."[201]

But there is a distinction between Baltimore and Ferguson. For decades, Baltimore has had Black mayoral administrations. Some might have expected that under African American municipal control there would have been less African American displacement, concentrated poverty, and neighborhood racial inequality. However, political scientists Adolph Reed, and others including John Arena, Karen Ferguson, Andra Gillespie, Frederick Harris, Christopher Mele, Ravi Perry, Clarence Stone, and Philip Thompson, note that African American control over municipal power does not always equate to benefits for low-income African Americans.[202] These scholars discuss how race and class interests can interact to prevent African American municipal leaders from executing policies that deeply alter the entrenched racial inequality and context of low-income African American communities. Mayor Schmoke did not structure the conditions leading up to the concentration of distress in the city's high-rise public housing. Those circumstances can be largely attributed to Baltimore's white-controlled Baltimore power structure.[203] Schmoke did think he could change conditions for some low-income African Americans by razing the high-rises, and he did. He partly thought "promoting the social and spatial displacement of the least advantaged" would "actually *help* the poorest by offering them new opportunities elsewhere."[204] However, he could not change the systemic challenges some of these families faced in and around Sandtown.

Schmoke noted that Baltimore is a "tale of two cities."[205] If you are white you have a better chance of success than if you are Black, and that is regardless of who is your mayor. We have seen this situation play out in other Black-governed municipalities, such as Newark, Washington, DC, Atlanta, and New Orleans, where low-income African Americans have not been helped much by Black mayoral representation.[206] These cities, with Black municipal representation, were the "hollow prizes" for those seeking racial equality.[207]

Mayor Schmoke knocked down Baltimore's public housing projects, but he tried to make his impact on the lives of low-income children. He worked hard to promote a climate of reading and learning by reforming the public school system.[208] In the end his efforts did little to improve the Baltimore public school system outcomes, although he did help the school system function from a financial standpoint.[209] Also, rather than implementing zero tolerance policing, he advocated for community policing and the removal of punitive laws for petty drug crimes, an unpopular stance at the time.[210]

Given the political and crime climate, his white successor was primed to put in punitive measures to lower violent offenses. Thus, the public housing demolition during the Schmoke administration and increased aggressive policing during the O'Malley tenure was a recipe for disaster and what Lawrence Anderson deemed a type of "double disrespect" for low-income people.[211] This toxic mix of displacing people and then hitting them over the head with aggressive policing contributed to the buildup of intense resentment.

Some scholars insist uprisings are fueled by frustrations and rage.[212] The rage is partly attributed to what Ta-Nehisi Coates identified. He claims the rage bubbles up from being "naked before the elements of the world. . . . The nakedness is not an error, nor pathology. The nakedness is a correct and intended result of policy, the predictable upshot of people forced for centuries to live under fear. The law did not protect us. And now, in your time, the law has become an excuse for stopping and frisking you, which is to say, for furthering the assault on your body."[213] In Baltimore, the rage might be worse or at least different than what occurred in other cities, like Ferguson. In Charm City, a greater number of the people pulling the policy inequality strings, knocking down the public housing, giving out corporate tax breaks to stimulate gentrification, and enforcing the zero tolerance policing were African American.

Class conflict is central to the situation in Baltimore. Elite African Americans were part of the city's political system that deployed slow violence. Often the interests of the Black elite conflict with Black working-class communities. We witnessed this in Atlanta's urban renewal. Historian Karen Ferguson, in writing about the erection of public housing in Atlanta in the 1940s, states, "[B]lack reform elites enthusiastically supported the program, even though it ushered in a decades-long orgy of urban renewal which cut huge swathes out of working-class [B]lack neighborhoods and uprooted thousands of [B]lack Atlantans."[214] She continues, "Black elite–sanctioned federal slum-clearance and housing programs actually victimized legions of poor [B]lack Atlantans and deepened their marginalization instead of helping them into the mainstream."[215] She adds, "Members of the city's so-called underclass can trace their continued exclusion from the public life of the city back to the enormous social, economic, and political barriers to African American progress during the Jim Crow era, which [B]lack reformers were most often unable and sometimes unwilling to lift for the poorest members of the [B]lack community."[216] This is still true today. In fact, Black municipal leadership "is associated with moderately greater scales of public housing removal in the 1990s and 2000s," compared to cities with white-directed governing.[217]

Intraracial conflict is real, but white racism cannot be denied in Baltimore or elsewhere in America. White racism created the "L" and the Black Butterfly through restrictive covenants, redlining, and the placement of public housing.[218] When the public housing went down, Mayor O'Malley instituted aggressive policing in the "ring of blight" to launch his statewide political career. White-controlled banks proliferated toxic subprime loans in the city's Black neighborhoods. White racism is deep-seated in Baltimore and is important for understanding the legacy of segregated Black neighborhoods, but these inequalities are replicated and advanced under Baltimore's Black political leadership. So, now what? Hope and change? Defund the police? How can we address the roots of the revolts? In the next chapter, I discuss some concrete policy positions to ameliorate conditions associated with unrest.

III   *Breaking the Cycle*

8 *Revisiting Theories and Racial Policy Responses*

Riots are coming, they are already here, more are on the way, no one doubts it. They deserve an adequate theory.

Author JOSHUA CLOVER

Between 2014 and 2020, the Great Rebellion tore through metropolitan America; however, very few people saw this wave of fierce discontent coming.[1] In fact, in 2012, urban historian Michael Katz published *Why Don't American Cities Burn?* He claimed the United States had made significant progress since the 1970s, compared to other Western European countries, in increasing the size of the Black middle class and the number of African American political officials. Katz posited that these factors helped to explain why large-scale, Black-led unrest, despite persistent racial inequality, did not occur more widely in the United States in the 1980s, 1990s, and 2000s. With the election of America's first Black president, Barack Obama, in November 2008, one might have expected the 2010s to have been relatively calm. However, during this period, the magnitude and intensity of Black political pushback surpassed the African American upheaval of the 1960s.[2] Why?

I sought to answer this critical question by investigating where the Great Rebellion began: Ferguson and Baltimore. Other scholars argued that the uprisings in these cities were mainly about unjust policing.[3] While I knew aggressive policing was a critical component, I wanted to better understand how other factors, both historical and contemporary, contributed to these revolts. When I asked key leaders in these cities to unpack the undercurrents of unrest, people spoke about abusive policing, but they also elevated other important circumstances.

We know there is more to the contemporary U.S. uprising narrative than policing. Low-income African Americans are frustrated, and aggressive policing is just one cause of their agonies. Repeated policies of slow violence resulting in segregation, divestment, displacement, and gentrification undergird the racial and spatial neighborhood inequality that produces brutal policing in particular places.[4] Being consistently displaced by state policies and condemned to high-poverty, aggressively surveilled neighborhoods while watching public resources bolster white spaces is a damaging dose of disrespect, and it brings on intense feelings of anger and resentment among low-income African Americans. These unsettling feelings are typically repressed as people go on with their daily routines of life. But at certain moments, painful policing can trigger the unleashing of repressed racial trauma that sits just beneath the surface in enduring American Black ghettos.

In the 1960s, we considered how our urban renewal policies segregated, displaced, and destroyed Black communities to create racially unequal metropolitan environments leading to the Great Uprisings (1963–72).[5] Yet, this urban renewal analysis was mainly missing from our assessment of the contemporary Great Rebellion,[6] and it cannot be ignored. In the 1990s, 2000s, and 2010s, a new round of urban renewal, related to HOPE VI grants, TIFs, and subprime lending, destroyed Black communities and displaced millions of people.[7] These contemporary housing and community development policies, and others, such as LIHTCs and Housing Choice

Vouchers, were ongoing forms of slow violence that helped shift and segregate the locations of urban and suburban poverty. Then local political decisions were made to punitively and exploitatively police poverty. When slow policy violence combined with sudden police violence, it sent Ferguson and Baltimore into revolts as people forcefully fought back not only against the police, but also against an ongoing cycle of racial and spatial repression.

Revisiting Past Theories

There are at least five major uprising theories: contact theory (demographic shifts), absolute deprivation (poverty concentration), relative deprivation (expectations), situational theory (police behavior), and flashpoint theory (contextual and situational). These explanations have relevance, but no singular one sufficiently explains the Ferguson and Baltimore revolts. I critique each one in turn.

Contact theory emphasizes demographic shifts. Black poverty moved to new locations like the suburbs, and white people moved to the inner city. This "great inversion" put people in contact with one another in places and ways that had rarely occurred in the past.[8] But what partly explains these population movements are state-supported housing and community development policies, like HOPE VI grants, TIFs, LIHTCs, and Housing Choice Vouchers. The implementation of these policies is associated with a slight decrease in racial segregation in some cities,[9] but racial inequality remains, and tensions rise as populations typically segregated from each other are in close contact and interact with one another.

Some scholars and policymakers point to concentrated poverty as the prime undercurrent of unrest.[10] It was thought that concentrated poverty made everyday living conditions so difficult that individuals in high-poverty places would fight back against the systems they believed neglected their neighborhoods. Yet if poverty concentration alone triggered unrest, we should have experienced more uprisings between 1970 and 1990 as poverty concentration climbed in Black urban neighborhoods.[11] Instead, this period saw few revolts.[12]

We did have a greater concentration of poverty and absolute deprivation in the suburbs, and in the central city in the 2000s.[13] Between 2000 and 2013, the number of high-poverty census tracts increased from 2,510 to 4,412.[14] What helps to explain this? Housing policies that dismantled inner-city public housing projects and other policies, like LIHTCs and Housing Choice Vouchers, reconcentrated people in low-demand urban and suburban areas. The Great Recession (2007–9) also devastated Black and Brown communities by driving them further into poverty through foreclosures, evictions, and housing vacancy concentration.[15] Thus, a reconcentration and an intensification of poverty rather than stagnant-spatial poverty helps to explain this modern uproar.

The relative deprivation unrest argument remains germane.[16] This theoretical perspective explains uprisings through the difference between the inclusion expectations of a disadvantaged group and their perceived status in society. The increase in poverty concentration and restructuring of the metropolitan milieu partially coincided with increasing Black equity expectations due to the election of President Obama. National surveys one year before and after the historic Obama 2008 election reveal that the percentage of Blacks who said their lives were better off than in the previous years almost doubled from 20 percent to 39 percent. Additionally, the percentage of African Americans who believed the white/Black standard of living gap would decrease increased by 14 percentage points during this period. Moreover, the percent of African Americans who anticipated the future for Blacks in America would be better increased by 9 percentage points.[17]

Just when African American expectations were high, tremendous economic upheaval occurred, leading to rising racial inequality and

Black frustrations. Many low-income Black neighborhoods did not change much, became worse, or were gentrified. Baltimore's D. Watkins states, "His presidency was extremely inspiring, but really didn't deliver us from anything. . . . Gunshots still banged outside of our front doors every night."[18] He adds, "Nothing really changed in my neighborhood after he was elected."[19] "Obama gave me super hope back in '08, but then reality set in. . . . That Obama magic deflated just like Al—Roker or Sharpton."[20] The lack of perceived on-the-ground racial progress meant that some in the Black community, according to Baltimore-born author Ta-Nehisi Coates, "quietly seethe[d]" during the Obama years.[21] Thus, the difference between nationally raised racial equity expectations and persistent dire conditions in many low-income Black communities must be considered as an important context for understanding the contemporary round of U.S. revolts.

Situational theory explains why police behaviors are important before and during the unrest. Aggressive and unjust policing is a critical component of uprisings,[22] but police behaviors must be contextualized and connected to the restructuring of the urban environment. Poverty movement and police surveillance go hand in hand and are part of the ongoing cycle of racial and spatial repression.[23] When the original ghetto walls came down, new walls of police supervision and gentrified neighborhoods were erected. The abusive behaviors of the police are intertwined with housing and community development policies that shift poverty and stimulate gentrification. In Ferguson, the police were used to collect tax revenue from low-income Black and Brown people to fund investments in white and middle-income neighborhoods. Baltimore's police were used to wall off poor Black areas to protect the "Jewel," the Inner Harbor, and the nearby gentrifying neighborhoods. As scholar Daanika Gordon states, "The police embraced an active role in the city's growth politics; in doing so, their institutional activities reinscribed many long-standing race- and class-based inequalities that characterize segregation."[24]

Lastly, flashpoint theory brings in situational factors and contextualizes them. This theory stresses historical factors, but it does little to specify which contextual and current situational factors are most relevant and related. I posit that repeated and connected housing and community development policies that stimulate "twice-cleared communities" and "serial displacement" must be central to understanding our modern period of unrest.[25] Repeated acts of state-supported slow violence that destroy people's homelands are extremely harmful and frustrating circumstances for segments of Black America. We must include ongoing policy violence when theorizing the key undercurrents of unrest.

An Urban Renewal Unrest Framework

I have blended elements and perspectives from these important but incomplete theories and developed a historical and multilevel *urban renewal unrest framework*. In America, urban renewal consistently means Black removal. There was much residential upheaval in the 1940s, 1950s, and 1960s,[26] and there was much residential destruction and instability in the 1990s, 2000s and 2010s.[27] In the 1990s and 2000s people were forcefully moved under the HOPE VI legislation; then by TIFs, gentrification, and uneven urban development; and then by the Great Recession, subprime lending, and the foreclosure crisis. These conditions led to the displacement of millions of people, many of whom were African American.[28]

Residential upheaval and revolts are connected. When people do not have a home, they are pushed to their limit. Community destruction, or root shock, is destabilizing and symbolic of the level of care the nation has for certain groups.[29] Black communities retain a memory of the old urban renewal, and the new urban renewal only adds to cumulative collective pain and chronic displacement trauma.[30] When people are consistently pushed by public policy into even worse conditions, it is only a matter of time before they snap, rebel, and revolt.

Uprising conditions arise from ongoing multilevel policy decisions of exclusion, alienation, and unequal separation. Baltimore activist Errica Bridgeford explains that since the end of slavery "law and policies got put into place to make it difficult for Black people." From local policies of legalized segregation to federal HOLC and FHA policies of community disinvestment, to old and new urban renewal displacement policies, to poorly designed Housing Choice Voucher and LIHTC programs, there are constant legislative moves to suppress and segregate Black communities and people. The depleted conditions in the chronic ghetto are not a result of capital markets or shortcomings of the people who live there. These difficult conditions arise from tangible repeated federal, state, and local housing and community development policies.

The effects of state-supported slow policy violence are additive. A repeated cycle of racial and spatial repression, segregation, divestment, displacement, and gentrification is painful and pushes generations of low-income Black people from one poverty neighborhood to another and maintains white affluence and racial inequality.[31] As Baltimore City Council member John Bullock states, "U.S. cities reflect patterns of inequality that are patently cumulative."[32] Violent discriminatory housing and community development policies make life extremely difficult for low-income African Americans and support the existence of chronic ghettos filled with people suffering from chronic displacement trauma.

Slow policy violence and sudden police violence are interrelated. When the ghetto walls of public housing containment came down and people were displaced, new "walls" of policing supervision formed around the chronic ghetto. Relentless antagonistic policing in a depleted and excluded Black space ultimately results in a sudden tragic death and an explosion of the pent-up frustrations that have accumulated across time and space. When those suffering from intergenerational chronic displacement trauma are confined to the chronic ghetto and chronically and aggressively policed, we should expect nothing less than a consistent result: a revolt. The aggressive policing of low-income Black spaces ignites frustration fumes connected with decades long, ongoing slow violence.[33]

Understanding contemporary slow violence requires an intersectional race and class analysis. People often look to racial discrimination alone to explain policies of slow violence and frustrations in low-income Black communities.[34] Much of the slow violence during the old urban renewal, as well as the associated displacement, was race based. White businesses and political coalitions instituted policies of segregation, divestment, and Black community destruction, exemplified by restrictive covenants, redlining, detrimental transportation development, and isolated public housing placement.[35] These policies were put in place to segregate and isolate African Americans to "protect" white spaces. As the 1968 Kerner Report states, white society and institutions are primarily responsible for the conditions that led to African American frustrations and the uprising of the 1960s.

Since the 1960s, however, African Americans have made considerable inroads into high-level municipal offices.[36] Compared to the old urban renewal period, African Americans, particularly in urban areas, have more political representation.[37] This increased political representation was present in St. Louis and Baltimore in the 1990s, and even at the highest national office in the 2010s, yet disadvantaged community conditions that undergird unrest remain. In the 1990s and 2000s, Black displacement occurred on a massive scale with public housing destruction, mortgage foreclosures and evictions, and gentrification. During the Obama administration, white/Black economic inequality widened, poverty concentration increased, and police brutality continued.[38]

Some policy decisions made by African Americans at the local and federal levels exacerbated existing racial inequality. Black political leaders in St. Louis and Baltimore razed public housing and funneled public resources to white companies and communities, reinforcing racial and spatial inequality. President Obama's advisors advocated for the deployment of $787 billion from the America Recovery and Reinvestment Act of 2009 to "shovel-ready" projects to bail out municipalities and bankers, instead of allocating more resources to help minority homeowners who disproportionately suffered during the Great Recession.[39] Political scientist Preston Smith II notes, "It is not that Obama and his ilk do not want to help working-class and poor [B]lacks with their policies, it is just that less fortunate folks have to wait until bankers, real estate developers, and high tech firms have their interests secured first."[40] The incorporation of African American political actors complicates our modern unrest assessment, compared to the 1960s.

However, African American politicians' decisions must be placed in the proper unequal and highly racialized American historic context. Racial inequality, aided by policies of segregation, unequal lending, and Black community upheaval, is deeply entrenched in the modern metropolitan American landscape.[41] The racially unbalanced scales were tipped and tilted long before African American leaders came into office. Additionally, these Black leaders had to navigate persistent and constant racism. That the United States selected Trump to succeed Obama brings into sharp focus just how racist our country remains. St. Louis activist Black Strode notes that the Trump years were a "period of white backlash . . . [and] the unmasking of present-day white nationalism and white supremacy."[42] White racism makes it difficult for Black leaders to directly address policy dynamics that reproduce and maintain racial inequality. A nuanced and evolving race and class analysis is needed to understand the conditions that foment unrest.[43]

Shortcomings and Strengths

There are some important limits to my urban renewal unrest framework. My investigation of slow violence was restricted to certain policies in the twentieth and twenty-first centuries, and some scholars would argue that the conditions of racial inequality date back to enslavement and the founding of racialized capitalism in America.[44] Ta-Nehisi Coates insists, "To ignore the fact that one of the oldest republics in the world was erected on a foundation of white supremacy, to pretend that the problems of a dual society are the same as the problems of unregulated capitalism, is to cover the sin of national plunder with the sin of national lying."[45] I do not disagree with this claim, but my point was not to demonstrate the legacy of enslavement or racialized capitalism but rather to highlight how racial discrimination is embedded in our twentieth- and twenty-first-century policies of urban redevelopment. My unrest framework suggests we do not need to go too far back in history to clearly see the devastating and destructive impacts of urban redevelopment policies on African American communities. Nonetheless, my analysis of pent-up frustrations in the chronic ghetto and the concept of chronic displacement trauma must be linked with the legacy of enslavement, racialized capitalism, and other past forms of racial trauma.

My urban renewal unrest evaluation leaves out other modern factors that might explain contemporary racial and spatial inequality and Black frustrations. This unrest examination did not investigate the ongoing employment discrimination that could partly explain, beyond urban development policies, the spatial landscape of neighborhood segregation. I also did not cover how neighborhood separation overlaps racial inequalities in education, health, and incarceration that could help elucidate the mounting Black frustrations in low-income communities.[46] Nor did I assess how widely accessible videos of police killings might have exacerbated anger and resistance among protesters.[47] My aim was not to cover all factors associated with unrest; rather, it was to contribute a new, historically grounded policy perspective and framework on the formation of conditions connected to the Ferguson and Baltimore uprisings.

Nonetheless, my unrest framework does underscore the importance of new urban renewal displacement and gentrification as violent processes that contribute to racial inequality. While some researchers suggest that displacement and gentrification are not deserving of considerable attention, compared to concentrated poverty,[48] we must contemplate how these processes and outcomes are connected. Even though displacement and gentrification only impact a small proportion of a city's population, these processes signal who is valued and welcomed in certain city spaces and facilitate a reconcentration of poverty. The type of gentrification I documented is critical since it maintains neighborhood racial inequality and contributes to the conditions of unrest.

Another limitation relates to my qualitative research method. The people I met told me about their lives and their perceptions of why people forcefully took to the streets in Ferguson and Baltimore after Michael Brown and Freddie Gray were killed by the police. My urban renewal unrest framework comes from their testimonies and life histories, so it is grounded in the empirical realities of my participants. However, my data and findings are limited to my interview sample in these specific settings. I spoke with a diverse set of organizational leaders closely tied to the St. Louis region and Baltimore. If I had narrowed my sample or research scope to a distinct group, such as the police or community organizers,[49] or studied other unrest locations,[50] I might have obtained different insights.

My framework's strength is the detailing of the linkages over time among race, redevelopment policy, neighborhood inequality, and aggressive policing to explain the context of contemporary unrest. My findings do not provide causal claims among these categories, concepts, and outcomes. Further investigations should more rigorously compare and test these relationships across other domestic and international cities and episodes of unrest.

Certain elements of my unrest framework might not fully generalize to other circumstances around the world. Violent outbreaks might not consistently relate to the intersection of pent-up displacement frustrations and contemporary unjust aggressive policing. In other countries and contexts, excluded groups might suffer more from other ongoing traumas than state-supported residential displacement. For example, chronic cultural or political displacement might lead to deep-seated suffering that, when provoked by the aggressive policing or other circumstances, ignites unrest. Additionally, in the United States, intense social and physical exclusion and discrimination are largely linked to the legacy of Black enslavement. In other contexts, excluded groups experiencing chronic trauma might not be drawn along racial lines, but rather by other social categories including ethnicity, class, immigration status, religion, and gender.[51] However, it is quite likely that repressed factions that revolt in other contexts will have experienced profound alienation, exploitation, and exclusion supported by repeated state policies of slow and sudden violence.

Racial Policy Responses

Gunnar Myrdal, in his 1944 *An American Dilemma*, highlighted profound racial conflicts, power imbalances, and inequality despite our deep national desire to claim that we are a land of equal opportunity for all.[52] In the twenty-first century, with policies of slow violence, racial neighborhood inequality, and deadly police practices against African Americans, we continue to struggle with this dilemma. Profound and persistent racial inequality makes some African Americans question whether the American democracy and the American Dream are lies. St. Louis activist Blake Strode proclaims: "I think sometimes it takes time for people to realize that the . . . How to say this? That the *promise* that has been made has been broken, right? It's not a work-in-progress and we're on the right path, it's not the arc of history . . . bending toward justice, it's like . . . No, we were actually just lied to and manipulated and taken advantage of."[53] With these lies in mind, many people turn to the streets. How do we address our ongoing racial dilemma? My urban renewal investigation provides a roadmap for disrupting and dismantling violent policies that sustain racially unequal circumstances in metropolitan America.

First, we need to end racialized police brutality. Police brutality makes living in concentrated Black poverty not just difficult, but deadly and traumatizing. The police need to be community partners, not violent state patrollers. Instead of stop-and-frisk policing in Black and Brown communities, we need neighborhood policing strategies that treat people with dignity and respect.[54] This requires the police to repair and build trusting relations in low-income Black and Brown communities.[55]

However, this type of community policing can be challenging in environments of concentrated poverty, especially when violent public policies have created economically depleted environments where some people feel hopeless, demoralized, and vulnerable to gang violence.[56] Policies of slow violence lead to a situation where violent crime and abusive policing disproportionately coexist in certain low-income Black neighborhoods.[57] "Violence is not evenly distributed across the communities of a city but rather is concentrated in neighborhoods that experience multiple forms of disadvantage, from poverty to segregation to joblessness," notes Patrick Sharkey and Alisabeth Marsteller.[58] Thus, we must minimize neighborhood inequality if we are going to tackle the interrelated issues of neighborhood violence, police violence, and unrest. Instead of exclusively targeting police reforms, we need to restructure the urban and suburban context in which people live and the police operate.

We need cities and metropolitan regions where poverty is more evenly distributed so that intense poverty concentration does not occur. Some scholars have advocated using housing vouchers to move low-income people to lower-poverty "opportunity neighborhoods" to reduce concentrated poverty.[59] This "dispersal consensus" among urban poverty scholars rationalized the HOPE VI displacement and the use of LIHTC and Housing Choice Voucher programs to provide alternative housing options for low-income people.[60] While some displaced HOPE VI families ended up in opportunity neighborhoods, many relocated to other isolated, segregated poverty pockets, like Southeast Ferguson and West Baltimore, where they were brutally policed.[61] The Black displacement connected with our federal HOPE VI housing program of 1990s and 2000s laid part of the foundation for the unrest of the 2010s, just as the old urban renewal set critical conditions for the uprisings of the 1960s.[62]

If we want to minimize unrest, we must reimagine our housing and community development policies. Rather than facilitating displacement to "help" the poor, we need to stop Black serial displacement and advance racial equity through building community and stabilizing people's homes.[63] People need a stable "homeplace" in our society, not a segregated community in some unwanted territory that eventually gets gentrified and destroyed.

We need to acknowledge and correct our past racialized policy violence. The past informs the present, and there is a cumulative effect to America's history of racism. While it is challenging to calculate and politically address the legacy of four hundred years of enslavement on present-day racial inequality,[64] we can make concrete policy reforms to reduce the racial inequality maintained and reinforced by twentieth- and twenty-first-century urban redevelopment policies.

How do we start on this restorative redevelopment reform path? St. Louis community organizer Kayla Reed has some suggestions. She explains it is about "equitable development." She declares that the answers to addressing unrest must consider "how . . . we move the ball on actually rebuilding the north side of St. Louis, the south side of Chicago for Black people, by Black people [and] with Black people in mind."[65] Reed's thoughts parallel with ideas sociologist Mary Pattillo wrote in 2009 when she asked policymakers and scholars to consider how to invest in low-income Black neighborhoods "as is."[66] By "as is," she meant injecting needed resources in African American communities without triggering gentrification and displacement. Pattillo advocates for policies that acknowledge the strengths and "worthiness of poor and/or [B]lack residents and neighborhoods."[67] In 2016, scholar Marcus Hunter and his colleagues, including Pattillo, introduced the concept of "Black Placemaking" to further spur policymakers to cultivate Black community building, creativity, and joy as opposed to Black displacement and destruction.[68]

Reed also underscores that we need robust community-based organizations to hold white and Black elected officials to the racial equity agenda. She states, "Movement happens when there are strong organizations holding visionary candidates accountable to transformative vision. . . . And the Democrats get to leverage their 'center position,' but it's always been center-right. Right? And that has created this phenomenon in places like St. Louis, in Detroit, and Atlanta, where we have these Black politicians who are conservative, call themselves Democrats. And they are gatekeepers to power or influence, and . . . [in] opposition to [the equity] movement in a lot of these spaces." Reed suggests we need stable grassroots organizations in Black communities to hold African American and white politicians' feet to the racial equity fire.

The Difficulties of Establishing Racial Recognition and Equity

Police reforms have been made in both Baltimore and Ferguson,[69] yet white and Black political leaders are uncomfortable with having direct conversations about racial harm history and equitable development. My exchange with former Ferguson Third Ward city council member Fran Griffin illuminates this matter. I asked Ms. Griffin if the white political establishment in Ferguson was amenable to a conversation on past racial harms. She states, "They didn't want to have that conversation. . . . Let's acknowledge the elephant in the room."[70] She claims the elephant in Ferguson's room is "systemic racism," including white-led policy decisions related to the unequal conditions between South and West Florissant, and how these areas are distinctly policed. The difficulty of having frank racial discussions is not just in Ferguson; some of Baltimore's top Black politicians, and our first Black president, do not always want to directly address race. Historian Matthew Crenson notes that during his time as mayor Kurt Schomke "remained largely silent . . . [on] race."[71] Additionally, scholars have highlighted how, early in his first term, President Obama rarely acknowledged racial discrimination as a primary driver of American inequality, and often lofted "race-neutral" policy solutions.[72]

Tackling racial inequality can be tough, and some of our African American political leaders only replicate and perpetuate racial inequality. Race-neutral rhetorical language of "lift all boats" sometimes gets Black leaders elected but does little to change systemic and racially inequitable conditions.[73] If we are serious about tackling racial inequality, we must go beyond racial representation; we must elevate political leaders who will support *racial recognition* and *racialized policies*. We must acknowledge the harms of the past and break the redevelopment cycle of racial and spatial repression.[74]

Ferguson is resistant to acknowledging the racial wrongs of the past and addressing the unequal community conditions related to Brown's death. The apartment complex where Brown was shot has been ironically renamed Pleasant View Gardens, and one of the only traces of Brown's death is a faded yellow rectangle in the middle of the street where his bullet-filled body lay (figure 19). It seems as if

FIGURE 19. "Pleasant View" Gardens on Canfield Drive. Photo by author.

some Ferguson leaders want to bury the memory of Michael Brown and the unrest.

I spoke with Eric Osterberg, Ferguson's former city manager, and Elliot Liebson, the city's director of planning, about any plans to remember Brown's death and confront the revolt conditions. Mr. Osterberg explains: "When I first came here [in 2021] . . . Michael Brown Sr. reached out to me and said that he wanted to meet. The city council resoundingly is like, 'Don't do that.' And I'm like, 'Well, why?' . . . . So one of the things that I . . . want to do . . . I'm just looking for the right opening, is . . . memorializing Michael Brown and doing something as a city to recognize and embrace the history, but understand [it] . . . in a way that . . . reconciles with the past and confronts it . . . We have an abandoned swim club called The Bermuda Swim in town. . . . It used to be an all-white swimming pool. . . . Then Black families started moving into the neighborhood adjacent to it and then started showing up at the pool. White people stopped going.

And then they closed it down. And it's been abandoned and sitting there ever since. So, one of the things that . . . we could do, which . . . Michael Brown Sr. has put on the table, is acquiring that property . . . [and] giving it to his foundation. And then they would make a community center there. That would solve the issue of not having a community center that's disconnected in the middle of the white neighborhood, that's inaccessible to the rest of the community."[75]

I ask if there is resistance to this plan. Mr. Osterberg responds: "There is resistance. So, the perspective from city council and like even the mayor is . . . Mayor [Jones] said, 'Well, the Browns sued us.' And I said, 'Well, yeah, of course they sued you.' And they just have this perspective that the Browns just want to hurt the city and their reputation, and they're holding it back."[76] The swimming club, a hurtful memory of segregation and racial discrimination, remains unused with weeds growing around it. This was a missed opportunity for Ferguson to acknowledge the past and heal its raw racial wounds.

But what about Southeast Ferguson? Mr. Osterberg speaks about the city's redevelopment plans. We discuss the Ferguson Market, where Michael Brown stole the cigarillos, and the Canfield Green Apartment complex, now Pleasant View Gardens. He states, "So, part of the Great Streets project, one of the things that there's complete consensus on council about is that . . . And one of the drivers behind us applying for that grant is that what the city wants to accomplish is realigning Ferguson Avenue in a manner that cuts right through where Ferguson Market [now Elite Liquors] is. So then it will just . . . So then Ferguson Market won't be an eyesore to the community. Yeah, there's this tendency to, in addition to not actually having the conversations we need to have, to just try to distance ourselves from that history as well."[77] The city council made a political move to erase the Ferguson Market, and there are more extensive plans to redevelop the apartment complex area where Brown was killed.

I discuss the comprehensive plan for Southeast Ferguson with the city's director of planning, Elliot Liebson. Mr. Liebson describes it like this: "On West Florissant, on either side, becomes part of the re-development proposal. And we're not gonna kick folks out necessarily. There's a lot of good offices and businesses in here, there's no reason to kick them out. We want public storage gone, gone, gone. That is such a waste of space. Beauty supply house, eh. The liquor stores, gone, gone."[78] With a new federal Great Streets grant in hand, we will see if Ferguson can produce equitable development or whether the low-income African Americans who live in this city section will be gone.

Did Baltimore's established Black leadership do any better? No. In 2016, motivated by the uprisings, Maryland's white Republican governor, Larry Hogan, and Baltimore's African American Democratic mayor, Stephanie Rawlings-Blake, developed a plan known as Project CORE—Creating Opportunities for Renewal and Enterprise.[79] The state and city political leaders wanted to demolish as many of the city's vacant units as they could.[80] They launched the initiative from Sandtown-Winchester.[81] The four-year effort was expected to spend $84 million to raze four thousand vacant homes throughout Baltimore over two phases. CORE replicates the same old redevelopment policies that drive unrest. This was not redress; just more of the same old urban renewal mess.

But it gets worse. The Housing Authority of Baltimore City announced they would sell their remaining public housing units to private developers. Historian Howard Gillette details the situation: "In Baltimore, authorities [majority Black-controlled] first authorized the sale of 22 of the city's 38 public housing developments in 2014. In 2018, the city added the Gilmor Homes to the list of complexes for sale, some 4,500 units, more than 40 percent of the city's entire stock. As a preliminary step, it designated 6 buildings in the sprawling [Sandtown] complex for demolition, including the buildings on

FIGURE 20. Freddie Gray memorial near site of his arrest. Getty Images/photo by Chip Somodevilla.

Butler Court where Freddie Gray had been arrested three years earlier" (figure 20).[82] Just like Ferguson, Baltimore plans to erase the history of the uprising through knocking down affordable housing and redeveloping the site where Gray was arrested.

Raymond "Ray" Kelly anticipates these city actions will displace the current residents and eventually gentrify Sandtown. He states, "As opportunities become prevalent [this community] will be gentrified and it'll be a whole other work base. And because of transportation issues and all the other boundaries that Baltimore puts up for Black people, this community will be moved to another community. Project CORE come in and there'll be redevelopment [of the empty lots]." Kelly claims the vacant units are "holes in our history" and fears they will ultimately be filled with upper-income people.[83]

In St. Louis, more uneven development persists. After decades of abandonment, Pruitt-Igoe is finally slated for redevelopment. The city plans to redevelop the site where Pruitt-Igoe once stood using massive federal resources. The National Geospatial-Intelligence Agency's (NGA) $1.7 billion second headquarters will anchor the 97-acre site.[84] This federal agency employs over 14,500 people worldwide and uses geospatial intelligence from satellites and other technologies to assist in strategic military decisions. The agency's information was critical to the Gulf War in Iraq and the assassination of Osama bin Laden.[85]

The agency's website proclaims: "The Gateway Arch will be visible from our future north St. Louis campus, too. It will continue to project that bold spirit of Lewis and Clark. Just as their journey started from here to map our nation's future, NGA is charting the future of our agency in St. Louis."[86] This future is connected to the country's past of Native genocide and the displacement of African Americans from a place people once called home. The NGA investments are not redress, just a public commitment to continue serial displacement and the expansion of the American capitalist system worldwide. The NGA represents the "spirit of Lewis and Clark" by engaging in local development that takes advantage of a depleted Black space, like Pruitt-Igoe, and using advance technologies to exploit other nations.

Can We Legislate Love and Respect?

Baltimore's Erricka Bridgeford made a profound statement about how to improve the situation. She claims, "If white people loved Black people as much as they love Black culture none of this would be happening, right? . . . If you loved Black people that much our conditions would be very different. . . . And when they [white folks] move into the neighborhoods . . . that's gentrifying; if they loved the people who lived there it would dawn on them, 'What the fuck happened to all the people who was living here before I moved here?'" Bridgeford declares redevelopment policies destroyed Black communities and insists "all of those things need to be put back together and delivered in a quality way that shows people that they are *loved* and that they matter." As Bridgeford suggests, it comes down to how we deploy public resources in a way that says, "Black Lives Matter." I ask her if part of the solution is to reform policing and she responds instantly and affirmatively yes, but then says, "So even if we fix police-community relations, what about the rest of the stuff?"[87]

Scholar Marc Lamont Hill argues in his 2016 book that most Americans still see African Americans as "Nobody."[88] His book's argument refers to James Baldwin's claim that the uprisings of the 1960s were spawned by the politics of disrespect. Both Hill and Baldwin stress the roots of revolts were triggered by a white-led society that does not treat African Americans with respect and dignity. It was not knowing, not acknowledging, and not respecting Black people that allowed policymakers and police to kill African Americans through slow and sudden violence. As Hill states, "To be Nobody is to be subject to State violence."[89]

Elijah Anderson discusses the importance of "respect" in the inner city.[90] Anderson explains that, for low-income people of color, feeling respected and protecting their pride are often elevated concerns because a racist society constantly tells them there is something wrong with their way of life and the high-poverty neighborhoods they call home. Anderson notes, "The hard reality of the world of the street can be traced to the profound sense of alienation from mainstream society and its institutions felt by many poor inner-city [B]lack people, particularly the young."[91]

Lawrence Anderson, like Elijah Anderson, Marc Hill, and James Baldwin,[92] argues that much of the hurt in Baltimore's low-income African American communities is due to a lack of respect. He claims, "The people of Baltimore are tolerant of real life, because they live real life. What they're not tolerant of is real life that's disrespectful. Don't disrespect me. . . . Everybody can show respect. And sometimes, depending on people's touch with certain communities or whatever, they lose a sense of that."[93] Lawrence Anderson feels some of the city's elite Black leaders over time executed policies, like the razing of public housing and stop-and-frisk policing, that demonstrate a lack of humanity, dignity, and respect for working-class African Americans.

We need racial policy reforms that make people feel respected, stable, and valued in their homes and communities. We need to stop Black serial displacement and racially unequal neighborhood development. We need policies to alleviate chronic displacement trauma. We need to acknowledge the racial wrongs of the past and build, not tear down, the future. We need low-income African Americans to sense they are settled and equal members of society. We need to move from plantation futures of inequality to futures of sustained racial progress, equitable development, and homeplace. Instead of serial displacement, we need to make serial cumulative progress toward racial equality and healing. In the words of scholar Lawrence Brown, we need to "make Black neighborhoods matter."[94]

We need a series of policy proposals to uplift Black neighborhoods. We should reform the Housing Choice Voucher and LIHTC programs to reduce concentrated poverty, alter the Federal Housing Administration housing lending programs to get sustainable, low-cost loans to Black communities, modify the governing structure of TIF districts to mandate low-income people's participation in the decisions to deploy public tax dollars, reinstate one-for-one public housing unit replacement, and institute build-first principles in public housing redevelopment plans, particularly in gentrifying Black neighborhoods. These policy reforms will not only decrease displacement, but they will also diminish the American Dilemma, strengthen our democracy, and get us closer to achieving the core ideals of equality and justice for all.

This nation was born from riots and revolts protesting British taxation efforts, including the British Stamp Act. It was taxation without representation. But then white Americans "stamped" Blacks with violent racism, leading to unimaginable human suffering and economic exploitation.[95] The American legacy of enslavement and racial violence persists, not only through unjust policing, but by slow policy violence that advances Black community segregation, divestment, displacement, and gentrification. Until this cycle of neighborhood instability and inequality is properly acknowledged and rectified,[96] there will be unrest now, unrest tomorrow, unrest forever. No justice, no peace!

FIGURE 21. Charm City riders. Photo by author.

A Pandemic Methods Mess and Some Solutions

The COVID-pandemic lockdown between 2020 and 2021 made the qualitative research for this comparative-city project challenging. I had collected most of the Baltimore data in person in 2018 and 2019. I drove from the Washington, DC, area to walk the streets of Sandtown and talk with key city and community members. My graduate student research partner, Lawrence Anderson, drove up with me almost every trip. Lawrence is extremely knowledgeable of the Baltimore political landscape. He advised me that Baltimore was not like New York City, Chicago, or Washington, DC, some of the other sites where I had conducted my neighborhood research. He prepared me for the expectation that people might confront and question me about why I was in their community. He was not wrong, and on a couple of occasions I had to quickly explain my "storyline" to people on the street.[1] However, the primary research challenge was not walking, talking, and learning from people in person in Baltimore, it was pivoting to "online ethnography" when the pandemic struck.[2] I vividly remember being in Baltimore with my family on March 8, 2020. We ate a nice Italian dinner and saw the musical *Wicked* at the Hippodrome Theatre downtown. I did not return to Baltimore until June 6, 2021.

During the stay-at-home order, I assessed my Charm City data and collected Ferguson information online. I virtually walked the Ferguson streets via Google Maps, watched archived video broadcasts of city council meetings, and interviewed people through a web video platform. I worried whether I would obtain a sufficient understanding of the St. Louis region to be able to write this book. I found that virtual interviews, although informative, lacked the intimacy, trust, and tacit knowledge generation I had become accustomed to acquiring in person. It was not until I finally received my university's travel approval that I became confident I could pull off this two-city comparative research. In September 2021, I finally stepped foot in St. Louis and Ferguson and returned on several subsequent trips to interview new people and reconnect with people I had initially met online.

I trained to be a qualitative researcher under Herbert Gans. Gans taught me ethnographic methods of participant-observation and face-to-face interviews. I need to feel the pulse of the communities, cities, and regions I study. While "virtual ethnography" was a useful and necessary technique for capturing certain qualitative information,[3] I found that online observations and interviews did not replace the importance of face-to-face interactions and grounded pavement knowledge: what Willow Lung-Amam calls "shoe-leather research."[4] I had to walk the street where Brown was killed. I needed to have beers in the Ferguson Brewery and King of Soul Café, as well as conversations with people in everyday settings, to build "cognitive empathy," which is "the degree to which the researcher understands how those interviewed or observed view the world and themselves—from their perspectives."[5] For me, in-person experiences and interactions are the most reliable ways to build trust and understanding to collect information, interpret data, and make plausible claims.[6] Once I was able to establish my grounded bearings in both sites, the analysis and writing flowed, as did my confidence in the reliability and validity of my findings.

During the height of the pandemic, I changed my initial research design. I had originally planned to conduct a three-city comparison among Ferguson, MO; Baltimore, MD; and Charlotte, NC. These cities experienced unrest in 2014, 2015, and 2016 and were interesting comparative cases because they had different political and economic histories and economic trajectories. The pandemic made the three-city comparison infeasible if I wanted to even approximate my publication timeframe, which was already delayed due to the lockdown. In the summer of 2020, I made the difficult decision to go with a two-city comparison. I felt that the political (Black-led vs. white-led) and geographic (urban vs. suburban) differences between Baltimore and Ferguson made this a compelling, two-city comparative unrest investigation.[7]

Not only did I make the decision to change my research design in 2020, but I also considered adding a national component. I contemplated unpacking what these city cases in 2014 and 2015 meant for what transpired when George Floyd was murdered and unrest ripped across the country in the summer of 2020. I spent months following and assessing how conditions in the United States changed between 2015 and 2020. Despite this initial effort, I eventually decided it was best to remain focused on Ferguson and Baltimore in this manuscript. This was a tough decision, but a prudent one theoretically, empirically, and practically.[8] I avoid making definitive claims about what 2014 Ferguson and 2015 Baltimore mean for the 2020 unrest.[9]

However, I do expect some of my Ferguson and Baltimore findings to have "transferable" generalization to other unrest circumstances in the United States and beyond.[10] For instance, my theoretical *urban renewal unrest framework* can help international scholars assess how the history of slow violence, and the disruption of "home," can result in cumulating frustrations in places like London, Paris, Cape Town, and Rio.[11] I also anticipate that race and class interconnections will be critical to detailing the specific dynamics leading up to and outcomes associated with the multiracial pushback to police brutality we witnessed in 2020 in the United States and around the world. Of course, frustrations from the pandemic will be tied to what occurred in 2020,[12] and this health-related circumstance was absent from my 2014 and 2015 unrest analysis.

Beyond pandemic-related challenges, other important issues arose in my qualitative work. Qualitative researchers must consider the health and safety of their participants. I felt I was collecting powerful and important data from those I spoke with, but some of that information might put my participants in jeopardy with their employers. I pondered these possibilities and thought about how to effectively protect my participants while accurately communicating my study findings. However, I chose not to use pseudonyms unless my participants requested I do so. This project was about the politics of inequality in particular spaces, and I felt it was important to use the real names of people and places to effectively anchor the study. Each of the individuals I interviewed signed a consent form or gave me verbal permission, and I followed their instructions on whether to reveal their identities and words. Even though I obeyed the scientific human participant policies of qualitative research, I did, and still do, worry some of the material in this manuscript might harm some of my participants and possibly perpetuate stereotypes. My goal is to break stereotypes, but some readers might conclude that this work enhances rather than minimizes them. I can safely say that the people I interviewed took great pride in their cities and communities, and I hope many of them perceive that I accurately articulated some of the merits and complex challenges that exist in them.

I never reached the level of embeddedness and intimacy in Ferguson and Baltimore as I did in my prior ethnographic research,[13] but I worked hard to gain the trust of people in these cities and attempted to deeply understand these places through their perspectives. To help build trust and gain knowledge, I researched the history of these places intensively for over a year before stepping foot in them. I also started my investigation by interviewing academics with extensive city knowledge before I entered my sites. While in the field, I spoke with key people from different sectors of these cities including clergy, activists, politicians, civic leaders, small business owners, and city staff. The testimonies of people provided the data, along with archival records and descriptive statistics, that grounded the findings; but ultimately, I interpret what individuals said.

My positionality is important to this study.[14] I am a fifty-year-old, white, urban sociologist, father, and husband, who is very much an outsider to Baltimore and Ferguson. I grew up in a New York City suburb and have spent much of my adult life in Chicago, New York, and Washington, DC. These roles and experiences filter my observations and interpretations of events and words people told me. Throughout the data collection process and analysis, I constantly thought about (and documented) how my multiple characteristics influenced my actions and thought processes, as well as how participants reacted to me and my questions. While being conscious of my race, gender, class, and background biases, I hope I have accurately captured, interpreted, and communicated a slice of the realities of the multilevel, complex dynamics and forces that influenced unrest in these important places.

APPENDIX B

Select Descriptive Statistics

TABLE 1. St. Louis City Population Change, 1880–2020

Year	White	Black*	Total
1880	328,191	22,250	350,512
1900	539,385	35,516	575,238
1920	702,615	69,854	772,897
1940	706,794	108,765	816,048
1960	534,004	214,377	750,026
1980	242,576	206,386	452,085
2000	152,666	178,266	348,189
2020	132,292	129,814	301,578

Source: U.S. Census.

*In 1880 the field labeled "Colored" in the census data is being used; from 1900–1960 the field of "Negro" in the census data is being used; from 2000–2020 the field of "Black alone" is being used.

TABLE 2. St. Louis County Population Change, 1880–2020

Year	White	Black*	Total
1880	28,008	3,880	31,888
1900	48,511	3,526	52,037
1920	95,988	4,729	100,737
1940	261,840	13,311	274,230
1960	683,652	19,007	703,532
1980	855,106	110,179	975,036
2000	781,316	192,348	1,016,315
2020	632,283	246,642	1,004,125

Source: U.S. Census.

* In 1880 the field labeled "Colored" in the census data is being used; from 1900–1960 the field of "Negro" in the census data is being used; from 2000–2020 the field of "Black alone" is being used.

TABLE 3. Baltimore City Population Change, 1880–2020

Year	White	Black*	Total
1880	278,584	53,716	332,313
1900	429,123	79,258	508,957
1920	625,130	108,322	733,326
1940	692,705	165,843	859,100
1960	610,608	325,589	939,024
1980	345,113	431,151	787,775
2000	205,982	418,951	651,154
2020	157,392	339,328	589,579

Source: U.S. Census.

* In 1880 the field labeled "Colored" in the census data is being used; from 1900–1960 the field of "Negro" in the census data is being used; from 2000–2020 the field of "Black alone" is being used.

Notes

Preface

1. I use the terms *riots*, *unrest*, *uprisings*, and *revolts* interchangeably. I understand these labels are emotionally and politically charged and mean different things to different people. Each term also carries with it an assumed set of motivations for behaviors. My use of these terms is to communicate a set of chaotic behaviors among multiple people that resulted in severe property damage. I assume these behaviors are associated with multiple motivations, and I make no claims to fully understand what drove these acts. The book's aim is to help clarify and understand some of the structural conditions and circumstances associated with modern unrest in America. My understanding of unrest is outlined more clearly in chapter 1.

2. DiPasquale and Glaeser 1998; Gale 1996.

3. J. W. Johnson 1991; W. Johnson 2020; Lumpkins 2008; Rudwick 1982.

4. Sandburg (1969) 2015.

5. M. Jackson 2016.

6. Ellsworth 1992.

7. Park and Burgess 1925, p. 22.

8. Grills, Aird, and Rowe 2016.

9. Davis 2017; Hannah-Jones 2021; Kendi 2017; Marable 1983; Wilkerson 2020.

10. Myrdal 1944.

11. Bonilla-Silva 2018; Brown 2021; Hackworth 2019.

12. Levy 2018.

13. Harris and Wilkins 1988; Hinton 2021; Levy 2018; Zelizer 2016.

14. Jargowsky 1997. Unrest occurred in 1980 in Miami, in 1991 in Washington, DC's Mt. Pleasant neighborhood, in 1992 in Los Angeles's South Central area, in 1997 in East Nashville, in 2001 in Cincinnati's Over-the-Rhine community, and in 2009 in Oakland; see Bronson 2006; Gale 1996; Herman 2005; Modan 2007; and Websdale 2001. For more on the Oakland riots, see Jesse McKinley, "In California, Protests after Man Dies at Hands of Police," *New York Times*, January 8, 2009, www.nytimes.com/2009/01/09/us/09oakland.html.

15. Hyra 2008.

16. Katz 2012.

17. Dikeç 2007; Laurence and Vaïsse 2005; Moran 2012; Schneider 2014.

18. Hyra 2014; Wacquant 2008.

19. Katz 2012, p. 83.

20. Kelly McCleary and Darran Simon, "Anger over Earlier Police Shooting May Have Helped Fuel Violence in Memphis," CNN, June 14, 2019, www.cnn.com/2019/06/14/us/memphis-police-shooting-protests-frayser-neighborhood.

21. Abrams 2023.

22. Brown 2021, p. 10.

Introduction

1. Cobbina 2019. Clark's quote in Meier, Rudwick, and Bracey 2007, p. 107.

2. Boyles 2019; Freixas and Abbott 2019; Love 2016; S.M. Moore 2015; U.S. Department of Justice 2017.

3. Murch 2015; K.-Y. Taylor 2016.

4. J. Rios 2020; Hill 2016.

5. Cobbina 2019.

6. Lowery 2016; U.S. Department of Justice 2017.

7. U.S. Department of Justice 2017.

8. U.S. Department of Justice 2017. Also see Frances Robles and Julie Bosman, "Autopsy Shows Michael Brown Was Struck at Least 6 Times," *New York Times*, August 17, 2014.

9. Ryan Devereaux, "A Complete Guide to the Shooting of Michael Brown by Darren Wilson," *The Intercept*, November 20, 2014.

10. Boyles 2019; Lowery 2016; J. Rios 2020; U.S. Department of Justice 2017. Also see Murch 2015.

11. Boyles 2019; Hill 2016; Powell 2016; J. Rios 2020; Underhill 2016.

12. Quoted in Lowery 2016, p. 26.

13. Associated Press, "Protesters Rally after Black Teen's Shooting," August 10, 2014.

14. Boyles 2019, pp. 8–9.

15. Boyles 2020; J. Rios 2020.

16. Boyles 2020; Lowery 2016.

17. Boyles 2019, p. 9.

18. J. Rios 2020.

19. Lowery 2016.

20. Mark Snowiss, "Ferguson Riots Underscore Police Militarization in US," *Voice of America*, August 15, 2014.

21. Boyles 2019, 2020; Cobbina 2019; J. Rios 2020.

22. Cobbina 2019.

23. Lowery 2016; Mislán and Dache-Gerbino 2018; Nassauer 2019.

24. Quote in Lowery 2016, p. 24.

25. Murch 2015; K.-Y. Taylor 2016. It is important to note that Boyles (2020) and J. Rios (2020) have written that several Ferguson protesters did not appreciate the Black Lives Matters (BLM) representatives who came to Ferguson and St. Louis, as they felt the BLM organization used the Ferguson situation to bolster the group's own interests.

26. Hill 2016, p. 70; W. Moore 2020; Pietila 2018.

27. Cobbina 2019.

28. W. Moore 2020.

29. Video of Gray's arrest, www.baltimoresun.com/news/crime/bs-md-gray-video-moore-20150423-story.html (accessed May 16, 2022).

30. The Young Turks, "Latest Police Neglect Victim: Freddie Gray Dies of a Severed Spine," YouTube, www.youtube.com/watch?v=dlsvUAst2UQ (accessed October 4, 2023).

31. W. Moore 2020.

32. Cobbina 2019.

33. Cobbina 2019; Nassauer 2019.

34. Ron Snyder. "One Year Later: Looking Back at the Baltimore Riots," WBALTV11, April 28, 2016.

35. W. Moore 2020.

36. Quoted in W. Moore 2020, p. 18.

37. Allen 2022, p. 3.

38. W. Moore 2020.

39. Associated Press, "A Timeline of the Freddie Gray Riots in Baltimore." April 28, 2015. Also see W. Moore 2020.

40. Cobbina 2019.

41. Dikeç 2017.

42. Purge was a reference to the 2013 horror movie *The Purge*, where the main plot centered on a specific period when crimes could be committed without punishment.

43. Bell et al. 2018; Cobbina 2019; W. Moore 2020.

44. Kevin Rector. "What Happened at Mondawmin? Newly Obtained Documents Shed Light on Start of Baltimore Riot," *Baltimore Sun*, April 20, 2019. Also see W. Moore 2020.

45. In this book Sandtown-Winchester is a reference to what many Baltimoreans call Sandtown, a West Baltimore community bounded by North Avenue to the north, Pennsylvania Avenue to the east, West Lafayette Avenue to the south, and North Monroe Street to the west.

46. Emma Patti Harris, "Baltimore Riots: Damage and Incidents of Violence," *Baltimore Sun*, April 27, 2015; Scott Dance, "Baltimore Erupts," *Chicago Tribune*, April 28, 2015.

47. W. Moore 2020.

48. Quote in W. Moore 2020, p. 176.

49. Sabrina Toppa, "The Baltimore Riots Cost an Estimated $9 Million in Damages," *Time*, May 14, 2015.

50. Matt Furber, Audra D. S. Burch, and Frances Robles, "What Happened in the Chaotic Moments Before George Floyd Died," *New York Times*, May 29, 2020.

51. Robert Samuels and Toluse Olorunnipa, "His Final Hours," *Washington Post Magazine*, May 15, 2022.

52. Video of Floyd's murder by Darnella Frazier, www.youtube.com/watch?v=prZ-bYOUuZo (accessed May 25, 2022).

53. Abrams 2023. Also see Jiachuan Wu, Nigel Chiwaya, and Savannah Smith, "Map: Protests and Rallies for George Floyd Spread across the Country," NBC News, June 12, 2020, www.nbcnews.com/news/us-news/map-protests-rallies-george-floyd-spread-across-country-n1220976; and Weiyi Cai, Juliette Love, Jugal K. Patel, and Yuliya Parshina-Kottas, "George Floyd Protest," *New York Times*, May 31, 2020.

54. Kishi et al. 2021. Also see Erica Chenoweth and Jeremy Pressman, "This Summer's Black Lives Matter Protests Were Overwhelmingly Peaceful, Our Research Finds," *Washington Post*, October 16, 2020.

55. Soo Kim, "Protests Near Me—List of Cities Rioting, States Where National Guard Has Been Deployed," *Newsweek*, June 6, 2020.

56. Hinton 2021; Levy 2018. Levy estimates that between 1963 and 1972 there were 750 urban revolts in 525 U.S. cities. He estimates 73 million people lived in

communities that experienced uprisings during this period. Hinton estimates a higher level: she claims that between May 1968 and December 1972 960 Black communities experienced 1,949 separate uprisings.

57. Boyles 2015; Cobbina 2019; Hill 2016; Lowery 2016; Schneider 2014.

58. Cobbina 2019, p. 14.

59. Schneider 2014, p. 28.

60. Kramer and Remster 2022, p. 46.

61. Abu-Lughod 2007; DiPasquale and Glaeser 1998; Gale 1996; Lieberson and Silverman 1965; Sugrue 1996.

62. Interview 2020.

63. M. B. Katz 2012, p. 80.

64. K.-Y. Taylor 2016, p. 10.

65. Zelizer 2016, p. 1.

66. Herman 2017; Rose and Mohl 2012; Teaford 1990, 2006; Vale 2019.

67. Fullilove 2004; Gale 1996; Herman 2013; Sugrue 1996; Tager 2001.

68. Butler 2017; Camp and Heatherton 2016; A. J. Davis 2017; V. M. Rios 2011.

69. Cobbina 2019.

70. Colebrook 2020.

71. Cobbina 2019; Schneider 2014; Murch 2015.

72. Butler 2017; A. J. Davis 2017; Stevenson 2015.

73. Nixon 2011, p. 2.

74. Colebrook 2020, p. 496.

75. Cashin 2021; Fullilove and Wallace 2011.

76. E. Anderson 2022; Duneier 2016; Freeman 2019; Jargowsky 1997, 2015; Sharkey 2013; Wacquant 2008.

77. Brown 2021.

78. Massey and Denton 1993; Trounstine 2018.

79. Bustamante, Jashnani, and Stoudt 2019; Cahill et al. 2019; Grills, Aird, and Rowe 2016; Nixon 2011; Pain 2019; Pain and Cahill 2022; Slater 2021.

80. Pain 2019.

81. Fullilove 2004, p. 11.

82. Carter 2007; Fullilove 2004.

83. Dowd 2020; Kern 2022.

84. Kern 2022, p. 109.

85. Dowd 2020, p. 311.

86. Kern 2022, p. 109.

87. Dowd 2020; Grills, Aird, and Rowe 2016.

88. Dowd 2020, p. 305; Fullilove 2004; Kern 2022.

89. Grills, Aird, and Rowe 2016.

90. Brown 2021, p. 10.

91. Boyles 2019; Butler 2017; Cobbina 2019; Hill 2016; Lowery 2016; Nassauer 2019; Schneider 2017.

92. Alexander 2012; also see Wacquant 2009 and Western 2006.

93. Fullilove 2004; Hyra 2012.

94. Hyra 2012.

95. Hirsch 1998.

96. K. T. Jackson 1987; Massey and Denton 1993.

97. Fullilove 2004; Goetz 2013; C. Gordon 2019; Hackworth 2007, 2019; Hyra 2012; Schaller 2019; Vale 2013; R. Y. Williams 2004.

98. Smith et al. 2002.

99. Kneebone and Berube 2013; Rosen 2020; Rothstein 2015.

100. Cashin 2021; Ehrenhalt 2012; Immergluck 2022.

101. Sharp 2014.

102. Logan and Oakley 2017.

103. Hyra 2008, 2017; Schaller 2019.

104. Murch 2015.

105. Elliot-Cooper, Hubbard, and Lees 2020; Kern 2022.

106. Fullilove 2004.

107. Cobbina 2019; Crenson 2017; Mallach 2018; Stoker, Stone, and Worgs 2015; Johnson 2020.

108. Clarence Burns, Freeman Bosely Jr., and Ella Jones were the first African American mayors in Baltimore, St. Louis, and Ferguson respectively.

109. Coates 2018; R. Kennedy 2012.

110. Bristol 1991; C. Gordon 2019; Hansman 2017; W. Johnson 2020.

111. By Disneyfication, I refer to city action to promote economic development policies that cater to the interests of tourists and the tourism industry by providing an entertaining and safe environment. Some infrastructure associated with the Disneyfication of Baltimore's Inner Harbor area include the completion of Camden Yards baseball stadium in 1992, the M&T Bank football stadium in 1998, the Port Discovery Children's Museum in 1998, and the redeveloped and expanded National Aquarium in 2005 (Levine 2000).

112. Gillette 2022.

113. Hesse and Hooker 2017; D. Thompson 2017.

114. Clark's quote in Meier, Rudwick, and Bracey 2007, p. 114.

115. Dikeç 2017, p. 7.

116. D. Thompson 2017.

117. The massive protests and incidents of unrest following Floyd's death occurred while I was more than halfway done with this book, but these events have
greatly shaped the way I think about unrest. The events of 2020 also increased my
motivation and dedication to this research.

118. While I was writing much of this manuscript, my mother was dying of
pancreatic cancer. This situation should not have affected my analysis, but I
would be lying if I did not admit it did. Losing an extremely close loved one is difficult and it sparks emotions and anger. My mother was not shot by the police, but
her cancer angered and saddened me, and I cannot image the level of rage that
filled the mothers of Michael Brown and Freddie Gray.

119. Hyra 2008, 2017.

120. While I am not an unrest researcher, I wrote a 2012 *Urban Affairs Review*
journal article comparing the old to the new urban renewal periods. This article
serves as the basis for the historical comparison of the urban renewal periods impacting the cities and communities that have experienced contemporary unrest.
I also have investigated the pre-, during, and post–Great Recession periods and
their racial impact on African American communities (see Hyra and Rugh 2016).
The dynamics and outcomes associated with the Great Recession are important
components of the unrest narratives described in this book.

121. See Hyra 2008, 2017.

122. For more on my research method, see appendix A.

123. Clark's quote in Meier, Rudwick, and Bracey 2007, p. 108.

Chapter 1. Riots or Revolts?

1. Park's quote in Park and Burgess 1925, p. 19.

2. Gilje 1996, p. 1.

3. Gilje 1996; Tager 2001.

4. Gilje 1996, p. 1. Also see Osterweil 2020.

5. McLaughlin 2014, p. 12.

6. Hinton 2021; Sugrue 2008.

7. McLaughlin 2014, p. 12.

8. Cobb 2021.

9. Zelizer 2016, p. 1.

10. McLaughlin 2014, p. 12.

11. Hinton 2021; Levy 2018.

12. Tilly 2003.

13. McAdam 1999.

14. Feagin and Hahn 1973.

15. Meier and Rudwick 1976.

16. Abu-Lughod 2007.

17. Hayden 1967.

18. Abu-Lughod 2007.

19. Sugrue 2008, p. 334.

20. Sugrue 2008, p. 334.

21. Feagin and Hahn 1973. I cite these authors not because they support this perspective, but they extensively cover it in their book. Several theories play the "blame the victim game" by pinpointing the percent of African Americans or the Great Migration or the interactions between whites and Blacks as the cause of riots. These types of analyses lead to the conclusion that if Blacks had just stayed in the South, or if they were just better attuned to the dynamics of the city or had stayed in their own segregated neighborhoods, riots would not have happened. While it is important as a social scientist to assess the root factors associated with unrest, it is vital to understand how variable formation and links can lead to unjust explanations for riots.

22. Schneider 2014, p. 26.

23. Nassauer 2019.

24. Hill 2020, pp. 64 and 65.

25. Hinton 2021, p. 14.

26. Osterweil 2020, p. 13.

27. Moran and Waddington 2016, p. 8. For these authors, "Riots are usually volatile and ephemeral events, intense outbursts of emotionally-charged violence that rarely last beyond a few days."

28. Zelizer 2016, p. 8.

29. K. B. Clark 1965; Gale 1996; U.S. National Advisory Commission on Civil Disorders 1968.

30. Olzak, Shanahan, and McEneaney 1996.

31. Cobbina 2019; Hill 2016; Lowery 2016; Schneider 2014.

32. Katz 2012; Wacquant 2008.

33. Nassauer 2019.

34. Abu-Lughod 2007; Bustamante, Jashnani, and Stoudt 2019; Sugrue 1996.

35. Moran and Waddington 2016, p. 6.

36. Myrdal 1944.

37. E. Anderson 2022; Cashin 2021; Shapiro 2017.

38. Jung Hyun Choi, "Racial Homeownership Rates Vary across the Most Commonly Cited Datatsets. When and Why Should You Use Different Ones?" *Urban Wire*, December 8, 2021.

39. Liz Mineo, "Racial Wealth Gap May Be a Key to Other Inequalities," *Harvard Gazette*, June 3, 2021.

40. Shapiro 2017, p. 17.

41. Harris and Curtis 2018, p. 15.

42. Ansell 2021.

43. Abu-Lughod 2007, p. 3.

44. Abu-Lughod 2007, p. vii.

45. Dikeç 2017, p. 8.

46. U.S. National Advisory Commission on Civil Disorders 1968, p. 2.

47. U.S. National Advisory Commission on Civil Disorders 1968, p. 10.

48. Gale 1996, p. 2.

49. F.R. Harris 1988, p. 12.

50. Meier, Rudwick, and Bracey 2007, p. 109.

51. Meier, Rudwick, and Bracey 2007, p. 115.

52. Olzak, Shanahan, and McEneaney 1996, p. 603.

53. Olzak, Shanahan, and McEneaney 1996, p. 590.

54. Spilerman 1976, p. 771.

55. Herman 2005.

56. Herman 2005, p. 5.

57. Sugrue 1996.

58. Sugrue 1996, p. 11.

59. Sugure 1996, pp. 260–61.

60. Abu-Lughod 2007.

61. Ammon 2016; Bauman, Biles, and Szylvian 2000; Biles and Rose 2022; Connolly 2014; Fullilove 2004; Gioielli 2014; Halpern 1995; Hirsch 1998; Klemek 2011; Zipp 2010.

62. Hyra 2012.

63. Fullilove 2004, p. 4.

64. M. Anderson 1967, p. 54.

65. Goetz 2013; Hirsch 1998; Vale 2013.

66. Sugrue 1996, p. 50.

67. Tager 2001, p. 174. Also see Massey and Kanaiaupuni 1993 for an excellent quantitative analysis of the relationship between public housing placement and concentrated poverty.

68. Hirsch 1998, p. 243.

69. Teaford 2006, p. 140.

70. Rose and Mohl 2012, p. 97.

71. Tager 2001, p. 175.

72. Jacobs 1992, p. 278.

73. Fullilove 2004, p. 3.

74. Fullilove 2004, p. 11.

75. Fullilove 2004, p. 14.

76. Grills, Aird, and Rowe 2016, p. 336.

77. Herman 2017, p. 54.

78. Teaford 1990, p. 180.

79. Teaford 2006, p. 112.

80. Vale 2019, p. 41.

81. Feagin and Hahn 1973, pp. 6–28. I am aware that some might conclude that the way to prevent riots is to keep African American expectations low. That is not the point here; rather, it is to underscore that poverty and economic deprivation often do not lead to widespread unrest without some expectation that action will lead to change.

82. Sugrue 2008, p. 290.

83. Sugrue 2008.

84. McAdam 1999, p. 42.

85. McAdam 1999, p. 43.

86. U.S. National Advisory Commission on Civil Disorders 1968.

87. U.S. National Advisory Commission on Civil Disorders 1968, p. 11.

88. Ture and Hamilton 1992.

89. Meier, Rudwick, and Bracey 2007, pp. 111–12.

90. U.S. National Advisory Commission on Civil Disorders 1968, p. 11.

91. Levy 2018, p. 11.

92. Dikeç 2017; Katz 2012; Wacquant 2008.

93. Schneider 2014, p. 25.

94. Schneider 2014, p. 26.

95. U.S. National Advisory Commission on Civil Disorders 1968, p. 11.

96. James Baldwin, "A Report from Occupied Territory," *The Nation*, July 11, 1966.

97. Meier, Rudwick, and Bracey 2007, pp. 109–10.

98. Cobbina 2019.

99. For excellent books on the trajectory of African American ghettos, see Duneier 2016; Freeman 2019; and Hutchison and Haynes 2012.

100. Boyles 2015; Cobbina 2019; Hill 2016; Lowery 2016; Kramer and Remster 2022; Schneider 2014.

101. Nassauer 2019.

102. Moran and Waddington 2016.

103. Moran and Waddington 2016, p. 3.

104. Moran and Waddington 2016, p. 9.

105. Moran and Waddington 2016, p. 16.

106. Moran and Waddington 2016, p. 19.

107. Aspects of this model were used by Cobbina 2019 to assess the contemporary unrest in Ferguson and Baltimore and by Schneider 2014 in Paris and New York City. Both these scholars conclude police officers are the primary actors in stimulating unrest.

108. Hyra 2008.

109. Maciag 2015.

110. Addie 2008; Addie and Fraser 2019; Boston 2021; Brand 2022; Causa Justa :: Just Cause 2014; Chronopoulos 2016; Cliffton, Griesedieck, and Hassler 2018; Dikeç 2017; Gibbons 2023; Golash-Boza 2023; Gomez 2013; Hern 2017; Hyra 2008, 2017; Immergluck 2022; Kern 2022; Lloyd 2011; Moskowitz 2017; Payne and Greiner 2019; Richardson, Mitchell, and Franco 2019; Schlichtman, Patch, and Hill 2017; R. Shaw 2018; Smith and Graves 2005; Summers 2019; Sutton 2020; Swanstrom, Webber, and Metzger 2015; Tach 2014; Timberlake and Johns-Wolfe 2017; Tissot 2015.

111. Hyra 2012.

112. Chaskin and Joseph 2015; Wilson 1996.

113. Hyra 2012; Goetz 2013; Richardson, Mitchell, and Franco 2019; Vale 2013, 2019.

114. Goetz 2013, p. 121.

115. Hyra and Rugh 2016.

116. Center for Responsible Lending 2013; Immergluck 2015; Sassen 2014.

117. Hyra and Rugh 2016; Rugh and Massey 2010; Wyly, Atia, and Hammel 2004.

118. Glaude 2017, p. 17.

119. While it has been demonstrated that middle-income African American homeowners were hit worse than low-income African Americans by the foreclosure crisis (Thomas et al. 2018), my argument is that low-income communities of color were hit hard too. Many low-income communities of color have middle-income people in them who were negatively impacted by the subprime and foreclosure crisis (Moore 2016; Pattillo 2007), and this had a devastating effect in

certain African American communities, leading to further impoverishment or gentrification (Hyra and Rugh 2016; Immergluck 2022; Shapiro 2017; Stein 2019).

120. Sassen 2014, p. 120.

121. Eviction Lab's data available at https://evictionlab.org/map/?m=modeled&c=p&b=efr&s=all&r=states&y=2018&z=3.07&lat=34.85&lon=-84.68&lang=en (accessed October 4, 2023).

122. Fullilove 2004; Desmond and Kimbro 2015; Gibbons and Barton 2016; Hatch and Yun 2021; Huynh and Maroko 2014; Hyra, Moulden, Weted, and Fullilove 2019; Lim et al. 2017; Keene and Geronimus 2011.

123. Goetz 2013, pp. 121–22.

124. Gioielli 2014, p. 98.

125. Saegert, Fields, and Libman 2011, p. 390.

126. Fullilove 2004; Gale 1996; Gioielli 2014; Herman 2013; Sugrue 1996; Tager 2001; Zelizer 2016.

127. One exception, Dikeç 2017.

128. Dikeç 2017, pp. 5 and 12.

129. Vale 2013, p. 30.

130. Vale 2013, pp. 1 and 33.

131. Fullilove and Wallace 2011, p. 381.

132. Fullilove and Wallace 2011, pp. 383–84. Other authors have described displaced African Americans as "refugees;" see Abu-Lughod 2007 and Sassen 2014. Psychologist Monica Luci (2020: 262) documents how refugees often experience "a substantial loss [and] a multilevel rupture" from homeland displacement.

133. For an analysis of the relationship between serial displacement and segregation in Baltimore, see Brown 2021.

134. Brown 2021, p. 107.

135. Bustamante, Jashnani, and Stoudt's (2019: 1) concept of *cumulative dehumanization* inspired my horizontal and vertical unrest analysis. They defined cumulative dehumanization as "a web of vertical and horizontal, synthetic and dynamic processes, affectively and materially interwoven to produce an extreme, everyday state-sanctioned dehumanization—an ongoing, racialized dehumanization that is fundamentally cumulative, both temporally and spatially—with a profusion of consequences attached."

136. Colebrook 2020. This framework was also influenced by the excellent gentrification work of Brown 2021; Dantzler 2021; Golash-Boza 2023; Immergluck 2022; Rucks-Ahidiana 2022; and B. Williams 2016.

Chapter 2. Segregation, Divestment, and Serial Displacement

1. Opening quote in Purnell 2016, p. 159.
2. Till 2012.
3. Grills, Aird, and Rowe 2016.
4. Grills, Aird, and Rowe 2016, p. 336.
5. Boyles 2015, p. 17.
6. Lipsitz 2011; Rogers 2015.
7. W. Johnson 2020, p. 10.
8. Freeman 2019; Inwood 2010; Hyra 2008, 2017.
9. Wright 2004.
10. Wright 2004, p. 7.
11. Rogers 2015, p. 9.
12. Interview 2020.
13. St. Louis was named after King Louis IX of France, and the Spanish and French fought for control of the area before it was acquired by the United States in 1803 from the French for $15 million in the Louisiana Purchase (Primm 2010). In the mid-eighteenth century, the city was an important fur trading post (Mendelson and Quinn 1985).
14. Primm 2010, p. 453; Winch 2011, 2018; Wright 2002.
15. Burbank 1966; Dowden-White 2011; Kavanaugh 2017; Kienzle 2017; Lipsitz 1991; Primm 2010; J. Rios 2020; Sandweiss 2001; Wright 2002. Before the French and Spanish settled in the St. Louis area, it was Osages and Missouris, and other tribes that lived there. Prior to these tribes the St. Louis area, sometime between CE 1050 and 1400, was a Cahokia Mound city.
16. Heathcott and Dietz 2019; J. Rios 2020.
17. Gioielli 2014, p. 42; Primm 2010.
18. Primm 2010.
19. Kavanaugh 2017, p. 72.
20. Bracey 2016.
21. Kienzle 2017.
22. Kavanaugh 2017; Kienzle 2017; Lang 2009; Primm 2010; Winch 2018; Wright 2002.
23. Berlin 2010; Dowden-White 2011; Grossman 1989; Lemann 1991; Lumpkins 2008; Wilkerson 2011.
24. Lumpkins 2008, p. 77.
25. W. Johnson 2020; Primm 2010.

26. Burbank 1966; Jack 2007.

27. Jack 2007, p. 146.

28. Jack 2007, p. 146.

29. Jack 2007, p. 147.

30. Jack 2007, p. 148.

31. Burbank 1966.

32. J. Rios 2020.

33. Lang 2009; J. Rios 2020. The actor Ellie Kemper was once named the Queen of Love and Beauty at The Veiled Prophet Ball; see Kelsey Klotz, "Ellie Kemper's Veiled Prophet Debutante Ball Past Is More Than a Celebrity Scandal," NBC News, June 4, 2021, www.nbcnews.com/think/opinion/ellie-kemper-s-veiled-prophet-debutante-ball-past-more-celebrity-ncna1269569.

34. For St. Louis City and County population and racial demographic change, see appendix B.

35. Ervin 2019.

36. W. Johnson 2020.

37. Lang 2009.

38. Lang 2004; Primm 2010; Purdy 2012.

39. Ervin 2019; Lang 2009; Lipsitz 1995.

40. W. Johnson 2020, p. 233.

41. Quote in Primm 2010, p. 415.

42. Campbell 2013.

43. W. Johnson 2020; Primm 2010.

44. Lumpkins 2008.

45. Lumpkins 2008.

46. Gibson 2020; Lumpkins 2008; Wright 2002, 2004.

47. Massey and Denton 1993, p. 21.

48. Freixas and Abbott 2019, p. xix.

49. Oliveri 2015.

50. C. Gordon 2008; Massey and Denton 1993; Primm 2010; Schuessler 2019.

51. Dowden-White 2011; C. Gordon 2008; Oliveri 2015; Primm 2010; Rothstein 2015.

52. Primm 2010.

53. Dowden-White 2011.

54. C. Gordon 2008; Rothstein 2017.

55. C. Gordon 2008.

56. Lang 2004, p. 727.

57. Gioielli 2014; W. Johnson 2020.

58. Rothstein 2017.

59. K. T. Jackson 1987.

60. Oliveri 2015.

61. K. T. Jackson 1987.

62. K. T. Jackson 1987, pp. 200–201.

63. K. T. Jackson 1987, p. 201.

64. Aaronson, Hartley, and Mazumder 2021.

65. Hanchett 2003, p. 166.

66. Rothstein 2015, p. 187.

67. Oliveri 2015, p. 1060.

68. Dowden-White 2011; Lipsitz 1995; Wilkerson 2020.

69. Dowden-White 2011; Lang 2009.

70. Burbank 1966; Dowden-White 2011; Ervin 2019; Lang 2009; Lipsitz 1995.

71. Ervin 2019, p. 1.

72. 700 North 1st Street in Laclede's Landing, St. Louis's website: http://users.stlcc.edu/mfuller/laclede.html (accessed October 4, 2023).

73. Dowden-White 2011; W. Johnson 2020; Wright 2002, 2004.

74. Early 1998; W. Johnson 2020; Kavanaugh 2017; Lipsitz 1995; Primm 2010; Wright 2002.

75. Hyra 2012.

76. Primm 2010, p. 432.

77. Primm 2010.

78. Heathcott and Murphy 2005.

79. Campbell 2013; Heathcott and Murphy 2005.

80. Fred Kaplan, "The Twisted History of the Gateway Arch," *Smithsonian Magazine*, October 2015.

81. Heathcott and Murphy 2005.

82. W. Johnson 2020; Kavanaugh 2017; Kienzle 2017; Primm 2010.

83. Heathcott and Murphy 2005, p. 180.

84. Campbell 2013, pp. 30–31.

85. Sandweiss 2001, p. 233. Also see Campbell 2013 and W. Johnson 2020.

86. Campbell 2013; Lang 2004, 2009; Primm 2010.

87. Campbell 2013.

88. Sandweiss 2001.

89. Campbell 2013.

90. Kaplan, "Twisted History of the Gateway Arch."

91. Primm 2010.

92. Campbell 2013.

93. Campbell 2013, p. 43.

94. Primm 2010, p. 453.

95. Primm 2010.

96. For an excellent analysis of the development of the dome, see Lipsitz 2011, pp. 73–94.

97. Primm 2010.

98. Heathcott and Murphy 2005; Lipsitz 2011.

99. Atkins's quote in Freixas and Abbott 2019, p. 304.

100. Biles and Rose 2022.

101. C. Gordon 2008; Heathcott 2008; Heathcott and Murphy 2005; Judd 2000; Lang 2009; Mumford 2019; Primm 2010; Sandweiss 2001; Teaford 1990.

102. Heathcott and Murphy 2005, p. 160.

103. W. Johnson 2020, p. 292.

104. C. Gordon 2008, p. 162.

105. C. Gordon 2008, pp. 162–63. Also see Lang 2009. The LCRA, at the time, was the agency in charge of the city's slum removal program and it also combined the role of the St. Louis Housing Authority (SLHA) in providing subsidized housing.

106. Lang 2009.

107. Gibson 2020; Wright 2002.

108. Lang 2009.

109. Dowden-White 2011; Wright 2002.

110. Cummings 2004.

111. Lang 2009. Heathcott and Murphy (2005) estimated that a total of $135 million was spent on the Mill Creek Valley redevelopment. Also see Tim O'Neil, "Aug. 7, 1954: Decision to Clear Mill Creek Valley Changed the Face of the City," *St. Louis Post-Dispatch*, August 7, 2022.

112. Lang 2009. C. Gordon (2008) estimated the Mill Creek Valley redevelopment displacement at 16,000 people, while Ervin (2019) and Lipsitz (2011) reported 20,000 displaced. Heathcott and Murphy (2005) reported that 5,630 units were razed in the Mill Creek Valley redevelopment.

113. Gibson 2020.

114. Rose and Mohl 2012.

115. Heathcott and Murphy 2005.

116. Ervin 2019, p. 153.

117. Heathcott 2011, p. 83.

118. C. Gordon 2019. Also see Lipsitz 2011.

119. Heathcott and Murphy 2005, p. 159.

120. C. Gordon 2019, p. 89.

121. Lipsitz 1995, p. 207.

122. Ervin 2019.

123. Campbell 2013.

124. Lang 2009.

125. Lang 2009.

126. Lang 2009, p. 110.

127. Quote in Lang 2009, p. 108.

128. Lang 2009, p. 109.

129. Lang 2009, p. 108.

130. Lang 2009.

131. Walker Hamilton, "Saint Louis City Board of Aldermen Looking to Return Ward Reduction to the Public for a Re-Vote," *NextSTL*, May 1, 2018.

132. Interview 2020.

133. Interview 2020.

134. Boyles 2015; C. Gordon 2019; Wright 2000, 2002.

135. C. Gordon 2019, p. 54.

136. C. Gordon 2019.

137. C. Gordon 2019. Some displaced people would also move to public housing in Kinloch, another Black suburban enclave.

138. C. Gordon 2019. This suburban Black removal process also occurred in the Baltimore, Maryland region; see Cashin 2021.

139. Hyra 2012.

140. Heathcott 2008, p. 237.

141. Rainwater 1970.

142. W. Johnson (2020: 301) reports that nearly 20 percent of those displaced from Mill Creek Valley ended up living in Pruitt-Igoe. For more on St. Louis's public housing and Pruitt-Igoe, see Bristol 1991; Heathcott 2011; Montgomery 1985; and von Hoffman 2003.

143. Igoe was named after William Leo Igoe, former Missouri Congressman and chairman of the St. Louis Board of Police Commissioners.

144. Bristol 1991; Hansman 2017; Rainwater 1970.

145. Hansman 2017. Also see Chelsea Bailey, "Civil Rights Attorney Frankie Muse Freeman Dies at 101," NBC News, January 13, 2008, www.nbcnews.com /storyline/mlk-50/civil-rights-attorney-frankie-muse-freeman-dies-101-n837491.

146. Hansman 2017.

147. C. Gordon 2019; Primm 2010.

148. Quote from Montgomery 1985, p. 229.

149. Hansman 2017; Ladner 1995.

150. Meehan's quote in Bristol 1991, p. 165.

151. Rainwater 1970. Also see Ladner 1995.

152. Ervin 2019; Lipsitz 1995; von Hoffman 2003.

153. Montgomery 1985.

154. Hill 2016, p. 20.

155. Primm 2010, p. 462.

156. Primm 2010.

157. Hansman 2017.

158. Wilson 1996.

159. Primm 2010.

160. Rainwater 1970.

161. O. Newman 1973.

162. Rainwater 1970.

163. Campbell 2013, p. 140.

164. von Hoffman 2003.

165. Hansman 2017; Hill 2016.

166. Quote in Montgomery 1985, pp. 232–33.

167. Quote in Hansman 2017, p. 112.

168. Cummings 2004; C. Gordon 2008. St. Louis had over 378 neighborhood restrictive covenants; see Hansman 2017.

169. Wright 2002, p. 64; also see C. Gordon 2008.

170. Gioielli 2014.

171. Wright 2001.

172. Lipsitz 1991; Wright 2002.

173. Wills 2018.

174. Harmon's quote in Jeannette Cooperman, "A Conversation with Clarence Harmon," *St. Louis Magazine*, November 29, 2012.

175. Heathcott and Murphy 2005, p. 164.

176. Wilson 1996.

177. Heathcott and Murphy 2005; Primm 2010.

178. Harris and Metzger 2018; Heathcott and Murphy 2005; Lipsitz 2011; Primm 2010.

179. C. Gordon 2008.

180. Gioielli 2014; C. Gordon 2008, 2019; Wright 2001. For more on the Ville see, Adolphus Hardy's quotes in Freixas and Abbott 2019, pp. 85–86, and footnote 14 on p. 67.

181. Quote in Freixas and Abbott 2019, p. 320.

182. C. Gordon 2008, p. 4.

183. Freixas and Abbott 2019; C. Gordon 2008; Wilson 1996.

184. Lipsitz 2011.

185. Gioielli 2014, p. 67.

Chapter 3. Central Corridor Gentrification and Suburban Segregation

1. Metzger's quote in interview 2020.

2. Freixas and Abbott 2019; C. Gordon 2019.

3. Garvey 2019, pp. 171–72; for more on this divide, see Lipsitz 1991.

4. Alissa Walker, "How St. Louis' History of Private Streets Led to a Gun-Brandishing Couple," *CURBED*, June 29, 2020.

5. Florida 2018.

6. Gillette 2022; Heathcott and Murphy 2005.

7. Heathcott and Murphy 2005; Lipsitz 2011. To better understand how and why several city leaders turned to amenity politics, see Clark 2011 and Hyra 2017.

8. Brenner and Theodore 2002; Soss, Fording, and Schram 2011; Wacquant 2009.

9. Florida 2018.

10. Maciag 2015.

11. Boston 2021; Dantzler 2021; Helmuth 2019; Hyra 2008, 2017; Hyra et al. 2019; Immergluck 2022; Sutton 2020.

12. Hwang and Sampson 2014; Rucks-Ahidiana 2021, 2022.

13. Gibbons 2023.

14. Carlson 2020; Easton et al. 2020; Freeman 2019; Hwang and Ding 2020; Hyra 2008; Newman and Wyly 2006.

15. For instance, in 2018 Todd Swanstrom argued, "Today, however, the big disruptive challenge facing older industrial cities like St. Louis is not gentrification but depopulation and disinvestment—not re-urbanization but de-urbanization." This quote appears here: http://cityobservatory.org/is-st-louis-gentrifying/ (accessed October 4, 2023). Also see Swanstrom's remarks in Freixas and Abbott 2019 as well as Mallach 2018 and Swanstrom, Webber, and Metzger 2017.

16. Interview 2020.

17. Interview 2020.

18. Interview 2020.

19. In fact, Swanstrom, Webber, and Metzger (2017) published a study suggesting that most of St. Louis's redeveloping neighborhoods between 1970 and 2010 were in the near south, while none were in North City.

20. Swanstrom and Plöger 2022.

21. Freixas and Abbott 2019; W. Johnson 2020; Katz and Wagner 2014; Mallach 2018; Swanstrom, Webber, and Metzger 2017; Wesenberg 2004. Also see Evan Binns, "CORTEX Set to Unveil Next Stage of Development," *St. Louis Business Journal*, October 19, 2012.

22. Interview 2020.

23. Lees 2003.

24. W. Johnson 2020.

25. Schaller 2019.

26. Interview 2020.

27. Judd 2000, p. 957; Harris and Metzger 2018.

28. City Foundry STL's website: www.cityfoundrystl.com (accessed October 4, 2023).

29. The Lawrence Group's website: www.thelawrencegroup.com/city-foundry-st-louis-the-backstory/ (accessed October 4, 2023).

30. Harris and Metzger 2018.

31. Freixas and Abbott 2019; Harris and Metzger 2018.

32. Gioielli 2014; C. Gordon 2019; W. Johnson 2020.

33. Harris and Metzger 2018.

34. O'Connor 1999.

35. Oluku 2011.

36. Oluku 2011, p. 114.

37. U.S. Department of Housing and Urban Development's website: www.hud.gov/sites/documents/DOC_10014.PDF (accessed October 4, 2023).

38. Interview 2020.

39. Heathcott 2008.

40. Heathcott 2011.

41. Meehan 1975.

42. Freixas and Abbott 2019; Oluku 2011.

43. Oluku 2011.

44. St. Louis Housing Authority's website: www.slha.org/properties-amenities/king-louis-square/ (accessed October 4, 2023).

45. Mark Groth, "Groth Guide to Peabody Darst Webbe," *NextSTL*, December 13, 2021, https://nextstl.com/2021/12/peabody-darst-webbe/.

46. Author's analysis of U.S. Census data.

47. Freixas and Abbott 2019; W. Johnson 2020; Mallach 2018; Swanstrom and Plöger 2022; Swanstrom, Webber, and Metzger 2015; Wesenberg 2004.

48. Interview 2020.

49. Swanstrom, Webber, and Metzger 2017.

50. Swanstrom, Webber, and Metzger 2017, p. 342.

51. Swanstrom, Webber, and Metzger 2017.

52. Swanstrom, Webber, and Metzger 2017, p. 342.

53. Oluku 2011.

54. Quote appeared in Najeeb Hasan, "No Place Like Home," *Riverfront Times*, July 18, 2001.

55. Hasan, "No Place Like Home."

56. Swanstrom, Webber, and Metzger 2017; Swanstrom and Plöger 2022.

57. S.M. Moore 2017. Also see Alexis Stephens. "Mixed-Income Housing Grant Add a New Layer to St. Louis Development Saga." *NextCity.* February 23, 2015. For a national look at the connection between HOPE VI and gentrification, see Goetz 2013; Vale 2013; and Lees, Slater, and Wyly 2008.

58. Freixas and Abbott 2019; Oluku 2011.

59. Oluku 2011. Also see McCormack Baron Salazar's website: https://www.mccormackbaron.com/community-profiles/renaissance-place-at-grand (accessed October 4, 2023).

60. Oluku 2011.

61. Oluku 2011.

62. Oluku 2011, pp. 200–202.

63. Hackworth and Smith 2001.

64. Ella Faust, "First Look: High Low, a Literary Hub and Cafe, Now Open in Midtown," *Riverfront Times*, December 11, 2019.

65. Hyra 2012.

66. Goetz 2013, p. 121.

67. Goetz 2013, pp. 14–15.

68. Vale 2013, p. 1.

69. Oluku 2011.

70. Goetz 2013; Hyra 2012; Vale 2013.

71. W. Johnson 2020, p. 384.

72. Schulman 2012, pp. 161–66.

73. C. Gordon 2019.

74. Goetz 2013.

75. Lipsitz 2011.

76. Quote in Jeannette Cooperman, "A Conversation with Clarence Harmon," *St. Louis Magazine*, November 29, 2012.

77. Arena 2012; Drake Rodriguez 2021; Stone 1989.

78. Hyra 2008, 2012.

79. Interview 2021. This quote was from the second interview I conducted with Reed.

80. For more on Action St. Louis, see their website: https://actionstl.org (accessed October 4, 2023).

81. Interview 2021.

82. Till 2012, p. 3.

83. Fullilove 2004.

84. Till 2012, p. 3. Also see Grills, Aird, and Rowe's 2016 concept of "Emotional Emancipation Circles."

85. Ewing 2018, p. 127.

86. Slocum 2019, p. 10.

87. Dikeç 2017; W. Johnson 2020; Loewen 2006; Oliveri 2015; Rothstein 2015.

88. Oliveri 2015; J. Rios 2020; Wright 2000, 2001.

89. Cobbina 2019; Hirt 2014; W. Johnson 2020; Wright 2000. Also see the 2019 documentary film *Where the Pavement Ends*, www.janegillooly.com/where-the-pavement-ends/ (accessed October 4, 2023). After the death of Martin Luther King Jr., the Kinloch residents tore down the barrier.

90. W. Johnson 2020, p. 325.

91. Oliveri 2015.

92. Rothstein 2015.

93. Oliveri 2015.

94. Rothstein 2015.

95. Oliveri 2015; Ryan Schuessler, "Kinloch Connection: Ferguson Fueled by Razing of Historic Black Town," *Aljazeera*, August 20, 2014.

96. Walter and Kramer 1969.

97. C. Gordon 2019.

98. Cummings 2004; W. Johnson 2020; Walter and Kramer 1969; Wright 2000, 2002, 2004.

99. Mei-Ling Hopgood, "Taking Off: About 140 Families Begin Move from Housing Complexes under Airport Authority's Noise Plan," *St. Louis Post-Dispatch*, August 29, 1996; Margaret Gillerman, "Kinloch Sets Sights on Old Public Housing," *St. Louis Post-Dispatch*, February 18, 2002. Also see Wright 2000.

100. U.S. Department of Housing and Urban Development 1967.

101. Quote from U.S. Department of Housing and Urban Development 1967, p. 8.

102. Cambria et al. 2018; Cummings 2004; Wright 2002.

103. Schuessler, "Kinloch Connection."

104. Cobbina 2019. Also see Schuessler, "Kinloch Connection."

105. Oliveri 2015, p. 1067. Also see Ben Westhoff, "The City Next to Ferguson Is Even More Depressing," *Vice*, June 3, 2015.

106. Interview 2021.

107. Interview 2021.

108. Keene, Padilla, and Geronimus 2010.

109. Interview 2020.

110. Dikeç 2017, p. 115.

111. Rothstein 2015.

112. Dikeç 2007; M. B. Katz 2012; Schneider 2014.

113. Moran 2012; Wacquant 2008.

114. Dikeç 2007, 2017; M. B. Katz 2012.

115. K. T. Jackson 1987.

116. My point here is that urban and suburban conditions are connected. For more on this in the St. Louis metro, see Heathcott and Murphy 2005.

117. Ehrenhalt 2012.

118. Rothstein 2015, p. 203.

Chapter 4. Plantation Politics and Policing

1. J. Rios 2019. Charles Brown's quote in Freixas and Abbott 2019, p. 435.

2. T. M. Shaw 2015.

3. Cobbina 2019, p. 28.

4. Cobbina 2019; T. M. Shaw 2015. At this time about 67 percent of Ferguson's population was African American and 23 percent was white.

5. T. M. Shaw 2015.

6. Alexander 2012; A. J. Davis 2017; J. Rios 2019; Western 2006.

7. Cobbina 2019; W. Johnson 2020; Lowery 2016; Moran and Waddington 2016.

8. T. M. Shaw 2015.

9. Boyles 2019; Cobbina 2019; Pinard 2015; T. M. Shaw 2015.

10. Hesse and Hooker 2017, p. 454.

11. J. Rios 2019, 2020; Moran and Waddington 2016; Wang 2018.

12. Interview 2020.

13. Interview 2020.

14. For a great description of "plantation politics" see Clarence Page, "Plantation Politics Revisited, Again," *Chicago Tribune*, January 22, 2006.

15. Wright Austin 2006.

16. Wright Austin 2006, p. 41.

17. Grimshaw 1992.

18. McKittrick 2013.

19. McKittrick 2013, p. 3.

20. McKittrick 2013, p. 4.

21. Boyles 2020.

22. Cobbina 2019; Jordan 2015; Pinard 2015.

23. J. Rios 2019, p. 254.

24. Interview 2020.

25. Interview 2020.

26. Interview 2020.

27. Others describe Ferguson's political landscape as the "good old boys" system.

28. Interview 2020.

29. Interview 2021.

30. Mollenkopf and Swanstrom 2015.

31. Mollenkopf and Swanstrom 2015.

32. Interview 2020.

33. J. Rios 2019, 2020. Also see Radley Balko, "How Municipalities in St. Louis County, Mo., Profit from Poverty," *Washington Post*, September 3, 2014.

34. J. Rios 2020.

35. Interview 2022.

36. Interview 2020.

37. Knowles's quote in J. Rios 2020, p. 111. The quote was an excerpt of a television interview Mayor Knowles did with MSNBC anchor Tamron Hall on August 19, 2014.

38. Interview 2020.

39. Interview 2021.

40. Interview 2021.

41. Dantzler 2021; Jenkins and Leroy 2021; Marable 1983; Robinson 2021.

42. C. Gordon 2019, p. 121.

43. Interview 2020.

44. Shapiro 2017, p. 85. Also see Mallach 2018 and C. Gordon 2019.

45. Interview 2021.

46. Interview 2020.

47. Interview 2020.

48. Interview 2021.

49. St. Louis ranks as one of the most violent cities in America. See *World Population Review*'s website: https://worldpopulationreview.com/us-city-rankings/most-violent-cities-in-america (accessed October 4, 2023).

50. Interview 2020.

51. Clerge 2019; Gale 1987; Lacy 2007; Lewis-McCoy 2014; Orfield 1997; Pattillo 1999; Smithsimon 2022; Vicino 2008.

52. Interview 2020.

53. J. Rios 2019, p. 246.

54. E. Anderson 2012; Duneier 2016; Freeman 2019.

55. J. Rios 2019, p. 263.

56. E. Anderson 2022.

57. E. Anderson 2012, p. 67.

58. E. Anderson 2012, p. 80.

59. Muhammad 2019.

60. Interview 2020.

61. Lipsitz 2011, p. 51.

62. Lipsitz 2011, p. 55.

63. Interview 2020.

64. Dikeç 2017; S. M. Moore 2015.

65. Underhill 2016, p. 4.

66. S. M. Moore 2015. For a breakdown of Ferguson's racial geography and segregation, see the maps and figures in these news articles: Ben Casselman, "The Poorest Corner of Town," *Fivethirtyeight*, August 26, 2014, https://fivethirtyeight.com/features/ferguson-missouri/; and Philip Bump, "Visualizing the Rapid Racial Change in Ferguson over the Past Decade," *Washington Post*, March 12, 2015, www.washingtonpost.com/news/the-fix/wp/2014/08/14/visualizing-the-rapid-racial-change-in-ferguson-over-the-past-decade/.

67. Interview 2020.

68. S. M. Moore 2015.

69. Dikeç 2017, p. 18; W. Johnson 2020. In 2013, Ferguson's median household income was $38,685. However, there was a large racial gap where the white median household income was $53,614 and the Black median was $32,023. However, it is also important to note that the city contains both high income whites and Blacks who make over $100,000 (Purnell 2016).

70. S. M. Moore 2015.

71. S.M. Moore 2015. Others estimate that in 2010 African Americans constituted 67 percent of the Ferguson population (Cobbina 2019). These discrepancies stemmed from Cobbina using the 2010 census for her estimates, while Moore used the 2008–12 American Community Survey data.

72. McClure 2019a.

73. McClure 2010.

74. Schwartz 2015.

75. Dawkins 2011; McClure 2019a.

76. McClure 2010.

77. This claim is based on my analysis of the placement of LIHTCs in the St. Louis region by 2014. The data are available at www.huduser.gov/portal/datasets/lihtc/property.html (accessed October 4, 2023).

78. S.M. Moore 2015. Also see Philip Tegeler, "Affirmatively Furthering Fair Housing in the LIHTC Program: Recent Progress," https://prrac.org/pdf/Tegeler_HJN_LIHTC_presentation.pdf (accessed October 4, 2023).

79. Williams's quote in Freixas and Abbott 2019, pp. 78–79.

80. McClure 2019a.

81. Metzger 2014; Rosen 2020.

82. Schwartz 2015.

83. McClure 2019b.

84. Vouchers are distributed by PHAs to low-income people but only one in four who qualify receive one due to their limited supply.

85. Metzger et al. 2019.

86. Metzger et al. 2019.

87. Jesse Bogan and Walter Moskop, "As Low-Income Housing Boomed, Ferguson Pushed Back," *St. Louis Post-Dispatch*, October 19, 2014. The total number of vouchers issued (11,000) is less than the number actually used (12,200), and this might be due to the fact that vouchers can be issued elsewhere, like by housing authorities outside of St. Louis City and County and used in these geographies. Vouchers are portable and can be used anywhere they are accepted and are no longer tied to the place where they were issued. Only about 5 percent of households, on average, use their vouchers outside of the jurisdiction that issued them (Schwartz 2015).

88. Metzger et al. 2019. Also see Jesse Bogan and Walter Moskop, "As Low-Income Housing Boomed, Ferguson Pushed Back," *St. Louis Post-Dispatch*, October 19, 2014.

89. Interview 2020.

90. Jesse Bogan, "Troubled Ferguson Apartment Complexes Change Hands, But Owners' Plans Are Unknown," *St. Louis Post Dispatch*, May 4, 2018.

91. Jesse Bogan and Walter Moskop, "As Low-Income Housing Boomed, Ferguson Pushed Back," *St. Louis Post-Dispatch*, October 19, 2014.

92. Rothstein 2017, p. 192.

93. Pennington-Cross and Ho 2010; Quercia, Stegman, and Davis 2007.

94. Avery, Brevoort, and Canner 2008; Baradaran 2017; Barr, Dokko, and Keys 2011; Immergluck 2009; Massey et al. 2016; Reid et al. 2017; Reid and Laderman 2011.

95. Mallach 2018.

96. Oliveri 2015, p. 1068.

97. J. Rios 2020, p. 72.

98. J. Rios 2019, p. 248.

99. W. Johnson 2020, p. 415.

100. Oliveri 2015; Shapiro 2017.

101. Interview 2020.

102. Hyra et al. 2020; Shapiro 2017. Also see Jim Gallagher, "Blame Poverty, Age for Weak North County Home Market," *St. Louis Post-Dispatch*, August 18, 2013; and Matthew Goldstein, "Another Shadow in Ferguson as Outside Firms Buy and Rent Out Distressed Homes," *New York Times*, September 3, 2014.

103. Raineth Housing's website: https://rainethhousing.com (accessed February 3, 2021).

104. Interview 2020.

105. Mallach 2017, p. 168.

106. Interview 2020.

107. Interview 2021.

108. Saegert, Fields, and Libman 2011, p. 390.

109. K.-Y. Taylor 2019, p. 5.

110. Center for Responsible Lending 2013, www.responsiblelending.org/mortgage-lending/research-analysis/2013-crl-research-update-foreclosure-spillover-effects-final-aug-19-docx.pdf (accessed July 24, 2019). Also see, Baradaran 2017.

111. Shapiro 2017, p. 40.

112. Kochhar and Fry 2014.

113. Glaude 2017, p. 17.

114. W. Johnson 2020.

115. C. Gordon 2019, p. 130.

116. C. Gordon 2019.

117. W. Johnson 2020, p. 421.

118. J. Rios 2020, p. 1.

119. J. Rios 2020, p. 103.

120. T. M. Shaw 2015, p. 3.

121. T. M. Shaw 2015, p. 2.

122. C. Gordon 2019, p. 142.

123. J. Rios 2019, p. 282. Also see Radley Balko, "How Municipalities in St. Louis County, Mo., Profit from Poverty," *Washington Post*, September 3, 2014.

124. Interview 2020.

125. Interview 2020.

126. Interview 2020.

127. Max Ehrenfreund, "The Risks of Walking While Black in Ferguson," *Washington Post*, March 4, 2015.

128. Underhill 2016, pp. 9-10.

129. W. Johnson 2020, p. 420.

130. W. Johnson 2020, p. 420.

131. W. Johnson 2020, p. 421. Also see, City of Ferguson's Department of Finance 2013.

132. Cobbina 2019, p. 55.

133. Boyles 2015. This would be the second major redevelopment of the area as it was "upgraded" in 1972, which placed public housing in the area (C. Gordon 2019).

134. Boyles 2015; Wright 2004.

135. C. Gordon 2019.

136. C. Gordon 2019; W. Johnson 2020.

137. W. Johnson 2020, p. 390.

138. C. Gordon 2019.

139. Boyles 2015; C. Gordon 2019; W. Johnson 2020. Also see Jaclyn Brenning, "Kirkwood's Journey: Separating Myths and Realities about Meacham Park, Thornton, Part 2," St. Louis Public Radio, February 7, 2010.

140. The DESCO Group's website: www.descogroup.com/company /about-109 (accessed October 4, 2023).

141. C. Gordon 2019.

142. W. Johnson 2020. Also see Gil Stuenkel, "Kirkwood, Ferguson TIFs Spark Projects," *St. Louis Business Journal*, October 29, 2000.

143. Boyles 2015.

144. W. Johnson 2020.

145. Boyles 2015.

146. Quote from *St. Louis Post-Dispatch* article cited in C. Gordon 2019, p. 117.

147. Boyles 2015; W. Johnson 2020.

148. C. Gordon 2019.

149. Boyles 2015.

150. Gil Stuenkel, "Kirkwood, Ferguson TIFs Spark Projects," *St. Louis Business Journal*, October 29, 2000. Also, see a comprehensive list of St. Louis region TIF projects at www.teamtifstl.com/wp-content/uploads/2017/01/Summary-of-TIF-Redevelopment-Projects-for-the-City-of-St-Louis.pdf (accessed July 9, 2020).

151. Betsy Riley, "Ferguson TIF Commission Passes $25 Million Project," *St. Louis Business Journal*, March 9, 1997.

152. W. Johnson 2020, p. 425. Also see Riley. "Ferguson TIF Commission Passes $25 Million Project," and Stuenkel. "Kirkwood, Ferguson TIFs Spark Projects."

153. Interview 2020.

154. Judd and Swanstrom 2015. In the St. Louis metropolitan region, there is a tremendous amount of political fragmentation and there exist near ninety municipalities (Jones 2000). These cities competed with one another for businesses to bolster their commercial tax base, and TIFs are widely used to help attract businesses.

155. J. Rios 2019, p. 292.

156. C. Gordon 2008.

157. W. Johnson 2020, p. 394.

158. W. Johnson 2020, pp. 425–26.

159. Interview 2020.

160. Missouri Department of Revenue, 2014 *Annual Report Summary: Local Tax Increment Financing Projects in Missouri*, Missouri Department of Revenue, February 1, 2015, https://dor.mo.gov/pdf/2014TIFAnnualReport.pdf. Also see the Office of Missouri State Auditor's website: https://auditor.mo.gov/TIF/View-Tif/772 (accessed October 4, 2023).

161. W. Johnson 2020, p. 429. Eventually the city did use some of the downtown TIF funds for the renovation of the city's police station and the expansion of its court complex (W. Johnson 2020, p. 430).

162. Walter Johnson, "Ferguson's Fortune 500 Company," *The Atlantic*, April 26, 2015.

163. J. Rios 2020, p. 19.

164. Interview 2020.

165. Interview 2020.

166. Lowery 2016; Nassauer 2019.

167. Interview 2020.

168. Interview 2020.

169. Interview 2020.

170. Jordan 2015. Also see Jonathan Topaz and Lucy McCalmont, "Obama Sending Holder to Ferguson," *Politico*, August 18, 2014.

171. Clerge 2019, p. xxii.

172. Cobbina 2019, p. 6.

173. J. Rios 2019, p. 236.

174. J. Rios 2019, p. 237. Also see Owens, Rodriguez, and Brown 2020.

175. J. Rios 2019, p. 237.

176. Interview 2020.

177. J. Rios 2019, p. 264.

178. Lang 2009.

179. Perry 2013.

180. Interview 2020.

181. Interview 2020.

182. Nassim Benchaabane, "St. Louis County Wins $18.2 Million Federal Grant for Improvements to West Florissant Avenue," *St. Louis Post-Dispatch*, November 16, 2021.

183. City of Ferguson, "Our Ferguson, 2040: A Comprehensive Planning Effort to Outline a Long Range Vision for the City of Ferguson," https://development-strategies.com/project/our-ferguson-2040-comprehensive-plan/ (accessed December 30, 2023).

184. Interview 2020.

185. Nick Kassoff, "Fran Griffin by Josh Privitt," *Ferguson Observer*, March 26, 2022.

186. Nick Kassoff, "A New Direction for Ferguson," *Ferguson Observer*, April 6, 2022.

187. Interview 2021.

188. Mele 2017, p. xiii.

189. Interview 2020.

Chapter 5. Ghetto Walls Go Up

1. Hicks's quote in Joie Chen, "Baltimore Senior: I Didn't Expect to See Rioting Here Twice in My Lifetime," *Aljazeera*, May 5, 2015.

2. During the research period of this book, I had the opportunity to go to Memphis and visit the Lorraine Hotel, where Martin Luther King Jr. was shot. It was a powerful experience to see the place where Dr. King had been assassinated.

I, along with Mindy Fullilove and Dominic Moulden, spoke on June 13, 2019, at Lorraine Hotel, which has been converted into the National Civil Rights Museum. The night of our talk an uprising erupted in Frayser, a North Memphis community, after the police shot and killed Brandon Webber, a twenty-year old African American man. It was a surreal experience to wake up the next day after our equitable development talk to learn the depressing news of the situation surrounding this unrest episode.

3. Levy 2011, pp. 4, 9–10; Levy 2018.

4. Levy 2011, p. 11. Others estimate that the total damage of the 1968 riots was $13.5 million in property damage, which is approximately $79 million in 2007 dollars. Michael Yockel, "100 Years: The Riots of 1968," *Baltimore Magazine*, May 2007.

5. Hill 2016, p. 70; W. Moore 2020; Pietila 2018.

6. Peter Herman, John Woodrow Cox, and Ashley Halsey, "After Peaceful Start, Protest of Freddie Gray's Death in Baltimore Turns Violent," *Washington Post*, April 25, 2018. Also see Brown 2021; Cobbina 2019; and W. Moore 2020.

7. W. J. Hennigan, Noah Bierman, and Joseph Tanfani, "Baltimore on Edge and on Alert," *Chicago Tribune*, April 29, 2015.

8. The Baltimore Development Corp. estimated that more than four hundred businesses had property damage or lost inventory from looting. See Daniel Leaderman, "93 Percent of Riot-Damaged Businesses Open Again, BDC Says," *The Daily Record*, November 24, 2015, and Deutsch 2017.

9. Sabrina Toppa, "The Baltimore Riots Cost an Estimated $9 Million in Damages," *Time*, May 14, 2015.

10. Levy 2018. Also see Mike Spies, "2 Maps That Explain the Baltimore Riots—1968 And Now," *Vocativ*, April 28, 2015.

11. While there are several dynamics related to persistent economic deprivation in low-income, African American communities (Jargowsky 1997; Massey and Denton 1993; Wilson 1996), this chapter's scope is mainly limited to urban renewal efforts.

12. S. Olson 1997.

13. Brown 2021; Crenson 2017; S. Olson 1997; Orr 1999.

14. McDougall 1993.

15. Crenson 2017, p. 164.

16. Gillette 1995.

17. Orr 1999.

18. Orr 1999, p. 21.

19. Orr 1999, p. 23.

20. S. Olson 1997.

21. McDougall 1993, p. 26; also see Crenson 2017.

22. Crenson 2017.

23. Crenson 2017, p. 175.

24. Orr 1999.

25. Crenson 2017, p. 173.

26. Orr 1999.

27. Crenson 2017, pp. 282–83.

28. Crenson 2017, p. 281.

29. Crenson 2017.

30. McDougall 1993, p. 37.

31. McDougall 1993, p. 44.

32. Orr 1999.

33. Orr 1999, p. 33.

34. Crenson 2017, p. 383.

35. Durr 2003. Also see appendix B.

36. Pietila 2010.

37. Orr 1999, p. 65.

38. Orr 1999; Pietila 2010.

39. Orr 1999, p. 31.

40. Brown 2021; Crenson 2017; Durr 2003; McDougall 1993; Orr 1999; Orser 1994; Pietila 2010.

41. McDougall 1993, p. 38.

42. Durr 2003, p. 86.

43. Orr 1999, p. 29.

44. Massey and Denson 1993.

45. Pietila 2010, p. 14.

46. Hirsch 2003; McDougall 1993; Orr 1999.

47. Borchert 1980.

48. Hayward 2008; Pietila 2010; R. Y. Williams 2004.

49. Hayward 2008, p. 50.

50. Crenson 2017; McDougall 1993; S. Olson 1997.

51. McDougall 1993.

52. Brown 2021.

53. Orr 1999, p. 30. Also see Brown 2021; S. Olson 1991; Power 1983, 2002.

54. McDougall 1993, p. 41.

55. Brown 2021.

56. McDougall 1993, p. 41.

57. McDougall 1993; Orr 1999; Pryor-Trusty and Taliaferro 2003; Jeremy Ashkens, Larry Buchanan, Alicia Desantis, Haeyoun Park, and Derek Watkins, "A Portrait of the Sandtown Neighborhood in Baltimore," *New York Times*, May 3, 2015. Sandtown-Winchester is defined using the city of Baltimore's designated neighborhood cluster boundaries, which for Sandtown-Winchester includes Harlem Park (Baltimore City Health Department 2017). The borders of the community consist of North Avenue to the north, Franklin Street to the south, North Monroe Street to the west, and Pennsylvania Avenue and North Fremont Avenue to the east. Some might consider this the Greater Sandtown-Winchester area.

58. Gioielli 2014; Nix and Weiner 2011.

59. Pietila 2010; Smithsimon 2022.

60. Pietila 2010, p. 8.

61. Pietila 2010.

62. Pietila 2010, p. 69.

63. Men of Sandtown's website: http://menofsandtown.org/history-of-sand-town/ (accessed September 16, 2018).

64. McDougall 1993, p. 42.

65. Brown 2021; Pietila 2010.

66. The HOLC's Baltimore map is available at https://jscholarship.library .jhu.edu/handle/1774.2/32621 (accessed October 4, 2022).

67. Durr 2003; Nix and Weiner 2011; Orser 1994; Pietila 2010; Vicino 2008.

68. McDougall 1993; Pietila 2010.

69. Crenson 2017; Gioielli 2014; Pietila 2018.

70. Lieb 2011.

71. Levy 2018.

72. Levy 2011; also see Spies, "2 Maps That Explain the Baltimore Riots."

73. Elfenbein, Hollowak, and Nix 2011.

74. Orr 1999, p. 36.

75. Cohen 2001; Marx 2008; Rosenblatt and DeLuca 2017; Stoker, Stone, and Worgs 2015. Also see Wenger, "Saving Sandtown-Winchester: Decade-Long, Multimillion-Dollar Investment Questioned," *Baltimore Sun*, May 10, 2015.

76. Ashkens et al., "Portrait of the Sandtown Neighborhood."

77. DeLuca and Rosenblatt 2013; Rosenblatt and Newman 2011.

78. R. E. Smith et al. 2002.

79. Cobbina 2019; Nassauer 2019; Schneider 2014.

80. Nick Mosby, *Nick Mosby for Mayor: New Energy. New Ideas*, YouTube, www.youtube.com/watch?v=hNlwxR-9uO8 (accessed October 4, 2023).

81. Interview 2019. For more on BUILD, visit their website: www.buildiaf.org (accessed October 4, 2023).

82. Lieb 2011; Mohl 2003; Rothstein 2017. The Interstate Highway Act of 1956 deployed nearly $25 billion for the development of expressways through urban areas. The federal government would pay 90 percent of the cost and would leave it to local policymakers to make the route decisions. See Rose and Mohl 2012.

83. Hyra 2012.

84. Hirsch 2003; O'Connor 1999; Rothstein 2017; R. Y. Williams 2004.

85. Lieb 2011, p. 55.

86. Mohl 2003. Likely over one million people were displaced to make room for the highway system (Rose and Mohl 2012).

87. Rose and Mohl 2012, p. 96. Also see Fullilove 2004.

88. Massey and Denton 1993.

89. Jesse Walker, "The Wound in West Baltimore: How City Planners Killed a Community," *Reason*, May 8, 2015. Also see Cashin 2021 and Rose and Mohl 2012.

90. Crenson 2017; Gioielli 2014; Lieb 2010.

91. Gomez 2013, p. 3. This is a phenomenon that Brett Williams discusses in Washington, DC, along the Anacostia Waterfront. For Williams, gentrification is preceded by a process of public abandonment (B. Williams 2016).

92. For more on the history of BUILD, see Bullock 2009 and Orr 1999.

93. I had the honor of interviewing Rev. Miles twice. He was an extremely dedicated person to improving conditions for low-income people in Baltimore. He passed away at the age of 72 on August 3, 2021. Jacques Kelly, "Bishop Douglas Miles, Activist Who Advocated for Baltimore's Impoverished Residents and Co-Headed BUILD, Dies," *Baltimore Sun*, August 4, 2021.

94. Interview 2019.

95. Crenson 2017, p. 461. Also see Baltimore Heritage's website: https://baltimoreheritage.org/history/race-and-place-in-greater-rosemont/ (accessed October 4, 2023).

96. Brown 2021; Hayward and Belfoure 1999; McDougall 1993; S. Olson 1997.

97. Hirsch 2003; R. Y. Williams 2004.

98. S. Olson 1997, p. 377.

99. Chris Gladora, "History: Housing Policy Segregation in Baltimore," *IndeyPendent Reader*, Summer 2006, issue 1. Also see Rose and Mohl 2012, p. 128, for a similar displacement estimate, as well as Hirsch 2003, pp. 68–69. Hirsch reports that between 1951 and 1971, 16,505 households were displaced in Baltimore; 81 percent of which were African American. Another source estimates that be-

tween 1951 and 1971 urban renewal displaced 25,000 households, a majority of which were African American (McDougall 1993, p. 56). Another source estimates that 38,000 people were displaced between 1951 and 1970 (Levy 2018, p. 133). And yet other estimate, between 1965 and 1980, puts the figure at 94,000 people (Pietila 2010, p. 219). A more recent yet slightly more conservative estimate puts the Baltimore Black displacement figure between 1940 and 2010 at 64,764 (Brown 2021, p. 97).

100. R. Y. Williams 2004, p. 103.

101. K. B. Clark 1965, p. 11. Clark states, "The dark ghetto's invisible walls have been erected by the white society by those who have power, both to confine those who have *no* power and to perpetuate their powerlessness."

102. Connolly 2014; Hirsch 1998; Roberto and Korver-Glenn 2021.

103. Hayward and Belfoure 1999, p. 171. Also see, Brown 2021 and R. Y. Williams 2004.

104. Hayward and Belfoure 1999, p. 173. The exception was the public housing built in Cherry Hill (Pietila 2010).

105. Pietila 2018; R. Y. Williams 2004.

106. Luke Broadwater and Talia Richman, "Baltimore May Demolish Part of Gilmor Homes, Move Residents From Crime-Riddled Public Housing," *Baltimore Sun*, January 10, 2018. Also see Baynard Woods, "Freddie Gray's Housing Complex Still Plagued by Poor Conditions and Abuse," *The Guardian*, April 30, 2016.

107. Fernández-Kelly 2015; R. Y. Williams 2004.

108. DeLuca, Clampet-Lundquist, and Edin 2016; Lieb 2011. Also see JoAnna Daemmrich, "Lafayette Courts Ends in 20 Seconds of Explosions, Cheers, Tears," *Baltimore Sun*, August 20, 1995. Flag House Courts, the Latrobe Homes, and Perkins Homes were originally designated as white-only projects but by 1964 they were predominantly African American. By 1969, these projects were over 90 percent African American (Hirsch 2003).

109. Brown 2021.

110. A Baltimore map depicting the public housing walls and the concentration of Black poverty near the downtown in 1960 can be found at the American Civil Liberties Union of Maryland's website: www.aclu-md.org/sites/default /files/field_documents/map3_1960.pdf (accessed October 4, 2023).

111. R. Y. Williams 2004. The HABC would also place most of its scattered site subsidized housing behind the walls of public housing in West and East Baltimore, which further impoverishes Sandtown-Winchester (*Thompson v. United States Department of Housing and Urban Development*, Civil Action No. MJG-95-

309 [D. Md. Jan. 10, 2006], map 6, www.aclu-md.org/sites/default/files/field_documents/map6_1990.pdf, accessed October 4, 2023).

112. R. Y. Williams 2004, p. 36.

113. Hirsch 2003, p. 7.

114. Orr 1999, p. 29.

115. Orr 1999, p. 29.

116. Brown 2021; Crenson 2017.

117. Crenson 2017; Gillette 2022; S. Olson 1997; Pietila 2010; C. F. Smith 1999.

118. Brown 2021; Bullock 2009; Crenson 2017; Hirsch 2003; Levine 2000; S. H. Olson 1997; Pietila 2010.

119. Hirsch 2003, p. 77.

120. Elfenbein, Hollowak, and Nix 2011.

121. Quote from Theodore Cornblatt, "Baltimore '68: Riots and Rebirth" collection. http://archives.ubalt.edu/bsr/oral-histories/transcripts/cornblatt.pdf. This Baltimore history project contains a wealth of information. I read many of the interviews from this project, which are available at http://archives.ubalt.edu/bsr/oral-histories/index.html (accessed October 4, 2023).

122. Quote in Elfenbein, Hollowak, and Nix 2011, p. 95. This is the edited volume that resulted from the "Baltimore '68: Riots and Rebirth" project.

123. Interview 2018.

124. U.S. National Advisory Commission on Civil Disorders 1968.

125. Elfenbein, Hollowak, and Nix 2011; Levy 2018.

126. Durr 2003; Pietila 2010.

127. Hirsch 2003; Massey and Denton 1993; Gomez 2013; Orr 1999; Pietila 2010; Rothstein 2017.

128. Lieb 2011, p. 52. The phrase "behind ghetto walls" references Lee Rainwater's 1970 classic study of the Pruitt-Igoe public housing project in St. Louis.

Chapter 6. Ghetto Walls Come Down

1. Interview 2018. Moore's quote in Luke Broadwater, "Thirty Years Later, the Issues Sound the Same," *Baltimore Sun*, https://digitaledition.baltimoresun.com/tribune/article_popover.aspx?guid=05c1a0c1-d1a9-415d-a219-a55daeb4ecf6 (accessed October 4, 2023).

2. Brown 2021.

3. Crenson 2017. Before the Inner Harbor was redeveloped, James Rouse, through the Greater Baltimore Committee, spearheaded the planning for the de-

velopment of the downtown Charles Center (see Gillette 2022; Harvey 2000; Levine 2000; Marx 2008; and S. H. Olson 1997).

4. Crenson 2017; Davis and Brocht 2002; Marx 2008; C. F. Smith 1999. Also see, Nick Gillepie, "Baltimore's Long History of Failed Development and Urban Renewal," *Reason*, April 28, 2015.

5. Gillette 2022; Gioielli 2014; Levine 2000.

6. Crenson 2017, p. 495.

7. Robert Sharoff, "Redevelopment Enriching Baltimore's Inner Harbor," *New York Times*, August 3, 1997. Also see Harvey 2000.

8. Crenson 2017; Judd and Swanstrom 2015.

9. R. Y. Williams 2004. Baltimore's public housing waitlist was once at forty-four thousand (C. F. Smith 1999).

10. Harvey 2000, pp. 140–41.

11. Crenson 2017, p. 501.

12. Crenson 2017, p. 501; Orr 1999, p. 36.

13. Harvey 2000, p. 133; Levine 2000, p. 138.

14. Crenson 2017; Gillette 2022; Levine 2000; Marx 2008; Olsen 2003; Teaford 1990; Wyly 2010.

15. Gillette 2022.

16. Bullock 2009, p. 53.

17. Olsen 2003; Pietila 2018. The Rouse Company also did some central city redevelopment in St. Louis (Primm 2010).

18. Crenson 2017, p. 492; Teaford 1990. For more on "festival developments," see Knox 1991.

19. Marx 2008.

20. Stoker, Stone, and Worgs 2015, p. 53. Also see C. F. Smith 1999.

21. Levine 2000, p. 129.

22. Levine 2000, p. 131.

23. Pietila 2018. Mayor Schmoke was the second Black mayor of Baltimore as Clarence H. "Du" Burns was appointed to finish out Schaefer's last year as mayor.

24. In 1980, Baltimore population became 54 percent African American, and political power started to shift from white to the new Black majority. This political power shift had begun under Mayor Schaefer when in 1984 he appointed Bishop L. Robinson as the city's first African American police commissioner.

25. Bullock 2009; Harvey 2000; Marx 2008; McDougall 1993; Özay 2021. Also see Enterprise's website: www.enterprisecommunity.org/about/what-we-do /our-history (accessed October 4, 2023).

26. Marx 2008; Rosenblatt and DeLuca 2017; Stoker, Stone, and Worgs 2015.

27. Rouse's quote in Marx 2008, p. 210.

28. Stoker, Stone, and Worgs 2015, p. 55. Also see Harvey 2000; Marx 2008; Pietila 2018; and Pill 2018. Other scholars would argue that the initiative over time did help to stabilize Sandtown; see DeLuca and Rosenblatt 2013 and Rosenblatt and DeLuca 2017.

29. Judd 2000, p. 955. Also see Teaford 1990 for more on the "messiah mayors."

30. Judd 2000, p. 955.

31. Harvey 2000, p. 141.

32. Levine 2000, p. 133.

33. R. Y. Williams 2004.

34. Interview 2018.

35. Chapin 2004.

36. Walters and Miserendino 2008.

37. Most of these funds were state gambling tax revenues, as opposed to city resources taken from Baltimore's capital or annual operating funds. However, city resources were used in the form of a land transfer (information obtained from my interview with former Baltimore Mayor Kurt Schmoke and Chapin 2004). For more information on the politics of the stadium deal, see Davis and Brocht 2002; Harvey 2000; and C. F. Smith 1999.

38. I literally mean bet on entertainment. In 2014, the $442 million Horseshoe Casino Baltimore was opened near the city's sports stadiums. This development expanded the Inner Harbor entertainment district. See Jeff Barker, "As Revenue Slides, Horseshoe Casino Baltimore Buys Up Nearby Land to Secure Its Future," *Baltimore Sun*, March 24, 2018; Luke Broadwater and Erica L. Green, "Maryland Casinos Are Pumping Out Billions for Education. So Why Are There School Budget Deficits?" *Baltimore Sun*, January 22, 2017; and Luke Broadwater, "Community Groups Criticize City Plan to Divert $3 Million in Casino Impact Funds," *Baltimore Sun*, August 19, 2014. For more on the use of casinos to boost economic development, see Mele 2017.

39. Wolman and Horak 2015.

40. Wolman and Horak 2015, p. 33. Also see Harvey 2000 and Taylor 2001 for information on the city's industrial and population declines during the 1970s and 1980s.

41. Brown 2021; Maciag 2015; Mallach 2018; W. Moore 2020; Pietila 2018; Richardson, Mitchell, and Franco 2019; Wyly 2010.

42. Maciag 2015. To access excellent Baltimore maps depicting this gentrification, see *Governing Magazine's* website: www.governing.com/archive/baltimore-gentrification-maps-demographic-data.html (accessed October 4, 2023).

43. Maciag 2015. Between 1990 and 2010, the percent of people in the city with a B.A. or higher increased from 16 percent to 24 percent (Wolman and Horak 2015). It seems many of these educated individuals located near the downtown.

44. Pietila 2018.

45. Baltimore Neighborhood Indicators Alliance–Jacob France Institute's dataset: https://bniajfi.org/vital_signs/data_downloads/ (accessed October 4, 2023). Here Sandtown-Winchester/Harlem Park refers to the Greater Sandtown community to include Harlem Park, which is just south of Sandtown-Winchester and stretches the original Sandtown-Winchester boundaries on the west from Pennsylvania Avenue to North Fremont Avenue and on south to West Franklin Street.

46. Levine 2000, p. 135, and Wyly 2010, p. 514, respectively.

47. DeLuca, Clampet-Lundquist, and Edin 2016, pp. xv–xvi.

48. Harbor Point's website: www.harborpoint.com/history (accessed October 4, 2023).

49. Otten 2019.

50. Mallach 2018.

51. Kern 2022; Schulman 2012.

52. Watkins 2016, p. 62.

53. Coates 2018, p. 86.

54. Brown 2021, p. 121.

55. Gomez 2013; Vicino 2008.

56. Brown 2021; Gomez 2013; Özay 2021.

57. Luke Broadwater, "Debt from Baltimore TIF Financing Deals Expected to Grow to Nearly $1 Billion," *Baltimore Sun*, November 9, 2017.

58. R. Y. Williams 2004.

59. Cisneros and Engdahl 2009, p. 3.

60. Venkatesh 2000, 2006, 2008.

61. Fernández-Kelly 2015; Hyra 2008.

62. Ervin 2017; Rodriguez 2021; R. Y. Williams 2004.

63. Hunt 2009; S. H. Olson 1997; Venkatesh 2000, 2006, 2008.

64. Quote in Cisneros and Engdahl 2009, p. vii.

65. DeLuca, Clampet-Lundquist, and Edin 2016; Jacobson 2007; S. H. Olson 1997; Rosen 2020; R. Y. Williams 2004.

66. Vale 2013, p. 30; R. Y. Williams 2004.

67. Jacobson 2007, p. 1. According to Jacobson's report, the demolition occurred while the Baltimore waitlist for public housing and Section 8 vouchers was at 29,477.

68. S. H. Olson 1997, p. 398.

69. Watkins 2016, p. 63.

70. U.S. Department of Housing and Urban Development, HOPE VI Revitalization Grants, FY 1993–2010, www.hud.gov/sites/documents/DOC_10014.PDF (accessed October 4, 2023).

71. Charles Belfoure, "In Baltimore, Public Housing Comes Full Circle," *New York Times*, March 19, 2000.

72. Lisa Akchin et al., "Heritage Crossing at 5: Successes and Challenges in a HOPE VI Development," report prepared by community planning graduate students, University of Maryland, Urban Studies and Planning Program, Spring Studio 2008.

73. For an excellent national study on HOPE VI and neighborhood redevelopment, see Tach and Emory 2017. These authors argue that HOPE VI public housing demolitions reduced neighborhood poverty through the direct displacement of low-income people rather than by attracting upper-income newcomers to mixed-income replacement housing. While this might be the national trend, I argue that, in Baltimore, HOPE VI developments, along with other state and city investments, displaced low-income people and eventually attracted upper-income people in and near central city areas, where public housing once stood. As noted, beyond the removal of public housing, there were other actions that displaced people and stimulated gentrification processes in and near Baltimore's "ring of blight." For instance, Johns Hopkins University partnered with the Annie E. Casey Foundation, the municipal government, and private real estate developers to redevelop eighty-eight acres in the city's mid-east section, just north of Johns Hopkins University Hospital. This major $1.8 billion redevelopment initiative, known as the East Baltimore Development, Inc. (EBDI), resulted in the displacement of 840 units, which likely removed twenty-six hundred people of color (Gomez 2013; Özay 2021; Pietila 2018).

74. Nix and Weiner 2011.

75. Natalie Sherman, "Lion Brothers Building to Open in December," *Baltimore Sun*, August 18, 2016. Also, see the BioPark's website: www.umbiopark.com /biopark (accessed October 4, 2023).

76. Quote from Sherman, "Lion Brothers Building to Open."

77. Interview 2018.

78. Meredith Cohn, "Redevelopment of West Baltimore's Poppleton Begins to Take Shape," *Baltimore Sun*, October 16, 2018; Cohn, "University of Maryland Bio-Park Plans 10-Story Gateway Tower on MLK Blvd," *Baltimore Sun*, June 27, 2019.

79. Bonds, Burnett, and Sissman 2018; Brown 2021; Gillette 2022. For more on Baltimore TIFs, see Broadwater, "Debt from Baltimore TIF Financing Deals."

80. Also see DeLuca, Clampet-Lundquist, and Edin 2016 and Rosen 2020.

81. R. E. Smith et al. 2002.

82. Pill 2018, p. 319.

83. Interview 2018.

84. Interview 2018.

85. Jacobs 1992, p. 278.

86. DeLuca, Clampet-Lundquist, and Edin 2016, pp. 30–36.

87. R. Y. Williams 2004.

88. Marx 2008, pp. 231–32.

89. Pietila 2018, p. 212. While the *Thompson v. HUD* case ordered the Housing Authority of Baltimore to only proceed with public housing demolitions if it relocated residents to less segregated census tracts, it did not accomplish its objects fully for all former residents. The demolition of the projects coincided with worse conditions in Sandtown. *Thompson v. United States Department of Housing and Urban Development*, Civil Action No. MJG-95-309 (D. Md. Jan. 10, 2006).

90. Brown 2021.

91. Lipsitz 2011.

92. Quotes in Coates 2018, pp. 207–8.

93. Quotes in Coates 2018, p. 208.

94. Massey and Rugh 2018, p. 302.

95. Coates 2018.

96. Interview 2018.

97. This figure might be a gross underestimation. In 2000, the U.S. Census count estimated that Baltimore had 42,480 vacant units; see Cohen 2001.

98. Ian Duncan, "In 2010, Baltimore had 16,800 Vacants. Eight Years and Millions of Dollars Later, the Number is Down to 16,500," *Baltimore Sun*, April 26, 2018. Also, see Terrence McCoy, "Baltimore Has More Than 16,000 Vacant Homes. Why Can't the Homeless Move In?" *Washington Post*, May 12, 2015.

99. Rosenblatt and Newman 2011.

100. Pietila 2018, p. 223.

101. C. F. Smith 1999, p. 221.

102. Florida 2018, pp. 97–98.

103. Interview 2018.

104. Interview 2018.

105. Interview 2018.

106. Crenson 2017.

107. Interview 2019.

108. U.S. National Advisory Commission on Civil Disorders 1968.

109. Vale 2013, p. 315.

110. Fullilove and Wallace 2011.

111. Interview 2019.

112. Brown 2021.

113. Levine 2000, p. 138.

Chapter 7. Watch Out for Broken Windows!

1. David Harvey's website: https://davidharvey.org/media/shortcv.pdf (accessed October 4, 2023). Opening quote in Harvey 2000, p. 257.

2. This is a reference to the title of Jeff Pegues's 2017 book on the contentious relationship between the police and Black America.

3. George L. Kelling and James Q. Wilson, "Broken Windows," *The Atlantic*, March 1982.

4. Welsh, Braga, and Bruinsma 2015.

5. Harcourt 2001, p. 7.

6. Harcourt 2001; Sharkey 2018.

7. Butler 2017; Camp and Heatherton 2016; Davis 2017; Haldipur 2019; Harcourt 2001; V. M. Rios 2011; Schrader 2019; Stuart 2016.

8. Harcourt 2001, p. 7.

9. Haldipur 2019, p. xii.

10. Cisneros and Engdahl 2009; Hunt 2009; Vale 2019; Venkatesh 2000, 2006, 2008.

11. DeLuca, Clampet-Lundquist, and Edin 2016; Goetz 2013; Rosen 2020; R. Y. Williams 2004; Vale 2013.

12. Chaskin and Joseph 2015; Goetz 2013; Hyra 2008.

13. Goetz 2013; Hyra 2008, 2012, 2017; Vale 2013, 2019.

14. Butler 2017; Camp and Heatherton 2016; Davis 2017; Haldipur 2019; Harcourt 2001; V. M. Rios 2011; Schrader 2019.

15. Bennett, Smith, and Wright 2006; Chaskin and Joseph 2015; Goetz 2013; Hackworth 2007; Hunt 2009; Rodriguez 2021; Vale 2013; R. Y. Williams 2004.

16. Some noteworthy exceptions include Fassin 2013; Wacquant 2008; and Websdale 2001.

17. Foucault 1995; Wacquant 2009.

18. E. Anderson 2022; D. Gordon 2022.

19. U.S. Department of Justice 2017.

20. U.S. Department of Justice 2017. The report declared on page 3, "There is reasonable cause to believe that BPD engages in a pattern or practice of conduct that violates the Constitution or federal law. BPD engages in a pattern or practice of: (1) making unconstitutional stops, searches, and arrests; (2) using enforcement strategies that produce severe and unjustified disparities in the rates of stops, searches and arrests of African Americans; (3) using excessive force; and (4) retaliating against people engaging in constitutionally-protected expression."

21. Quote from the *Voices of Baltimore: Black, White & Gray* series, https://video.mpt.tv/video/mpt-digital-studios-voices-baltimore-kwame-rose/ (accessed October 4, 2023).

22. U.S. Department of Justice 2017.

23. Cobbina 2019.

24. The NAACP Legal Defense Fund's National Police Funding Database for Baltimore: https://policefundingdatabase.org/explore-the-database/settlements/?settlements=Baltimore%2C+Maryland&settlement-location=3c40e57d-12da-4b36-b9d5-8c135d468176#settlements-table (accessed October 4, 2023).

25. The NAACP Legal Defense Fund's National Police Funding Database for Ferguson: https://policefundingdatabase.org/explore-the-database/settlements/?settlements=Ferguson%2C+Missouri&settlement-location=9ebe08cb-5fe5-4c3a-9dec-7134470a27eb#settlements-table [accessed October 4, 2023].

26. The NAACP Legal Defense Fund's National Police Funding Database for St. Louis: https://policefundingdatabase.org/explore-the-database/settlements/?settlements=St.+Louis%2C+Missouri&settlement-location=d7edc121-e910-4820-a44b-8b5ef5ce9184#settlements-table [accessed October 4, 2023].

27. For another example of city policing to maintain segregation, see D. Gordon 2022.

28. Laniyonu 2018, p. 903.

29. Vargas 2016. Robert Vargas argues that street violence in Chicago is related to a strong, mainly white-led centralized Democratic party that aimed to maintain power through strategic gerrymandering. I argue that a weak Democratic party is also associated with street violence. In Baltimore, too much pluralism and a lack of central control relates to why the police have so much autonomy and why city political leaders find it difficult to get collective action to solve deeply entrenched city challenges. The lack of political collective action and bureaucratic agency control partly relate to why the streets in certain communities are violent.

30. The West Baltimore Commission on Police Misconduct and the No Boundaries Coalition 2016, p. 6.

31. U.S. Department of Justice 2017.

32. Moskos 2008, p. 30.

33. Moskos 2008, p. 55.

34. Watkins 2019, p. 67.

35. U.S. Department of Justice 2017, p. 157.

36. West Baltimore Commission on Police Misconduct and the No Boundaries Coalition 2016, p. 15.

37. West Baltimore Commission on Police Misconduct and the No Boundaries Coalition 2016, p. 14. For more documentation of Baltimore police brutality, see U.S. Department of Justice 2017.

38. Interview 2018.

39. D. Watkins's quote from the *Voices of Baltimore: Black, White & Gray* series, https://video.mpt.tv/video/mpt-digital-studios-voices-baltimore-d-watkins/ (accessed October 4, 2023).

40. Quote in Bell et al. 2018, p. 9.

41. Sharkey 2018, p. xxi.

42. Also see Haldipur 2019.

43. Interview 2018.

44. Interview 2018.

45. Woods and Soderberg 2020. Also see Charlie Gile, "Seven Baltimore Cops Indicted on Federal Racketeering Charges," U.S. News, March 1, 2017, and CBS Baltimore, "Inside The GTTF: What Happened to the Officers in Baltimore's Biggest Police Corruption Scandal," April 29, 2022, https://www.cbsnews.com/baltimore/news/inside-the-gttf-what-happened-to-the-officers-in-baltimores-biggest-police-corruption-scandal/.

46. Pietila 2018, p. 229.

47. Jessica Lussenhop, "Rogue Baltimore Police Unit Ringleader Wayne Jenkins Sentenced," BBC News, June 7, 2018; Jon Schuppe, "Disgraced Baltimore Officer Says Detective Slain Before Testifying Was Also Corrupt," U.S. News, February 5, 2018.

48. Browning, Marshall, and Tabb 2002; Colburn and Adler 2005.

49. Levine 2000, p. 126.

50. L. N. Moore 2002; H. A. Thompson 2017.

51. Orr 1999.

52. Pietila 2018.

53. Crenson 2017.

54. Orr 1999.

55. Crenson 2017; Pietila 2018; R. B. Taylor 2001.

56. R. B. Taylor 2001.

57. Golash-Boza 2023.

58. Narrative Collapse website. "A History of Murder Rates in Maryland and Baltimore since 1975," https://narrative-collapse.com/narrative-collapse-370/ (accessed October 4, 2023).

59. R. B. Taylor 2001.

60. Interview 2018.

61. R. B. Taylor 2001, pp. 60, 372.

62. Pietila 2018.

63. R. B. Taylor 2001.

64. Francis X. Clines, "A Divisive Mayoral Race in Baltimore." *New York Times*, August 8, 1999; Gerard Shields, "O'Malley Is Wooing Zero-Tolerance Gurus," *Baltimore Sun*, October 2, 1999. Also see U.S. Department of Justice 2017.

65. Wacquant 2009.

66. Hill 2016.

67. Shankar Vedantam, "How a Theory of Crime and Policing Was Born, and Went Terribly Wrong," NPR's *Hidden Brain*, November 1, 2016.

68. Conor Friedersdorf, "Applying 'Broken Windows' to the Police," *The Atlantic*, December 8, 2014. Also see Hill 2016; R. B. Taylor 2001; and Wacquant 2009.

69. Paul Schwartzman and John Wagner, "As Baltimore Mayor, Critics Say, O'Malley's Police Tactics Sowed Distrust," *Washington Post*, April 25, 2015.

70. Crenson 2017.

71. Clines, "Divisive Mayoral Race."

72. The alignment between some African American support for a white candidate in Baltimore is nothing new and dates to the 1970s when Du Burns supported the Donald Shaefer mayoral ticket while two other African American candidates were running for this position. See Crenson 2017 and Orr 1999.

73. R. B. Taylor 2001; U.S. Department of Justice 2017.

74. U.S. Department of Justice 2017, p. 41.

75. U.S. Department of Justice 2017, p. 17.

76. Narrative Collapse website, "History of Murder Rates."

77. Graham Vyse, "Will Democrats Ever Care about Martin O'Malley?" *The New Republic*, March 16, 2017.

78. Interview 2018.

79. Interview 2019.

80. Watkins 2019, p. 96.

81. Carter 2007; Dowd 2020; Fullilove 2004; Fullilove and Wallace 2011; Goetz 2013; Kern 2022; Pain 2019.

82. R.B. Taylor 2001, p. 13.

83. Sharkey 2018, p. 79. Also see Sharkey's 2013 work *Stuck in Place* and David Hardy's 2010 book *Living the Drama* to better understand the impact of neighborhood violence on children and youth. Moreover, see E. Anderson 1999 for his in-depth description of the "code of the street;" in particular his understanding of the "violent fallout" of the drug trade in inner-city, low-income communities of color. He explains that the result of the drug trade "is a constant sense of uncertainty, a belief that anything [violent] can happen at any time" (p. 118).

84. *Baltimore Sun*, "Baltimore Homicides," https://homicides.news.baltimoresun.com/?range=2022 (accessed October 4, 2023). Baltimore ranks as one of the most violent cities in America. See *World Population Review's* website: https://worldpopulationreview.com/us-city-rankings/most-violent-cities-in-america (accessed October 4, 2023).

85. D.M. Kennedy 2012.

86. Quote from DeLuca, Clampet-Lundquist, and Edin 2016, p. 27.

87. Emily Esfahani Smith, "Baltimore's Ceasefire Program Strives to Create Peace amid the Violence—At Least for a Weekend," *Washington Post*, February 8, 2019.

88. Interview 2018.

89. For more on the impact and experience of violence on youth in Baltimore, see DeLuca, Clampet-Lundquist, and Edin 2016 and Watkins 2016, 2017, and 2019. For an exceptional analysis of the impact of violence on inner-city youth, see Harding 2010.

90. Interview 2018.

91. Quote from Tim Prudente, "'Nobody Kill Anybody': Murder-Free Weekend Urged in Baltimore," *Baltimore Sun*, July 18, 2017.

92. Interview 2018.

93. Watkins 2016, 2017, 2019.

94. Watkins 2019, p. 6.

95. Watkins quote from the *Voices of Baltimore: Black, White & Gray* series.

96. Kevin Rector, "Dropped Out, Re-Enrolled, Set to Graduate and Then Shot Dead: A 19-Year-Old Is Mourned in Baltimore," *Baltimore Sun*, March 22, 2017. Also see Pietila 2018.

97. Timothy Williams, "In Baltimore, Anguish over a Record-Breaking Homicide Rate," *New York Times*, January 17, 2018.

98. Kevin Rector, "These Baltimore Students Aren't Afraid of Mass Shootings. They're Facing Gun Violence in Their Everyday Lives," *Baltimore Sun*, March 1, 2018.

99. Interview 2018.

100. Paul Schwartzman, "Weary of Scandal and Violence, Baltimore's Residents Ask: 'Why Do We Stay?'" *Washington Post*, April 6, 2019.

101. Crenson 2017; Pietila 2018.

102. Crenson 2017, p. 4.

103. Tim Swift, "Man Killed in Altercation with Squeegee Kids Identified as Father of 3 from Hampden," FoxNews, July 8, 2022.

104. King, Drabinski, and Davis 2019.

105. Interview 2018.

106. Watkins 2019, p. 6.

107. Crenson 2017, p. 5.

108. Order & Chaos Coffee's website: www.orderchaoscoffee.com (accessed October 4, 2023).

109. Brown 2021.

110. Pietila 2018.

111. Interview 2018. Also see Crenson 2017.

112. Grimshaw 1992; Walter 1988.

113. Ballotpedia's website: https://ballotpedia.org/Municipal_elections_in_ Baltimore,_Maryland_(2016)#Primary (accessed October 4, 2023).

114. Crenson 2017, p. 395.

115. Crenson 2017, p. 396.

116. Asch and Musgrove 2017; Barras 1998; Gillespie 2012.

117. Crenson 2017, p. 396.

118. Interview 2018. For more on Embry, see Orr 1999 and C. F. Smith 1999.

119. Erie 1988; Merton 1957.

120. Luke Broadwater, "Inside Catherine Pugh's Home in Ashburton: How the Mayor of Baltimore Gave Up the Fight and Decided to Resign," *Baltimore Sun*, May 4, 2019.

121. "Former Baltimore Mayor Pugh's Scandal over 'Healthy Holly' Books: Full Coverage," *Baltimore Sun*, June 13, 2019.

122. U.S. Department of Justice, U.S. Attorney's Office, District of Maryland, "Former Baltimore Mayor Catherine Pugh Sentenced to Three Years in Federal Prison for Fraud Conspiracy and Tax Charges," February 27, 2020, www.justice .gov/usao-md/pr/former-baltimore-mayor-catherine-pugh-sentenced-three-years-federal-prison-fraud.

123. Crenson 2017, p. 3.

124. Bullock 2009.

125. Pill 2018, p. 322.

126. Kahn and McComas 2021; R. B. Taylor 2001; Wolman and Horak 2015.

127. Pill 2018; Stoker, Stone, and Worgs 2015.

128. Interview 2018.

129. Logan and Molotch 2007; Merton 1957; Stone 1989.

130. Dahl 1961.

131. Crenson 2017.

132. Orr 1999, p. 44.

133. Bullock 2009, p. 102; C. F. Smith 1999.

134. C. F. Smith 1999.

135. Crenson 2017.

136. C. F. Smith 1999.

137. Crenson 2017, p. 499. Also see Levine 2000; Pietila 2018; C. F. Smith 1999.

138. Levine 2000, p. 129.

139. Quote from Crenson 2017, p. 500.

140. Orr 1999; Pietila 2018.

141. Orr 1999.

142. Orr 1999, p. 52.

143. Orr 1999, p. 51.

144. Bullock 2009; Crenson 2017; Orr 1999.

145. Elfenbein, Hollowak, and Nix 2011.

146. Crenson 2017, p. 397.

147. Interview 2019.

148. Interview 2019.

149. Pietila 2018.

150. Pietila 2018, p. 210.

151. Orr 1999; Pietila 2018.

152. C. F. Smith 1999.

153. Pietila 2018, p. 210.

154. Orr 1999; C. F. Smith 1999.

155. Davis and Brocht 2002; Levine 2000; C. F. Smith 1999.

156. Brown 2021; Davies and Pill 2012; C. F. Smith 1999.

157. Orr 1999; Pietila 2018; Pill 2018; Thomson 2021.

158. Pietila 2018, p. 200.

159. Pietila 2018.

160. C.F. Smith 1999.

161. Abell Foundation's website: https://abell.org/trustees-and-staff/robert-c-embry-jr/ (accessed October 4, 2023).

162. Orr 1999.

163. Pietila 2018.

164. Pill 2018, p. 328.

165. Pill 2018, p. 320.

166. Interview 2018.

167. Interview 2018.

168. Pill 2018, p. 320.

169. Interview 2018.

170. Brown 2021; Orr 1999.

171. Interview 2018.

172. Lipsky 2010.

173. Interview 2018.

174. Watkins 2017.

175. Deutsch 2017.

176. Chepesiuk 2014.

177. The crews in Baltimore more closely resemble the fragmented organizational structure described in Boston by sociologist David Hardy. In Hardy's book *Living the Drama* (2010: 54), which focuses on youth violence in Boston's high poverty neighborhoods, he states, "Most of the groups are not actively engaged in criminal activities such as 'corporate' drug dealing for collective economic benefit." In Baltimore, the violence among crews does for the most part center on drug territories but it is not organized like Chicago as a collective corporate structure and is more informal like Boston. In Baltimore anyone, like Watkins, can become their own corner CEO.

178. Interview 2019.

179. For more on Baltimore's gang/drug culture, see Deutsch 2017; Pietila 2018; and Simon and Burns 1998.

180. For two excellent books on the relationship between churches and inner-city community conditions, see McRoberts 2005 and Owens 2007.

181. For an interesting take on the relationship between political and street structures and conflict in Chicago, see Vargas 2016.

182. Crenson 2017, p. 5. While Crenson calls them gangs, others in Baltimore prefer the term "neighborhood networks" (see D.M. Kennedy 2012, p. 108). I would call them crews, a term popular in Washington, DC.

183. Braga et al. 2001; D.M. Kennedy 2012.

184. Smith, "Baltimore's Ceasefire Program"; Justin Fenton, "Star Criminologist Hopes to Make Difference in Return to Baltimore," *Baltimore Sun*, February 15, 2014.

185. D.M. Kennedy 2012, p. 107.

186. Brown 2021, p. 2.

187. Dahl 1961; Stone 1989. Economic and political slack refers to extra resources that are strategically used by civic and business institutions and certain individuals to forge collaboration and partnerships to solve large urban challenges.

188. Steil et al. 2018; Wilson 1996.

189. Interview 2018.

190. This fragmentation can be witnessed among the city's community organization entities and community development corporations. John Bullock (2009: 61) claims that, "although there are many community groups in Baltimore, they tend not to be organized in a collective manner."

191. Interview 2019.

192. Pill 2018.

193. Cisneros and Engdahl 2009.

194. Interview 2018.

195. Interview 2019.

196. Interview 2019.

197. Interview 2019.

198. Harvey 2000, p. 133. "Baltimore is, for the most part, a mess. Not the kind of enchanting mess that makes cities such interesting places to explore, but an awful mess."

199. Interview 2019.

200. Harvey 2000; D.M. Kennedy 2012.

201. D. Watkins quote from the *Voices of Baltimore: Black, White & Gray* series.

202. Arena 2012; Ferguson 2002; Gillespie 2012; F. Harris 2012; Mele 2017; Perry 2013; Reed 1999; Stone 1989; J.P.I. Thompson 2006.

203. Brown 2021; Orr 1999.

204. Vale 2013, p. 5.

205. Interview 2018.

206. Arena 2012; Ferguson 2002; Gillespie 2012; Hyra 2017; Immergluck 2022; Stone 1989.

207. Friesema 1969; Kraus and Swanstrom 2001.

208. Crenson 2017.

209. Orr 1999.

210. R. B. Taylor 2001.

211. Interview 2018.

212. K. B. Clark 1965; Dikeç 2017.

213. Coates 2015, p. 17.

214. Ferguson 2002, p. 187.

215. Ferguson 2002, p. 188.

216. Ferguson 2002, p. 268.

217. Owens, Rodriguez, and Brown 2021, p. 342. Also see Morel et al. 2022.

218. Brown 2021; Cashin 2021; Pietila 2010; Rothstein 2017.

Chapter 8. Revisiting Theories and Racial Policy Responses

1. Opening quote in Clover 2019, p. 1.

2. Hinton 2021.

3. Boyles 2015; Cobbina 2019; Hill 2016; Lowery 2016; Nassauer 2019; Schneider 2017.

4. Nixon 2011; Pain and Cahill 2022.

5. Abu-Lughod 2007; Gale 1996; Hinton 2021; Levy 2018; Sugrue 1996.

6. Two exceptions were Brown 2021 and Dikeç 2017.

7. Fullilove 2004; Goetz 2013; Hepburn, Louis, and Desmond 2023; Immergluck 2015; Sassen 2014; Schaller 2019.

8. Ehrenhalt 2012.

9. Hartman and Squires 2010; Glaeser and Vigdor 2012.

10. Gale 1996; Harris and Wilkins 1988.

11. Jargowsky 1997.

12. Katz 2012.

13. Jargowsky 2015; Kneebone and Berube 2013.

14. Jargowsky 2015.

15. Hyra and Rugh 2016; Immergluck 2015; Shapiro 2017.

16. Dikeç 2017; Katz 2012; Wacquant 2008.

17. The Pew Research Center conducted these surveys. www.pewsocial-trends.org/2010/01/12/blacks-upbeat-about-black-progress-prospects/ (accessed October 4, 2023).

18. Watkins 2019, p. 40.

19. Watkins 2019, p. 123.

20. Watkins 2016, pp. 105, 150.

21. Coates 2018, p. 124.

22. Cobbina 2019; Hill 2016; Nassauer 2019.

23. Cahill et al. 2019; D. Gordon 2022; Johnson and Patterson 2022; Laniyonu 2018; Logan and Oakley 2017; Sharp 2014; Wacquant 2009.

24. D. Gordon 2022, p. 7.

25. Fullilove and Wallace 2011; Vale 2013.

26. M. Anderson 1967.

27. Goetz 2013; Sassen 2014.

28. Fullilove 2004; Goetz 2013; Hepburn, Louis, and Desmond 2023; Immergluck 2015; Sassen 2014; Schaller 2019.

29. Fullilove 2004; Pain 2019; Till 2012.

30. Bustamante, Jashnani, and Stoudt 2019; Carter 2007; Dowd 2020; Slater 2021.

31. Bustamante, Jashnani, and Stoudt 2019.

32. Bullock 2009, p. 3.

33. Grills, Aird, and Rowe 2016.

34. Massey and Denton 1993; Rothstein 2017.

35. C. Gordon 2019; Fullilove 2004; Hirsch 1998; Massey and Denton 1993; Loewen 2006; Rothstein 2017.

36. Gillespie 2012; F. Harris 2012.

37. Hyra 2012.

38. Chait 2017; DeFilippis 2016; Glaude 2017; Harris and Curtis 2018; Jargowsky 2015; Stevenson 2015.

39. Bratt and Immergluck 2016; Chait 2017; Congressional Budget Office 2015; Silver 2016. The Obama Great Recession recovery policies were vastly unequal: almost $1.2 trillion for bankers and local governments and only $15 billion spent on borrowers.

40. P. H. Smith 2016, p. 69.

41. Kendi 2017.

42. Interview 2021.

43. Arena 2012; Ferguson 2002; Gillespie 2012; Mele 2017.

44. Kendi 2017; Marable 1983; Robinson 2021.

45. Coates 2018, p. 198.

46. Alexander 2012; Ansell 2021; Ewing 2018; Norwood 2016; Western 2006.

47. Bonilla and Rosa 2015; Hinton 2021.

48. Cortright and Mahmoudi 2014; Mallach 2018.

49. Boyles 2019; Cobbina 2019; Mislán and Dache-Gerbino 2018.

50. Dikeç 2017.

51. Abrams 2023; Dikeç 2017; Moran and Waddington 2016; Wacquant 2008.

52. Myrdal 1944.

53. Interview 2021.

54. R. B. Taylor 2001.

55. Meares and Tyler 2017.

56. D. M. Kennedy 2012; Moskos 2008.

57. Travis and Western 2017.

58. Sharkey and Marsteller 2022, p. 349.

59. Chetty, Hendren, and Katz 2016; DeLuca, Clampet-Lundquist, and Edin 2016; Desmond 2017.

60. Imbroscio 2008.

61. Oakley, Ruel, and Reid 2013; R. E. Smith et al. 2002; Turner, Popkin, and Rawlings 2009.

62. Fullilove 2004; Gale 1996; Herman 2017; Sugrue 1996; Tager 2001; Teaford 1990, 2006; Vale 2019; Zelizer 2016.

63. Fullilove 2004.

64. Coates 2018; Craemer 2015; Darity and Mullen 2020.

65. Interview 2021.

66. Pattillo 2009, p. 31.

67. Pattillo 2009, p. 33.

68. Hunter et al. 2016. Additionally, Hunter and Robinson published a 2018 book advancing a perspective to focus responsible public investments in Black communities to minimize Black displacement and destruction and maximize Black joy and asset-rich "Chocolate Cities." Also see Brand 2022 and her Black Mecca futures concept.

69. Cobbina 2019.

70. Interview 2021.

71. Crenson 2017, p. 510.

72. Dawson 2011; F. Harris 2012, p. x.

73. Arena 2012; Dawson 2011; F. Harris 2012; Mele 2017.

74. Mckesson 2018.

75. Interview 2022.

76. Interview 2022.

77. Interview 2022.

78. Interview 2022.

79. For more on CORE, see the Maryland Department of Housing and Community Development's website: https://dhcd.maryland.gov/projectcore/pages/default.aspx (accessed October 4, 2023). Also see Gillette 2022.

80. Gillette 2022.

81. Natalie Sherman, "New Program Aimed at Old Baltimore Vacants Problem Gets Slow Start," *Baltimore Sun*, September 24, 2016.

82. Gillette 2022, p. 33.

83. Interview 2018.

84. National Geospatial-Intelligence Agency's website: www.nga.mil/about /About_N2W.html (accessed October 4, 2023).

85. National Geospatial-Intelligence Agency's website: www.nga.mil /history/Geoint_in_the_Gulf_War.html and www.nga.mil/about/history.html (accessed October 4, 2023).

86. National Geospatial-Intelligence Agency's website: www.nga.mil /history/NGA_St_Louis_Heritage.html (accessed October 4, 2023).

87. Interview 2018.

88. Hill 2016.

89. Hill 2016, p. xvii.

90. E. Anderson 1992, 1999.

91. E. Anderson 1999, p. 34.

92. Baldwin 1961; E. Anderson 1992, 1999, 2022; Hill 2016.

93. Interview 2018.

94. Brown 2021, p. 16.

95. Kendi 2017; Marable 1983; Robinson 2021.

96. Brown 2021; Cashin 202; Coates 2018; Gale 1996.

Appendix A. A Pandemic Methods Mess and Some Solutions

1. Schatzman and Strauss 1973, p. 24.

2. Boellstorff et al. 2012; Pink et al. 2016.

3. Boellstorff et al. 2012; Hine 2015; Pink et al. 2016.

4. Lung-Amam 2017, p. 13.

5. Small and Calarco 2022, p. 23.

6. Schatzman and Strauss 1973.

7. For excellent readings on historical, comparative research designs, see Mahoney and Rueschemeyer 2003 and Yin 2018. For examples of different historical and contemporary comparative unrest research designs and data collection methods, see Abrams 2023; Abu-Lughod 2007; Cobbina 2019; Dikeç 2017; Herman 2017; Hinton 2021; and Levy 2018.

8. In 2021, Joseph Gibbons and I started a national quantitative investigation of the city-level characteristics associated with the likelihood of peaceful protests turning violent.

9. For an insightful book on the protest and unrest events of 2020, see Abrams 2023.

10. Emerson 2001, pp. 302–4.

11. Dikeç 2007, 2017; Fassin 2013; Hesse and Hooker 2017; Márquez and Rana 2017; Moran 2012; Moran and Waddington 2016; Ndu 2022; Schneider 2014, 2017.

12. Abrams 2023.

13. Hyra 2008, 2017.

14. Reyes 2020.

References

Aaronson, D., Hartley, D., and Mazumder, B. (2021). The Effects of the 1930s HOLC "Redlining" Maps. *American Economic Journal: Economic Policy*, 13(4), 355–92.

Abrams, B. (2023). *The Rise of the Masses: Spontaneous Mobilization and Contentious Politics*. University of Chicago Press.

Abu-Lughod, J. L. (2007). *Race, Space, and Riots in Chicago, New York, and Los Angeles*. Oxford University Press.

Addie, J.-P. D. (2008). The Rhetoric and Reality of Urban Policy in the Neoliberal City: Implications for Social Struggle in Over-the-Rhine, Cincinnati. *Environment and Planning A*, 40, 2674–92.

Addie, J.-P. D., and Fraser, J. C. (2019). After Gentrification: Social Mix, Settler Colonialism, and Cruel Optimism in the Transformation of Neighbourhood Space. *Antipode*, 51(5), 1369–94.

Alexander, M. (2012). *The New Jim Crow: Mass Incarceration in the Age of Colorblindness*. The New Press.

Allen, D. (2022). *No Justice, No Peace: From the Civil Rights Movement to Black Lives Matter*. Legacy Lit.

Ames, A., Evans, M., Fox, L., Milam, A., Petteway, R., and Rutledge, R. (2011). *Neighborhood Health Profile: Sandtown-Winchester/Harlem Park*. Baltimore City Health Department.

Ammon, F. R. (2016). *Bulldoze: Demolition and Clearance of the Postwar Landscape*. Yale University Press.

Anderson, E. (1992). *Streetwise: Race, Class, and Change in an Urban Community*. University of Chicago Press.

——— (1999). *Code of the Street: Decency, Violence, and the Moral Life of the Inner City*. W. W. Norton.

——— (2012). Toward Knowing the Iconic Ghetto. In R. Hutchinson and B. D. Haynes (eds.), *The Ghetto: Contemporary Global Issues and Controversies*, 67–82. Westview Press.

——— (2022). *Black in White Space: The Enduring Impact of Color in Everyday Life*. University of Chicago Press.

Anderson, M. (1967). *The Federal Bulldozer*. McGraw-Hill.

Ansell, D. A. (2021). *The Death Gap: How Inequality Kills*. University of Chicago Press.

Arena, J. (2012). *Driven from New Orleans: How Nonprofits Betray Public Housing and Promote Privatization*. University of Minnesota Press.

Asch, C. M., and Musgrove, G. D. (2017). *Chocolate City: A History of Race and Democracy in the Nation's Capital*. University of North Carolina Press.

Avery, R. B., Brevoort, K. P., and Canner, G. B. (2008). The 2007 HMDA Data. *The Federal Reserve Board Bulletin*, 94.

Baldwin, J. (1961). *Nobody Knows My Name*. Dial Press.

Baltimore City Health Department. (2017). *Baltimore City 2017 Neighborhood Health Profile: Sandtown-Winchester/Harlem Park*.

Baltimore Neighborhood Indicators Alliance. (2018). *Spring 2018 Vital Signs 16*.

Baradaran, M. (2017). *The Color of Money: Black Banks and the Racial Wealth Gap*. The Belknap Press of Harvard University Press.

Barr, M. S., Dokko, J. K., and Keys, B. J. (2011). Exploring the Determinants of High-Cost Mortgages to Homeowners in Low- and Moderate-Income Neighborhoods. In S. Wachter and M. Smith (eds.), *The American Mortgage System: Crisis and Reform*, 60–86. University of Pennsylvania Press.

Barras, J. R. (1998). *The Last of the Black Emperors: The Hollow Comeback of Marion Barry*. Bancroft Press.

Bauman, J. F., Biles, R., and Szylvian, K. M. (2000). *From Tenements to the Taylor Homes: In Search of an Urban Housing Policy in Twentieth-Century America*. Penn State University Press.

Bell, M., Clemens, H., DeLuca, S., Dernberger, B., Edin, K., and Young, A. (2018). *Set-Up City: The Voices of Baltimore Youth after the April 2015 Unrest*. Poverty and Inequality Research Lab at Johns Hopkins University.

Bennett, L., Smith, J. L., and Wright, P. A. (2006). *Where Are Poor People to Live? Transforming Public Housing Communities*. Routledge.

Berlin, I. (2010). *The Making of African America: The Four Great Migrations*. Penguin Books.

Biles, R., and Rose, M.H. (2022). *A Good Place to Do Business: The Politics of Downtown Renewal Since 1945*. Temple University Press.

Boellstorff, T., Nardi, B., Pearce, C., and Taylor, T.L. (eds.) (2012). *Ethnography and Virtual Worlds: A Handbook of Method*. Princeton University Press.

Bonds, J.M., Burnett, A.A., and Sissman, E. (2018). Community Finance in East Baltimore: A Study of Phase One Redevelopment and Financing. *Community Development Department*, 3.

Bonilla, Y., and Rosa, J. (2015). #Ferguson: Digital Protest, Hashtag Ethnography, and the Racial Politics of Social Media in the United States. *American Ethnologist*, 42(1), 4–17.

Bonilla-Silva, E. (2018). *Racism without Racists: Color-Blind Racism and the Persistence of Racial Inequality in America*. Rowman & Littlefield.

Borchert, J. (1980). *Alley Life in Washington: Family, Community, Religion, and Folklife in the City, 1850–1970*. University of Illinois Press.

Boston, A.T. (2021). Manufacturing Distress: Race, Redevelopment, and the EB-5 Program in Central Brooklyn. *Critical Sociology*, 47(6), 961–76.

Boyles, A.S. (2015). *Race, Place, and Suburban Policing: Too Close for Comfort*. University of California Press.

——— (2019). *You Can't Stop the Revolution: Community Disorder and Social Ties in Post-Ferguson America*. University of California Press.

——— (2020). Racial-Spatial Politics: Policing Black Citizens in White Spaces and a 21st-Century Uprising. *American Ethnologist*, 47(2), 150–54.

Bracey, C.A. (2016). Michael Brown, Dignity, and Déjà Vu: From Slavery to Ferguson and Beyond. In K.J. Norwood (ed.), *Ferguson's Fault Lines: The Race Quake That Rocked a Nation*, 1–16. American Bar Association.

Braga, A.A., Kennedy, D.M., Waring, E.J., and Piehl, A.M. (2001). Problem-Oriented Policing, Deterrence, and Youth Violence: An Evaluation of Boston's Operation Ceasefire. *Journal of Research in Crime and Delinquency*, 38(3), 195–225.

Brand, A.L. (2022). Black Mecca Futures: Re-Membering New Orleans's Claiborne Avenue. *Journal of Urban Affairs*, 44(6), 808–21.

Bratt, R.G., and Immergluck, D. (2016). Housing Policy and the Mortgage Foreclosure Crisis during the Obama Administration. In J. DeFilippis (ed.), *Urban Policy in the Time of Obama*, 79–98. University of Minnesota Press.

Brenner, N., and Theodore, N. (2002). *Spaces of Neoliberalism: Urban Restructuring in North America and Western Europe*. Blackwell Publishers.

Bristol, K.G. (1991). The Pruitt-Igoe Myth. *Journal of Architectural Education*, 44(3), 163–71.

Bronson, P. (2006). *Behind the Lines—The Untold Story of the Cincinnati Riots.* Chilidog Press.

Brown, L. T. (2021). *The Black Butterfly: The Harmful Politics of Race and Space in America.* Johns Hopkins University Press.

Browning, R. P., Marshall, D. R., and Tabb, D. H. (2002). *Racial Politics in American Cities.* Pearson.

Bullock, J. T. (2009). *BUILD to WIN: Community Organizing, Power, and Participation in Local Governance.* Digital Repository at the University of Maryland.

Burbank, D. T. (1966). *Reign of the Rabble: The St. Louis General Strike of 1877.* A. M. Kelley.

Bustamante, P., Jashnani, G., and Stoudt, B. G. (2019). Theorizing Cumulative Dehumanization: An Embodied Praxis of "Becoming" and Resisting State-Sanctioned Violence. *Social and Personality Psychology Compass,* 13(1), 1–13.

Butler, P. (2017). *Chokehold: Policing Black Men.* The New Press.

Cahill, C., Stoudt, B. G., Torre, M. E., X, D., Matles, A., Belmonte, K., Djokovic, S., Lopez, J., and Pimentel, A. (2019). "They Were Looking at Us Like We Were Bad People": Growing Up Policed in the Gentrifying, Still Disinvested City. *ACME: An International Journal for Critical Geographies,* 18(5), article 5.

Cambria, N., Fehler, P., Purnell, J. Q., and Schmidt, B. (2018). *Segregation in St. Louis: Dismantling the Divide.* Washington University in St. Louis.

Camp, J. T., and Heatherton, C. (eds.) (2016). *Policing the Planet: Why the Policing Crisis Led to Black Lives Matter.* Verso.

Campbell, T. (2013). *The Gateway Arch: A Biography.* Yale University Press.

Carlson, H. J. (2020). Measuring Displacement: Assessing Proxies for Involuntary Residential Mobility. *City & Community,* 19(3), 573–92.

Carter, R. T. (2007). Racism and Psychology and Emotional Injury: Recognizing and Assessing Race-Based Traumatic Stress. *The Counseling Psychologist,* 25(1), 13–105.

Cashin, S. (2021). *White Space, Black Hood: Opportunity Hoarding and Segregation in the Age of Inequality.* Beacon Press.

Causa Justa :: Just Cause (2014). *Development without Displacement: Resisting Gentrification in the Bay Area.*

Center for Responsible Lending (2013). 2013 *Update: The Spillover Effect of Foreclosures.*

Chait, J. (2017). *Audacity: How Barack Obama Defied His Critics and Created a Legacy That Will Prevail.* Custom House.

Chapin, T.S. (2004). Sports Facilities as Urban Redevelopment Catalysts: Baltimore's Camden Yards and Cleveland's Gateway. *Journal of the American Planning Association*, 70(2), 193–209.

Chaskin, R.J., and Joseph, M.L. (2015). *Integrating the Inner City: The Promise and Perils of Mixed-Income Public Housing Transformation*. University of Chicago Press.

Chepesiuk, R. (2014). *Black Gangsters of Chicago*. Barricade Books.

Chetty, R., Hendren, N., and Katz, L.F. (2016). The Effects of Exposure to Better Neighborhoods on Children: New Evidence from the Moving to Opportunity Experiment. *American Economic Review*, 106(4), 885–902.

Chronopoulos, T. (2016). African Americans, Gentrification, and Neoliberal Urbanization: The Case of Fort Greene, Brooklyn. *Journal of African American Studies*, 20(3), 294–322.

Cisneros, H.G., and Engdahl, L. (eds.) (2009). *From Despair to Hope: Hope VI and the New Promise of Public Housing in America's Cities*. Brookings Institution Press.

Clark, K.B. (1965). *Dark Ghetto: Dilemmas of Social Power*. Harper & Row.

Clark, T.N. (ed.). (2011). *The City as an Entertainment Machine*. Lexington Books.

Clerge, O. (2019). *The New Noir: Race, Identity, and Diaspora in Black Suburbia*. University of California Press.

Cliffton, R., Griesedieck, C., and Hassler, A. (2018). Gentrification in Charlottesville. Unpublished paper. https://libraopen.lib.virginia.edu/downloads/kk91fk65d.

Clover, J. (2019). *Riot. Strike. Riot: The New Era of Uprisings*. Verso Books.

Coates, T.-N. (2015). *Between the World and Me*. Spiegel & Grau.

—— (2018). *We Were Eight Years in Power: An American Tragedy*. One World.

Cobb, J. (2021). *The Essential Kerner Commission Report*. Liveright.

Cobbina, J.E. (2019). *Hands Up, Don't Shoot: Why the Protests in Ferguson and Baltimore Matter, and How They Changed America*. NYU Press.

Cohen, J.R. (2001). Abandoned Housing: Exploring Lessons from Baltimore. *Housing Policy Debate*, 12(3), 415–48.

Colburn, D.R., and Adler, J.S. (eds.) (2005). *African-American Mayors: Race, Politics, and the American City*. University of Illinois Press.

Colebrook, C. (2020). Fast Violence, Revolutionary Violence: Black Lives Matter and the 2020 Pandemic. *Journal of Bioethical Inquiry*, 17(4), 495–99.

Congressional Budget Office. (2015). *Estimated Impact of the American Recovery and Reinvestment Act on Employment and Economic Output in 2014*.

Connolly, N. D. B. (2014). *A World More Concrete: Real Estate and the Remaking of Jim Crow South Florida*. University of Chicago Press.

Cortright, J., and Mahmoudi, D. (2014). *Lost in Place: Why the Persistence and Spread of Concentrated Poverty—Not Gentrification—Is Our Biggest Urban Challenge*. CityObservatory.

Craemer, T. (2015). Estimating Slavery Reparations: Present Value Comparisons of Historical Multigenerational Reparation Policies. *Social Science Quarterly*, 96(2), 639–55.

Crenson, M. A. (2017). *Baltimore: A Political History*. Johns Hopkins University Press.

Cummings, S. (2004). African American Entrepreneurship in the St. Louis Metropolitan Region: Inner City Economics and Dispersion to the Suburbs. In B. Baybeck and T. Jones (eds.), *St. Louis Metromorphosis: Past Trends and Future Directions*, 143–70. Missouri Society Press.

Dahl, R. A. (1961). *Who Governs? Democracy and Power in an American City*. Yale University Press.

Dantzler, P. A. (2021). The Urban Process under Racial Capitalism: Race, Anti-Blackness, and Capital Accumulation. *Journal of Race, Ethnicity and the City*, 2(2), 113–34.

Darity, W. A., and Mullen, A. K. (2020). *From Here to Equality: Reparations for Black Americans in the Twenty-First Century*. University of North Carolina Press.

Davies, J. S., and Pill, M. (2012). Hollowing Out Neighbourhood Governance? Rescaling Revitalisation in Baltimore and Bristol. *Urban Studies*, 49(10), 2199–217.

Davis, A. J. (ed.) (2017). *Policing the Black Man: Arrest, Prosecution, and Imprisonment*. Pantheon.

Davis, K., and Brocht, C. (2002). *Subsidizing the Low Road: Economic Development in Baltimore*. Good Jobs First. www.goodjobsfirst.org/wp-content/uploads/docs/pdf/balt.pdf.

Dawkins, C. J. (2011). *Exploring the Spatial Distribution of Low Income Housing Tax Credit Properties*. Assisted Housing Research Cadre Report, University of Maryland.

Dawson, M. C. (2011). *Not in Our Lifetimes: The Future of Black Politics*. University of Chicago Press.

DeFilippis, J. (ed.) (2016). *Urban Policy in the Time of Obama*. University of Minnesota Press.

DeLuca, S., Clampet-Lundquist, S., and Edin, K. (2016). *Coming of Age in the Other America*. Russell Sage Foundation.

DeLuca, S., and Rosenblatt, P. (2013). *Sandtown-Winchester—Baltimore's Daring Experiment in Urban Renewal: 20 Years Later, What Are the Lessons Learned?* The Abell Foundation.

Desmond, M. (2017). *Evicted: Poverty and Profit in the America City*. Crown.

Desmond, M., and Kimbro, R.T. (2015). Eviction's Fallout: Housing, Hardship, and Health. *Social Forces*, 94(1), 295–324.

Dettling, L.J., Hsu, J.W., Jacobs, L., Moore, K.B., Thompson, J.P., and Llanes, E. (2017). Recent Trends in Wealth-Holding by Race and Ethnicity: Evidence from the Survey of Consumer Finances. *FEDS Notes*. Board of Governors of the Federal Reserve System.

Deutsch, K. (2017). *Pill City: How Two Honor Roll Students Foiled the Feds and Built a Drug Empire*. St. Martin's Press.

Dikeç, M. (2007). *Badlands of the Republic: Space, Politics and Urban Policy*. Blackwell Publishing.

——— (2017). *Urban Rage: The Revolt of the Excluded*. Yale University Press.

DiPasquale, D., and Glaeser, E.L. (1998). The Los Angeles Riot and the Economics of Urban Unrest. *Journal of Urban Economics*, 43(1), 52–78.

Dowd, A. (2020). Displacement Trauma: Complex States of Personal, Collective and Intergenerational Fragmentation and Their Intergenerational Transmission. *Journal of Analytical Psychology*, 65(2): 300–324.

Dowden-White, P.A. (2011). *Groping toward Democracy: African American Social Welfare Reform in St. Louis, 1910–1949*. University of Missouri Press.

Drake Rodriguez, A. (2021). *Diverging Spaces for Deviants: The Politics of Atlanta's Public Housing*. University of Georgia Press.

Duneier, M. (2016). *Ghetto: The Invention of a Place, the History of an Idea*. Farrar, Straus and Giroux.

Durr, K.D. (2003). *Behind the Backlash: White Working-Class Politics in Baltimore, 1940–1980*. Univesity of North Carolina Press.

Early, G. (ed.) (1998). *"Ain't But a Place": An Anthology of African American Writings about St. Louis*. Missouri Historical Society Press.

Easton, S., Lees, L., Hubbard, P., and Tate, N. (2020). Measuring and Mapping Displacement: The Problem of Quantification in the Battle against Gentrification. *Urban Studies*, 57(2), 286–306.

Ehrenhalt, A. (2012). *The Great Inversion and the Future of the American City*. Knopf.

Elfenbein, J.I., Hollowak, T.L., and Nix, E.M. (eds.) (2011). *Baltimore '68: Riots and Rebirth in an American City*. Temple University Press.

Elliott-Cooper, A., Hubbard, P., and Lees, L. (2020). Moving beyond Marcuse: Gentrification, Displacement, and the Violence of Un-Homing. *Progress in Human Geography*, 44(3), 492–509.

Ellsworth, S. (1992). *Death in a Promised Land: The Tulsa Race Riot of 1921.* Louisiana State University Press.

Emerson, R. M. (2001). *Contemporary Field Research: Perspectives and Formulations.* Waveland Press.

Erie, S. P. (1988). *Rainbow's End: Irish-Americans and the Dilemmas of Urban Machine Politics, 1840–1985.* University of California Press.

Ervin, K. K. (2019). *Gateway to Equality: Black Women and the Struggle for Economic Justice in St. Louis.* University Press of Kentucky.

Ewing, E. L. (2018). *Ghosts in the Schoolyard: Racism and School Closings on Chicago's South Side.* University of Chicago Press.

Fassin, D. (2013). *Enforcing Order: An Ethnography of Urban Policing.* Wiley.

Feagin, J. R., and Hahn, H. (1973). *Ghetto Revolts: The Politics of Violence in American Cities.* Macmillan.

Ferguson, K. (2002). *Black Politics in New Deal Atlanta.* University of North Carolina Press.

Fernández-Kelly, P. (2015). *The Hero's Fight: African Americans in West Baltimore and the Shadow of the State.* Princeton University Press.

Florida, R. (2018). *The New Urban Crisis: How Our Cities Are Increasing Inequality, Deepening Segregation, and Failing the Middle Class—And What We Can Do about It.* Basic Books.

Foucault, M. (1995). *Discipline & Punish: The Birth of the Prison* (A. Sheridan, trans.). Vintage Books.

Freeman, L. (2019). *A Haven and a Hell: The Ghetto in Black America.* Columbia University Press.

Freixas, C., and Abbott, M. (eds.) (2019). *Segregation by Design.* Springer.

Friesema, P. H. (1969). Black Control of Central Cities: The Hollow Prize. *Journal of the American Institute of Planners*, 35(2), 75–79.

Fullilove, M. T. (2004). *Root Shock: How Tearing Up City Neighborhoods Hurts America, and What We Can Do about It.* One World/Ballantine.

Fullilove, M. T., and Wallace, R. (2011). Serial Forced Displacement in American Cities, 1916–2010. *Journal of Urban Health*, 88(3), 381–89.

Gale, D. E. (1987). *Washington, D.C.: Inner-City Revitalization and Minority Suburbanization.* Temple University Press.

—— (1996). *Understanding Urban Unrest: From Reverend King to Rodney King.* SAGE.

Garvey, P. (2019). Secret Socialist Lover. In R. Schuessler (ed.), *The St. Louis Anthology*. Belt Publishing.

Gibbons, J. (2023). Examining the Long-Term Influence of New Deal Era Redlining on Contemporary Gentrification. *Urban Studies*, 1–19. https://doi.org/10.1177/00420980231160469.

Gibbons, J., and Barton, M. S. (2016). The Association of Minority Self-Rated Health with Black versus White Gentrification. *Journal of Urban Health*, 93(6), 909–22.

Gibson, V. (2020). *The Last Children of Mill Creek*. Belt Publishing.

Gilje, P. A. (1996). *Rioting in America*. Indiana University Press.

Gillespie, A. (2012). *The New Black Politician: Cory Booker, Newark, and Post-Racial America*. NYU Press.

Gillette, H., Jr. (1995). *Between Justice and Beauty: Race, Planning, and the Failure of Urban Policy in Washington, D.C.* Johns Hopkins University Press.

—— (2022). *The Paradox of Urban Revitalization: Progress and Poverty in America's Postindustrial Era*. University of Pennsylvania Press.

Gioielli, R. R. (2014). *Environmental Activism and the Urban Crisis: Baltimore, St. Louis, Chicago*. Temple University Press.

Glaeser, E. L., and Vigdor, J. L. (2012). *The End of the Segregated Century: Racial Separation in America's Neighborhoods, 1890–2010*. Manhattan Institute.

Glaude, E. S., Jr. (2017). *Democracy in Black: How Race Still Enslaves the American Soul*. Crown.

Goetz, E. G. (2013). *New Deal Ruins: Race, Economic Justice, and Public Housing Policy*. Cornell University Press.

Golash-Boza, T. (2023). *Before Gentrification: The Creation of DC's Racial Wealth Gap*. University of California Press.

Gomez, M. B. (2013). *Race, Class, Power, and Organizing in East Baltimore: Rebuilding Abandoned Communities in America*. Lexington Books.

Gordon, C. (2008). *Mapping Decline: St. Louis and the Fate of the American City*. University of Pennsylvania Press.

—— (2019). *Citizen Brown: Race, Democracy, and Inequality in the St. Louis Suburbs*. University of Chicago Press.

Gordon, D. (2022). *Policing the Racial Divide: Urban Growth Politics and the Remaking of Segregation*. NYU Press.

Grills, C. N., Aird, E. G., and Rowe, D. (2016). Breathe, Baby, Breathe: Clearing the Way for the Emotional Emancipation of Black People. *Cultural Studies ↔ Critical Methodologies*, 16(3), 333–43.

Grimshaw, W.J. (1992). *Bitter Fruit: Black Politics and the Chicago Machine, 1931–1991*. University of Chicago Press.

Grossman, J.R. (1989). *Land of Hope: Chicago, Black Southerners, and the Great Migration*. University of Chicago Press.

Hackworth, J. (2007). *The Neoliberal City: Governance, Ideology, and Development in American Urbanism*. Cornell University Press.

—— (2019). *Manufacturing Decline: How Racism and the Conservative Movement Crush the American Rust Belt*. Columbia University Press.

Hackworth, J., and Smith, N. (2001). The Changing State of Gentrification. *Journal of Economic and Human Geography*, 92(4), 464–77.

Haldipur, J. (2019). *No Place on the Corner: The Costs of Aggressive Policing*. NYU Press.

Halpern, R. (1995). *Rebuilding the Inner City*. Columbia University Press.

Hanchett, T.W. (2003). The Other "Subsidized Housing": Federal Aid to Suburbanization, 1940s–1960s. In F.F. Bauman, R. Biles, and K.M. Szylvian (eds.), *From Tenements to the Taylor Homes: In Search of an Urban Housing Policy in Twentieth-Century America*, 163–79. Pennsylvania State University Press.

Hannah-Jones, N. (2021). *The 1619 Project: A New Origin Story*. One World.

Hansman, B. (2017). *Pruitt-Igoe*. Arcadia Publishing.

Harcourt, B.E. (2001). *Illusion of Order: The False Promise of Broken Windows Policing*. Harvard University Press.

Harding, D.J. (2010). *Living the Drama: Community, Conflict, and Culture among Inner-City Boys*. University of Chicago Press.

Harris, F. (2012). *The Price of the Ticket: Barack Obama and the Rise and Decline of Black Politics*. Oxford University Press.

Harris, F., and Curtis, A. (2018). *Healing Our Divided Society*. Temple University Press.

Harris, F.R. (1988). The 1967 Riots and the Kerner Commission. In F.R. Harris and R.W. Wilkins (eds.), *Quiet Riots: Race and Poverty in the United States*, 5–15. Pantheon.

Harris, F.R., and Wilkins, R.W. (eds.) (1988). *Quiet Riots: Race and Poverty in the United States*. Pantheon.

Harris, N., and Metzger, M.W. (2018). St. Louis's "Team TIF": A Community-Academic Partnership for Tax Incentive Reform. *Journal of Urban Affairs*, 40(6), 863–86.

Hartman, C., and Squires, G. (eds.) (2010). *The Integration Debate: Competing Futures for American Cities*. Routledge.

Harvey, D. (2000). *Spaces of Hope*. University of California Press.

Hatch, M. E., and Yun, J. (2021). Losing Your Home Is Bad for Your Health: Short- and Medium-Term Health Effects of Eviction on Young Adults. *Housing Policy Debate*, 31(3–5), 469–89.

Hayden, T. (1967). *Rebellion in Newark: Official Violence and Ghetto Response*. Random House.

Hayward, M. E. (2008). *Baltimore's Alley Houses: Homes for Working People since the 1780s*. Johns Hopkins University Press.

Hayward, M. E., and Belfoure, C. (1999). *The Baltimore Rowhouse*. Princeton Architectural Press.

Heathcott, J. (2008). The City Quietly Remade: National Programs and Local Agendas in the Movement to Clear the Slums, 1942–1952. *Journal of Urban History*, 34(2), 221–42.

—— (2011). In the Nature of a Clinic: The Design of Early Public Housing in St. Louis. *Journal of the Society of Architectural Historians*, 70(1), 82–103.

Heathcott, J., and Dietz, A. (2019). *Capturing the City: Photographs from the Streets of St. Louis, 1900–1930*. Missouri Historical Society Press.

Heathcott, J., and Murphy, M. A. (2005). Corridors of Flight, Zones of Renewal: Industry, Planning, and Policy in the Making of Metropolitan St. Louis, 1940–1980. *Journal of Urban History*, 31(2), 151–89.

Helmuth, A. S. (2019). "Chocolate City, Rest in Peace": White Space-Claiming and the Exclusion of Black People in Washington, DC. *City & Community*, 18(3), 746–69.

Hepburn, P., Louis, R., and Desmond, M. (2023). Beyond Gentrification: Housing Loss, Poverty, and the Geography of Displacement. *Social Forces*. https://apps.crossref.org/pendingpub/pendingpub.html?doi=10.1093%2Fsf%2Fsoad123.

Herman, M. A. (2005). *Fighting in the Streets: Ethnic Succession and Urban Unrest in Twentieth-Century America*. Peter Lang Inc., International Academic Publishers.

—— (2017). *Summer of Rage: An Oral History of the 1967 Newark and Detroit Riots*. New ed. Peter Lang Inc., International Academic Publishers.

Hern, M. (2017). *What a City Is For: Remaking the Politics of Displacement*. The MIT Press.

Hesse, B., and Hooker, J. (2017). Introduction: On Black Political Thought inside Global Black Protest. *South Atlantic Quarterly*, 116(3), 443–56.

Hill, M. L. (2016). *Nobody: Casualties of America's War on the Vulnerable, from Ferguson to Flint and Beyond*. Atria Books.

—— (2020). *We Still Here: Pandemic, Policing, Protest, and Possibility*. Haymarket Books.

Hine, C. (2015). *Ethnography for the Internet: Embedded, Embodied and Everyday*. Routledge.

Hinton, E. (2021). *America on Fire: The Untold History of Police Violence and Black Rebellion Since the 1960s*. Liveright.

Hirsch, A. R. (1998). *Making the Second Ghetto: Race and Housing in Chicago 1940–1960*. University of Chicago Press.

—— (2003). *Public Policy and Residential Segregation in Baltimore, 1900–1968*. Baltimore: Langsdale Library, Special Collections Department.

Hirt, S. A. (2014). *Zoned in the USA*. Cornell University Press.

hooks, b. (1990). *Yearning: Race, Gender, and Cultural Politics*. South End Press.

Hunt, D. B. (2009). *Blueprint for Disaster: The Unraveling of Chicago Public Housing*. University of Chicago Press.

Hunter, M. A., Pattillo, M., Robinson, Z. F., and Taylor, K.-Y. (2016). Black Placemaking: Celebration, Play, and Poetry. *Theory, Culture & Society*, 33(7–8), 31–56.

Hunter, M. A., and Robinson, Z. F. (2018). *Chocolate Cities: The Black Map of American Life*. University of California Press.

Hutchison, R., and Haynes, B. D. (eds.) (2012). *The Ghetto: Contemporary Global Issues and Controversies*. Routledge.

Huynh, M., and Maroko, A. R. (2014). Gentrification and Preterm Birth in New York City, 2008–2010. *Journal of Urban Health*, 91(1), 211–20.

Hwang, J., and Ding, L. (2020). Unequal Displacement: Gentrification, Racial Stratification, and Residential Destinations in Philadelphia. *American Journal of Sociology*, 126(2), 354–406.

Hwang, J., and Sampson, R. J. (2014). Divergent Pathways of Gentrification: Racial Inequality and the Social Order of Renewal in Chicago Neighborhoods. *American Sociological Review*, 79(4), 726–51.

Hyra, D. S. (2008). *The New Urban Renewal: The Economic Transformation of Harlem and Bronzeville*. University of Chicago Press.

—— (2012). Conceptualizing the New Urban Renewal: Comparing the Past to the Present. *Urban Affairs Review*, 48(4), 498–527.

—— (2014). Revisiting the US Black and French Red Belts: Parallel Themes and a Shared Dilemma. In C. C. Yeakey, V. T. Sanders Thompson, and A. Wells (eds.), *Urban Ills: Twenty-First Century Complexities of Urban Living in Global Context, Vol. I*, 297–328. Lexington Books.

—— (2017). *Race, Class, and Politics in the Cappuccino City*. University of Chicago Press.

Hyra, D., Fullilove, M., Moulden, D., and Silva, K. (2020). *Contextualizing Gentrification Chaos: The Rise of the Fifth Wave*. Metropolitan Policy Center.

Hyra, D., Moulden, D., Weted, C., and Fullilove, M. (2019). A Method for Making the Just City: Housing, Gentrification, and Health. *Housing Policy Debate*, 29(3), 421–31.

Hyra, D., and Rugh, J.S. (2016). The US Great Recession: Exploring Its Association with Black Neighborhood Rise, Decline and Recovery. *Urban Geography*, 37(5), 700–726.

Hyra, D.S., Squires, G.D., Renner, R.N., and Kirk, D.S. (2013). Metropolitan Segregation and the Subprime Lending Crisis. *Housing Policy Debate*, 23(1), 177–98.

Imbroscio D. (2008). "[U]Nited and Actuated by Some Common Impulse of Passion": Challenging the Dispersal Consensus in American Housing Policy Research. *Journal of Urban Affairs*, 30(2), 111–30.

Immergluck, D. (2009). *Foreclosed: High-Risk Lending, Deregulation, and the Undermining of America's Mortgage Market*. Cornell University Press.

—— (2015). *Preventing the Next Mortgage Crisis: The Meltdown, the Federal Response, and the Future of Housing in America*. Rowman & Littlefield.

—— (2022). *Red Hot City: Housing, Race, and Exclusion in Twenty-First Century Atlanta*. University of California Press.

Inwood, J.F. (2010). Sweet Auburn: Constructing Atlanta's Auburn Avenue as a Heritage Tourist Destination. *Urban Geography*, 31(5), 573–94.

Jack, B.M. (2007). *The St. Louis African American Community and the Exodusters*. University of Missouri Press.

Jackson, K.T. (1987). *Crabgrass Frontier: The Suburbanization of the United States*. Oxford University Press.

Jackson, M. (2016). Music, Race, Desegregation, and the Fight for Equality in the Nation's Capital. In D. Hyra and S. Prince (eds.), *Capital Dilemma: Growth and Inequality in Washington, DC*, 27–44. Routledge.

Jacobs, J. (1992). *The Death and Life of Great American Cities*. Vintage.

Jacobson, J. (2007). *The Dismantling of Baltimore's Public Housing: Housing Authority Cutting 2,400 Homes for the Poor from Its Depleted Inventory; A 15-Year Trend Shows a Decrease of 42 Percent in Occupied Units*. Abell Foundation.

Jargowsky, P.A. (1997). *Poverty and Place: Ghettos, Barrios, and the American City*. Russell Sage Foundation.

——— (2015). *The Architecture of Segregation: Civil Unrest, the Concentration of Poverty, and Public Policy*. The Century Foundation.

Jenkins, D., and Leroy, J. (eds.) (2021). *Histories of Racial Capitalism*. Columbia University Press.

Johnson, J. W. (1991). *Black Manhattan*. De Capo Press.

Johnson, L. T., and Patterson, E. J. (2022). The Policing of Subway Fare Evasion in Postindustrial Los Angeles. *Punishment & Society*, 24(3), 457–76.

Johnson, W. (2020). *The Broken Heart of America: St. Louis and the Violent History of the United States*. Basic Books.

Jones, E. T. (2000). *Fragmented by Design: Why St. Louis Has So Many Governments*. Palmerston & Reed Publishing.

Jordan, S. P. (2015). Federalism, Democracy, and the Challenge of Ferguson. *Saint Louis University Law Journal*, 59(4–7), 1103–16.

Judd, D. (2000). Strong Leadership. *Urban Studies*, 37(5–6), 951–61.

Judd, D. R., and Swanstrom, T. (2015). *City Politics: The Political Economy of Urban America*. Pearson.

Kahn, M. E., and McComas, M. (2021). *Unlocking the Potential of Post-Industrial Cities*. Johns Hopkins University Press.

Katz, B., and Wagner, J. (2014). *The Rise of Innovation Districts: A New Geography of Innovation in America*. Brookings Institution.

Katz, M. B. (2012). *Why Don't American Cities Burn?* University of Pennsylvania Press.

Kavanaugh, M. O. (2017). *Hidden History of Downtown St. Louis*. The History Press.

Keene, D. E., and Geronimus, A. T. (2011). "Weathering" HOPE VI: The Importance of Evaluating the Population Health Impact of Public Housing Demolition and Displacement. *Journal of Urban Health*, 88(3), 417–435.

Keene, D. E., Padilla, M. B., and Geronimus, A. T. (2010). Leaving Chicago for Iowa's "Fields of Opportunity": Community Dispossession, Rootlessness, and the Quest for Somewhere to "Be OK." *Human Organization*, 69(3), 275–84.

Kendi, I. X. (2017). *Stamped from the Beginning: The Definitive History of Racist Ideas in America*. Nation Books.

Kennedy, D. M. (2012). *Don't Shoot: One Man, A Street Fellowship, and the End of Violence in Inner-City America*. Bloomsbury USA.

Kennedy, R. (2012). *The Persistence of the Color Line: Racial Politics and the Obama Presidency*. Vintage Books.

Kern, L. (2022). *Gentrification Is Inevitable and Other Lies*. Verso.

Kienzle, V. B. (2017). *Lost St. Louis*. The History Press.

King, N. P., Drabinski, K., and Davis, J. C. (eds.) (2019). *Baltimore Revisited: Stories of Inequality and Resistance in a U.S. City*. Rutgers University Press.

Kishi, R., Stall, H., Wolfson, A., and Jones, S. (2021). *A Year of Racial Justice Protests: Key Trends in Demonstrations Supporting the BLM Movement*. The Armed Conflict Location & Event Data Project (ACLED). https://acleddata. com/acleddatanew/wp-content/uploads/2021/05/ACLED_ Report_A-Year-of-Racial-Justice-Protests_May2021.pdf.

Klemek, C. (2011). *The Transatlantic Collapse of Urban Renewal: Postwar Urbanism from New York to Berlin*. University of Chicago Press.

Kneebone, E., and Berube, A. (2013). *Confronting Suburban Poverty in America*. Brookings Institution Press.

Knox, P. L. (1991). The Restless Urban Landscape: Economic and Sociocultural Change and the Transformation of Metropolitan Washington, DC. *Annals of the Association of American Geographers*, 81(2), 181–209.

Kochhar, R., and Fry, R. (2014). *Wealth Inequality Has Widened Along Racial, Ethnic Lines Since End of Great Recession*. Pew Research Center.

Kramer, R., and Remster, B. (2022). The Slow Violence of Contemporary Policing. *Annual Review of Criminology*, 5(1), 43–66.

Kraus, N., and Swanstrom, T. (2001). Minority Mayors and the Hollow-Prize Problem. *PS: Political Science and Politics*, 34(1), 99–105.

Lacy, K. (2007). *Blue-Chip Black: Race, Class, and Status in the New Black Middle Class*. University of California Press.

Ladner, J. A. (1995). *Tomorrow's Tomorrow: The Black Woman*. University of Nebraska Press.

Lang, C. (2004). Between Civil Rights and Black Power in the Gateway City: The Action Committee to Improve Opportunities for Negroes (Action), 1964–75. *Journal of Social History*, 37(3), 725–54.

——— (2009). *Grassroots at the Gateway: Class Politics and Black Freedom Struggle in St. Louis, 1936–75*. University of Michigan Press.

Laniyonu, A. (2018). Coffee Shops and Street Stops: Policing Practices in Gentrifying Neighborhoods. *Urban Affairs Review*, 54(5), 898–930.

Laurence, J., and Vaïse, J. (2005). *Understanding Urban Riots in France*. Brookings Institution.

Lees, L. (2003). Super-Gentrification: The Case of Brooklyn Heights, New York City. *Urban Studies*, 40(12), 2487–509.

Lees, L., Slater, T., and Wyly, E. (2008). *Gentrification*. Routledge.

Lemann, N. (1991). *The Promised Land: The Great Black Migration and How It Changed America*. Knopf.

Levine, M.V. (2000). 'A Third-World City in the First World': Social Exclusion, Racial Inequality, and Sustainable Development in Baltimore, Maryland. In M. Polèse and R. Stren (eds.), *The Social Sustainability of Cities: Diversity and the Management of Change, 123-56*. University of Toronto Press.

Levy, P.B. (2011). The Dream Deferred: The Assassination of Martin Luther King, Jr., and the Holy Week Uprisings of 1968. In J.I. Elfenbein, T.L. Hollowak, and E.M. Nix (eds.), *Baltimore '68: Riots and Rebirth in an American City, 3-25*. Temple University Press.

—— (2018). *The Great Uprising: Race Riots in Urban America during the 1960s*. Cambridge University Press.

Lewis-McCoy, R.L. (2014). *Inequality in the Promised Land: Race, Resources, and Suburban Schooling*. Stanford University Press.

Lieb, E. (2011). "White Man's Lane": Hollowing Out the Highway Ghetto in Baltimore. In J.I. Elfenbein, T.L. Hollowak, and E.M. Nix (eds.), *Baltimore '68: Riots and Rebirth in an American City, 51-69*. Temple University Press.

Lieberson, S., and Silverman, A.R. (1965). The Precipitants and Underlying Conditions of Race Riots. *American Sociological Review*, 30(6), 887-98.

Lim, S., Chan, P.Y., Walters, S., Culp, G., Huynh, M., and Gould, L.H. (2017). Impact of Residential Displacement on Healthcare Access and Mental Health among Original Residents of Gentrifying Neighborhoods in New York City. *PloS One*, 12(12), e0190139.

Lipsitz, G. (1991). *The Sidewalks of St. Louis: Places, People, and Politics in an American City*. University of Missouri.

—— (1995). *A Life in the Struggle: Ivory Perry and the Culture of Opposition*. Temple University Press.

—— (2011). *How Racism Takes Place*. Temple University Press.

Lipsky, M. (2010). *Street-Level Bureaucracy, 30th Anniversary Edition: Dilemmas of the Individual in Public Service*. Russell Sage Foundation.

Lloyd, R. (2011). East Nashville Skyline. *Ethnography*, 12(1), 114-45.

Loewen, J.W. (2006). *Sundown Towns: A Hidden Dimension of American Racism*. Touchstone.

Logan, J.R., and Molotch, H. (2007). *Urban Fortunes: The Political Economy of Place*. 20th anniversary ed. with a new preface. University of California Press.

Logan, J.R., and Oakley, D. (2017). Black Lives and Policing: The Larger Context of Ghettoization. *Journal of Urban Affairs*, 39(8), 1031-46.

Love, B. L. (2016). Good Kids, Mad Cities: Kendrick Lamar and Finding Inner Resistance in Response to FergusonUSA. *Cultural Studies ↔ Critical Methodologies*, 16(3), 320–23.

Lowery, W. (2016). *They Can't Kill Us All: Ferguson, Baltimore, and a New Era in America's Racial Justice Movement*. Little, Brown.

Luci, M. (2020). Displacement as Trauma and Trauma as Displacement in the Experience of Refugees. *Journal of Analytical Psychology*, 65(2), 260–80.

Lumpkins, C. L. (2008). *American Pogrom: The East St. Louis Race Riot and Black Politics*. Ohio University Press.

Lung-Amam, W. (2017). *Trespassers?: Asian Americans and the Battle for Suburbia*. University of California Press.

Maciag, M. (2015). Gentrification in America Report. *Governing Magazine*.

Mahoney, J., and Rueschemeyer, D. (eds.) (2003). *Comparative Historical Analysis in the Social Sciences*. Cambridge University Press.

Mallach, A. (2018). *The Divided City: Poverty and Prosperity in Urban America*. Island Press.

Marable, M. (1983). *How Capitalism Underdeveloped Black America: Problems in Race, Political Economy and Society*. South End Press.

Márquez, J. D., and Rana, J. (2017). Black Radical Possibility and the Decolonial International. *South Atlantic Quarterly*, 116(3), 505–28.

Marx, P. (2008). *Jim Rouse: Capitalist/Idealist*. University Press of America.

Massey, D., and Kanaiaupuni, S. (1993). Public Housing and the Concentration of Poverty. *Social Science Quarterly*, 74, 109–22.

Massey, D. S., and Denton, N. A. (1993). *American Apartheid: Segregation and the Making of the Underclass*. Harvard University Press.

Massey, D. S., and Rugh, J. S. (2018). The Great Recession and the Destruction of Minority Wealth. *Current History*, 117(802), 298–303.

Massey, D. S., Rugh, J. S., Steil, J. P., and Albright, L. (2016). Riding the Stagecoach to Hell: A Qualitative Analysis of Racial Discrimination in Mortgage Lending. *City Community*, 15(2), 118–36.

McAdam, D. (1999). *Political Process and the Development of Black Insurgency, 1930–1970*. University of Chicago Press.

McClure, K. (2010). Are Low-Income Housing Tax Credit Developments Locating Where There Is a Shortage of Affordable Units? *Housing Policy Debate*, 20(2), 153–71.

—— (2019a). What Should Be the Future of the Low-Income Housing Tax Credit Program? *Housing Policy Debate*, 29(1), 65–81.

——— (2019b). The Allocation of Rental Assistance Resources: The Paradox of High Housing Costs and High Vacancy Rates. *International Journal of Housing Policy*, 19(1), 69–94.

McDougall, H. (1993). *Black Baltimore: A New Theory of Community*. Temple University Press.

Mckesson, D. (2018). *On the Other Side of Freedom: The Case for Hope*. Penguin.

McKittrick, K. (2013). Plantation Futures. *Small Axe: A Caribbean Journal of Criticism*, 17(3 (42)), 1–15.

McLaughlin, M. (2014). *The Long, Hot Summer of 1967: Urban Rebellion in America*. Palgrave Macmillan.

McRoberts, O.M. (2005). *Streets of Glory: Church and Community in a Black Urban Neighborhood*. University of Chicago Press.

Meares, T., and Tyler, T. (2017). Policing: A Model for the Twenty-First Century. In A.J. Davis (ed.), *Policing the Black Man: Arrest, Prosecution, and Imprisonment*. Pantheon.

Meehan, E.J. (1975). *Public Housing Policy: Convention versus Reality*. Center for Urban Policy Research, Rutgers University.

Meier, A., and Rudwick, E. (1976). *From Plantation to Ghetto*. Hill and Wang.

Meier, A., Rudwick, E., and Bracey, J. (eds.) (2007). *Black Protest in the Sixties*. Markus Wiener.

Mele, C. (2017). *Race and the Politics of Deception: The Making of an American City*. NYU Press.

Mendelson, R.E., and Quinn, M.A. (1985). Residential Patterns in a Midwestern City: The St. Louis Experience. In B. Checkoway and C.V. Patton (eds.), *The Metropolitan Midwest: Policy Problems and Prospects for Change, 151–70*. University of Illinois Press.

Merton, R.K. (1957). *Social Theory and Social Structure*. Free Press.

Metzger, M.W. (2014). The Reconcentration of Poverty: Patterns of Housing Voucher Use, 2000 to 2008. *Housing Policy Debate*, 24(3), 544–67.

Metzger, M.W., Bender, A., Flowers, A., Murugan, V., and Ravindranath, D. (2019). Step by Step: Tenant Accounts of Securing and Maintaining Quality Housing with a Housing Choice Voucher. *Journal of Community Practice*, 27(1), 31–44.

Mislán, C., and Dache-Gerbino, A. (2018). The Struggle for 'Our Streets': The Digital and Physical Spatial Politics of the Ferguson Movement. *Social Movement Studies*, 17(6), 676–96.

Modan, G.G. (2007). *Turf Wars: Discourse, Diversity, and the Politics of Place*. Wiley-Blackwell.

Mohl, R. A. (2003). Planned Destruction: The Interstates and Central City Housing. In F. F. Bauman, R. Biles, and K. M. Szylvian (eds.), *From Tenements to the Taylor Homes: In Search of an Urban Housing Policy in Twentieth-Century America, 226–45*. Pennsylvania State University Press.

Mollenkopf, J., and Swanstrom, T. (2015). The Ferguson Moment: Race and Place. NYU Furman Center. https://furmancenter.org/research/iri/essay /the-ferguson-moment-race-and-place.

Montgomery, R. (1985). Pruitt-Igoe: Policy Failure or Societal Symptom. In B. Checkoway and C. V. Patton (eds.), *The Metropolitan Midwest: Policy Problems and Prospects for Change, 229–43*. University of Illinois Press.

Moore, N. Y. (2016). *The South Side: A Portrait of Chicago and American Segregation*. Picador.

Moore, L. N. (2002). *Carl B. Stokes and the Rise of Black Political Power*. University of Illinois Press.

Moore, S. M. (2015). Southeast Ferguson: The Transformation Opportunity or Is Decent and Affordable Good Enough? *Journal of Affordable Housing & Community Development Law*, 24(2), 257–66.

—— (2017). Ferguson: Undoing the Damage of the Past—Creating Community Wealth. *Journal of Affordable Housing and Community Development Law*, 25(3), 297–308.

Moore, W. (2020). *Five Days: The Fiery Reckoning of an American City*. One World.

Moran, M. (2012). *The Republic and the Riots: Exploring Urban Violence in French Suburbs, 2005–2007*. Peter Lang AG, Internationaler Verlag der Wissen-schaften.

Moran, M., and Waddington, D. (2016). *Riots: An International Comparison*. Palgrave Macmillan.

Morel, D., Rodriguez, A. D., Sidney, M., Garay, N. B., and Straub, A. (2022). Measuring and Explaining Stalled Gentrification in Newark, New Jersey: The Role of Racial Politics. *Urban Affairs Review*, 58(6), 1585–1621.

Moskos, P. (2008). *Cop in the Hood: My Year Policing Baltimore's Eastern District*. Princeton University Press.

Moskowitz, P. (2017). *How to Kill a City: Gentrification, Inequality, and the Fight for the Neighborhood*. Nation Books.

Muhammad, K. G. (2019). *The Condemnation of Blackness: Race, Crime, and the Making of Modern Urban America*, with a new preface. Harvard University Press.

Mumford, E. P. (2019). American Urban Housing and Racial Integration Before 1968. In C. Freixas and M. Abbott (eds.), *Segregation by Design: Conversations and Calls for Action in St. Louis, 37–61*. Springer.

Murch, D. (2015). Ferguson's Inheritance. *Jacobin Magazine*.

Myrdal, G. (1944). *An American Dilemma: The Negro Problem and Modern Democracy*. Harper & Brothers.

Nassauer, A. (2019). *Situational Breakdowns: Understanding Protest Violence and Other Surprising Outcomes*. Oxford University Press.

Ndu, T. (2022). *Symbolic vs. Neighbourhood Politics: Stigma, Diversity and Collective Anti-Gentrification Resistance on Tottenham's Broadwater Farm Estate*. Thesis, University of Leicester.

Newman, K., and Wyly, E. K. (2006). The Right to Stay Put, Revisited: Gentrification and Resistance to Displacement in New York City. *Urban Studies*, 43(1), 23–57.

Newman, O. (1973). *Defensible Space: People and Design in the Violent City*. Architectural Press.

Nix, E. M., and Weiner, D. R. (2011). Pivot in Perception: The Impact of the 1968 Riots on Three Baltimore Business Districts. In J. I. Elfenbein, T. L. Hollowak, and E. M. Nix (eds.), *Baltimore '68: Riots and Rebirth in an American City, 180–207*. Temple University Press.

Nixon, R. (2011). *Slow Violence and the Environmentalism of the Poor*. Harvard University Press.

Norwood, K. J. (ed.) (2016), *Ferguson's Fault Lines: The Race Quake That Rocked a Nation*. American Bar Association.

Oakley, D., Ruel, E., and Reid, L. (2013). "It Was Really Hard. . . . It was Alright. . . . It Was Easy." Public Housing Relocation Experiences and Destination Satisfaction in Atlanta. *Cityscape*, 15(2), 173–92.

O'Connor, A. (1999). Swimming against the Tide: A Brief History of Federal Policy in Poor Communities. In R. F. Ferguson and W. T. Dickens (eds.), *Urban Problems and Community Development, 77–121*. Brookings Institution Press.

Oliveri, R. C. (2015). Setting the Stage for Ferguson: Housing Discrimination and Segregation in St. Louis. *Missouri Law Review*, 80(4), 1053–75.

Olsen, J. (2003). *Better Places, Better Lives: A Biography of James Rouse*. Urban Land Institute.

Olson, K. (1991). Old West Baltimore: Segregation, African-American Culture, and the Struggle for Equality. In E. Fee, L. Shopes, and L. Zeidman (eds.), *The Baltimore Book: New Views of Local History, 57–78*. Temple University Press.

Olson, S. H. (1997). *Baltimore: The Building of an American City*. Johns Hopkins University Press.

Oluku, U. A. (2011). "A Comparative Analysis of the Effectiveness of the HOPE VI Program in Revitalizing Conventional Public Housing Sites: A Multiple

Case Study in St. Louis." Dissertation, University of Missouri–St. Louis. https://irl.umsl.edu/dissertation/433.

Olzak, S., Shanahan, S., and McEneaney, E. H. (1996). Poverty, Segregation, and Race Riots: 1960 to 1993. *American Sociological Review*, 61(4), 590–613.

Orfield, M. (1997). *Metropolitics: A Regional Agenda for Community and Stability*. Brookings Institution Press.

Orr, M. (1999). *Black Social Capital: The Politics of School Reform in Baltimore*, 1986–1999. University Press of Kansas.

Orser, W. E. (1994). *Blockbusting in Baltimore: The Edmondson Village Story*. University Press of Kentucky.

Osterweil, V. (2020). *In Defense of Looting: A Riotous History of Uncivil Action*. Bold Type Books.

Otten, R. E. (2019). Under Armour's Global Headquarters and the Redevelopment of South Baltimore. In N. P. King, K. Drabinski, and J. C. Davis (eds.), *Baltimore Revisited: Stories of Inequality and Resistance in a U.S. City, 306-14*. Rutgers University Press.

Owens, M. L. (2007). *God and Government in the Ghetto: The Politics of Church-State Collaboration in Black America*. University of Chicago Press.

Owens, M. L., Rodriguez, A. D., and Brown, R. A. (2021). "Let's Get Ready to Crumble": Black Municipal Leadership and Public Housing Transformation in the United States. *Urban Affairs Review*, 57(2), 342–72.

Özay, E. (2021). *Urban Renewal and School Reform in Baltimore: Rethinking the 21st Century Public School*. Routledge.

Pain, R. (2019). Chronic Urban Trauma: The Slow Violence of Housing Dispossession. *Urban Studies*, 56(2), 385–400.

Pain, R., and Cahill, C. (2022). Critical Political Geographies of Slow Violence and Resistance. *Environment and Planning C: Politics and Space. Politics and Space*, 40(2), 359–72.

Park, R. E., and Burgess, E. W. (1925). *The City*. University of Chicago Press.

Pattillo, M. (1999). *Black Picket Fences: Privilege and Peril among the Black Middle Class*. University of Chicago Press.

—— (2009). Investing in Poor Black Neighborhoods "As Is." In M. A. Turner, S. J. Popkin, and L. Rawlings (eds.), *Public Housing and the Legacy of Segregation, 31-46*. Urban Institute Press.

Payne, A. A., and Greiner, A. L. (2019). New-Build Development and the Gentrification of Oklahoma City's Deep Deuce Neighborhood. *Geographical Review*, 109(1), 108–30.

Pegues, J. (2017). *Black and Blue: Inside the Divide between the Police and Black America*. Prometheus.

Pennington-Cross, A., and Ho, G. (2010). The Termination of Subprime Hybrid and Fixed-Rate Mortgages. *Real Estate Economics*, 38(3), 399–426.

Perry, R. K. (2013). *Black Mayors, White Majorities: The Balancing Act of Racial Politics*. University of Nebraska Press.

Pietila, A. (2010). *Not in My Neighborhood: How Bigotry Shaped a Great American City*. Ivan R. Dee.

———. (2018). *The Ghosts of Johns Hopkins: The Life and Legacy That Shaped an American City*. Rowman & Littlefield Publishers.

Pill, M. (2018). Philanthropic Foundations in the City Policy Process: A Perspective on Policy Capacity from the United States. In X. Wu, M. Howlett, and M. Ramesh (eds.), *Policy Capacity and Governance: Assessing Governmental Competences and Capabilities in Theory and Practice*, 313–35. Palgrave Macmillan.

Pinard, M. (2015). Poor, Black and "Wanted": Criminal Justice in Ferguson and Baltimore. *Howard Law Journal*, 58(3), 857–80.

Pink, S., Horst, H., Postill, J., Hjorth, L., Lewis, T., and Tacchi, J. (2016). *Digital Ethnography: Principles and Practice*. SAGE.

Powell, K. J. (2016). Making #BlackLivesMatter: Michael Brown, Eric Garner, and the Specters of Black Life—Toward a Hauntology of Blackness. *Cultural Studies ↔ Critical Methodologies*, 16(3), 253–60.

Power, G. (1983). Apartheid Baltimore Style: The Residential Segregation Ordinances of 1910–1913. *Maryland Law Review*, 42(2), 289–329.

———. (2002). Deconstructing the Slums of Baltimore. In J. I. Elfenbein, J. R. Breiham, and T. L. Hollowak (eds.), *From Mobtown to Charm City: New Perspectives on Baltimore's Past*, 47–63. Maryland Historical Society.

Primm, J. N. (2010). *Lion of the Valley: St. Louis, Missouri, 1764–1980*. Missouri Historical Society Press.

Pryor-Trusty, R., and Taliaferro, T. (2003). *Black America Series: African-American Entertainment in Baltimore*. Arcadia Publishing.

Purdy, H. L. (2012). *Historical Analysis of the Economic Growth of St. Louis: 1840–1945*. BiblioGov.

Purnell, J. Q. (2016). The Geography of Inequality: A Public Health Context for Ferguson and the St. Louis Region. In K. J. Norwood (ed.), *Ferguson's Fault Lines: The Race Quake That Rocked a Nation*, 145–65. American Bar Association.

Quercia, R. G., Stegman, M. A., and Davis, W. R. (2007). The Impact of Predatory Loan Terms on Subprime Foreclosures: The Special Case of

Prepayment Penalties and Balloon Payments. *Housing Policy Debate*, 18(2), 311–46.

Rainwater, L. (1970). *Behind Ghetto Walls: Black Families in a Federal Slum*. Routledge.

Reed, A., Jr. (1999). *Stirrings in the Jug: Black Politics in the Post-Segregation Era*. University of Minnesota Press.

Reid, C., and Laderman, E. (2011). Constructive Credit: Revisiting the Performance of Community Reinvestment Act Lending during the Subprime Crisis. In S. M. Wachter and M. M. Smith (eds.), *The American Mortgage System: Crisis and Reform, 159–80*. University of Pennsylvania Press.

Reid, C. K., Bocian, D., Li, W., and Quercia, R. G. (2017). Revisiting the Subprime Crisis: The Dual Mortgage Market and Mortgage Defaults by Race and Ethnicity. *Journal of Urban Affairs*, 39(4), 469–87.

Reyes, V. (2020). Ethnographic Toolkit: Strategic Positionality and Researchers' Visible and Invisible Tools in Field Research. *Ethnography*, 21(2), 220–40.

Richardson, J., Mitchell, B., and Franco, J. (2019). *Shifting Neighborhoods: Gentrification and Cultural Displacement in American Cities*. National Community Reinvestment Coalition.

Rios, J. (2019). Racial States of Municipal Governance: Policing Bodies and Space for Revenue in North St. Louis County, MO. *Minnesota Journal of Law & Inequality*, 37(2), 235–308.

——— (2020). *Black Lives and Spatial Matters: Policing Blackness and Practicing Freedom in Suburban St. Louis*. Cornell University Press.

Rios, V. M. (2011). *Punished: Policing the Lives of Black and Latino Boys*. NYU Press.

Roberto, E., and Korver-Glenn, E. (2021). The Spatial Structure and Local Experience of Residential Segregation. *Spatial Demography*, 9, 277–307.

Robinson, C. J. (2021). *Black Marxism: The Making of the Black Radical Tradition*. Revised and updated 3rd ed. University of North Carolina Press.

Rodriguez, A. D. (2021). *Diverging Space for Deviants: The Politics of Atlanta's Public Housing*. University of Georgia Press.

Rogers, J. (2015). *Ferguson Is America: Roots of Rebellion*. Mira Digital Publishing.

Rose, M. H., and Mohl, R. A. (2012). *Interstate: Highway Politics and Policy since 1939*. University of Tennessee Press.

Rosen, E. (2020). *The Voucher Promise: "Section 8" and the Fate of an American Neighborhood*. Princeton University Press.

Rosenblatt, P., and DeLuca, S. (2017). What Happened in Sandtown-Winchester? Understanding the Impacts of a Comprehensive Community Initiative. *Urban Affairs Review*, 53(3), 463–94.

Rosenblatt, P., and Newman, K. (2011). *The Impact of Foreclosure Waves on the City of Baltimore*. Report for Congressman Elijah Cummings. Johns Hopkins University.

Rothstein, R. (2015). The Making of Ferguson. *Journal of Affordable Housing & Community Development Law*, 24(2), 165–204.

—— (2017). *The Color of Law: A Forgotten History of How Our Government Segregated America*. Liveright.

Rucks-Ahidiana, Z. (2021). Racial Composition and Trajectories of Gentrification in the United States. *Urban Studies*, 58(13), 2721–41.

—— (2022). Theorizing Gentrification as a Process of Racial Capitalism. *City & Community*, 21(3), 173–92.

Rudwick, E. (1982). *Race Riot at East St. Louis, July 2, 1917*. University of Illinois Press.

Rugh, J.S., and Massey, D.S. (2010). Racial Segregation and the American Foreclosure Crisis. *American Sociological Review*, 75(5), 629–51.

Saegert, S., Fields, D., and Libman, K. (2011). Mortgage Foreclosure and Health Disparities: Serial Displacement as Asset Extraction in African American Populations. *Journal of Urban Health*, 88(3), 390–402.

Sandburg, C. ([1969], 2015). *Chicago Race Riots*. Revised ed. Houghton Mifflin Harcourt.

Sandweiss, E. (2001). *St. Louis: Evolution of American Urban Landscape*. Temple University Press.

Sassen, S. (2014). *Expulsions: Brutality and Complexity in the Global Economy*. Harvard University Press.

Schaller, S. F. (2019). *Business Improvement Districts and the Contradictions of Placemaking: BID Urbanism in Washington, D.C.* University of Georgia Press.

Schatzman, L., and Strauss, A. L. (1973). *Field Research: Strategies for a Natural Sociology*. Prentice-Hall.

Schlichtman, J. J., Patch, J., and Hill, M. L. (2017). *Gentrifier*. University of Toronto Press, Scholarly Publishing Division.

Schneider, C. L. (2014). *Police Power and Race Riots: Urban Unrest in Paris and New York*. University of Pennsylvania Press.

—— (2017). When Does Police Violence Cause Urban Unrest? *Metropolitics*. https://metropolitics.org/When-Does-Police-Violence-Cause-Urban-Unrest.html.

Schrader, S. (2019). *Badges without Borders: How Global Counterinsurgency Transformed American Policing*. University of California Press.

Schuessler, R. (2019). *The St. Louis Anthology*. Belt Publishing.

Schulman, S. (2012). *The Gentrification of the Mind: Witness to a Lost Imagination.* University of California Press.

Schwartz, A. F. (2015). *Housing Policy in the United States.* 3rd ed. Routledge.

Shapiro, T., Meschede, T., and Osoro, S. (2013). *The Roots of the Widening Racial Wealth Gap: Explaining the Black-White Economic Divide.* Institute on Assets and Social Policy.

Shapiro, T. M. (2017). *Toxic Inequality: How America's Wealth Gap Destroys Mobility, Deepens the Racial Divide, and Threatens Our Future.* Basic Books.

Sharkey, P. (2013). *Stuck in Place: Urban Neighborhoods and the End of Progress toward Racial Equality.* University of Chicago Press.

——— (2018). *Uneasy Peace: The Great Crime Decline, the Renewal of City Life, and the Next War on Violence.* W. W. Norton.

Sharkey, P., and Marsteller, A. (2022). Neighborhood Inequality and Violence in Chicago, 1965–2020. *University of Chicago Law Review,* 89(2), 349–81.

Sharp, E. B. (2014). Politics, Economics, and Urban Policing: The Postindustrial City Thesis and Rival Explanations of Heightened Order Maintenance Policing. *Urban Affairs Review,* 50(3), 340–65.

Shaw, R. (2018). *Generation Priced Out: Who Gets to Live in the New Urban America.* University of California Press.

Shaw, T. M. (2015). *The Ferguson Report: Department of Justice Investigation of the Ferguson Police Department / United States Department of Justice, Civil Rights Division.* The New Press.

Silver, H. (2016). National Urban Policy in the Age of Obama. In J. DeFilippis (ed.), *Urban Policy in the Time of Obama,* 11–44. University of Minnesota Press.

Simon, D., and Burns, E. (1998). *The Corner: A Year in the Life of an Inner-City Neighborhood.* Crown.

Slater, T. (2021). *Shaking Up the City: Ignorance, Inequality and the Urban Question.* University of California Press.

Slocum, K. (2019). *Black Towns, Black Futures: The Enduring Allure of a Black Place in the American West.* University of North Carolina Press.

Slooter, L. (2019). *The Making of the Banlieue: An Ethnography of Space, Identity and Violence.* Palgrave Macmillan.

Small, M. L., and Calarco, J. M. (2022). *Qualitative Literacy: A Guide to Evaluating Ethnographic and Interview Research.* University of California Press.

Smith, C. F. (1999). *William Donald Schaefer: A Political Biography.* Johns Hopkins University Press.

Smith, H., and Graves, W. (2005). Gentrification as Corporate Growth Strategy: The Strange Case of Charlotte, North Carolina and the Bank of America. *Journal of Urban Affairs*, 27(4), 403-18.

Smith, P.H. II. (2016). Obama, Race, and Urban Policy. In J. DeFilippis (ed.), *Urban Policy in the Time of Obama*, 65-78. University of Minnesota Press.

Smith, R.E., Naparstek, A., Popkin, S., Bartlett, L., and Bates, L. (2002). *Housing Choice for HOPE VI Relocatees*. Urban Institute.

Smithsimon, G. (2022). *Liberty Road: Black Middle-Class Suburbs and the Battle between Civil Rights and Neoliberalism*. NYU Press.

Soss, J., Fording, R.C., and Schram, S.F. (2011). *Disciplining the Poor: Neoliberal Paternalism and the Persistent Power of Race*. University of Chicago Press.

Spilerman, S. (1976). Structural Characteristics of Cities and the Severity of Racial Disorders. *American Sociological Review*, 41(5), 771-93.

Steil, J.P., Albright, L., Rugh, J.S., and Massey, D.S. (2018). The Social Structure of Mortgage Discrimination. *Housing Studies*, 33(5), 759-76.

Stein, S. (2019). *Capital City: Gentrification and the Real Estate State*. Verso.

Stevenson, B. (2015). *Just Mercy: A Story of Justice and Redemption*. One World.

Stoker, R.P., Stone, C.N., and Worgs, D. (2015). Neighborhood Policy in Baltimore. In C.N. Stone, and R.P. Stoker (eds.), *Urban Neighborhoods in a New Era: Revitalization Politics in the Postindustrial City*, 50-80. University of Chicago Press.

Stone, C.N. (1989). *Regime Politics: Governing Atlanta, 1946-1988*. University Press of Kentucky.

Stuart, F. (2016). *Down, Out, and Under Arrest: Policing and Everyday Life in Skid Row*. University of Chicago Press.

Sugrue, T.J. (1996). *The Origins of the Urban Crisis: Race and Inequality in Postwar Detroit*. Princeton University Press.

—— (2008). *Sweet Land of Liberty: The Forgotten Struggle for Civil Rights in the North*. Random House.

Summers, B.T. (2019). *Black in Place. The Spatial Aesthetics of Race in a Post-Chocolate City*. University of North Carolina Press.

Sutton, S. (2020). Gentrification and the Increasing Significance of Racial Transition in New York City 1970-2010. *Urban Affairs Review*, 56(1), 65-95.

Swanstrom, T., and Plöger, J. (2022). What to Make of Gentrification in Older Industrial Cities? Comparing St. Louis (USA) and Dortmund (Germany). *Urban Affairs Review*, 58(2), 526-62.

Swanstrom, T., Webber, H.S., and Metzger, M.W. (2017). Rebound Neighborhoods in Older Industrial Cities. In *Economic Mobility: Research & Ideas on*

Strengthening Families, Communities & the Economy, edited by the Federal
Reserve Bank of St. Louis and the Board of Governors of the Federal Reserve
System. Federal Reserve Bank.

Tach, L., and Emory, A. D. (2017). Public Housing Redevelopment, Neighborhood Change, and the Restructuring of Urban Inequality. *American Journal
of Sociology*, 123(3), 686–739.

Tach, L. M. (2014). Diversity, Inequality, and Microsegregation: Dynamics of
Inclusion and Exclusion in a Racially and Economically Diverse Community. *Cityscape*, 16(3), 13–45.

Tager, J. (2001). *Boston Riots: Three Centuries of Social Violence*. Northeastern
University Press.

Taylor, K.-Y. (2016). *From #BlackLivesMatter to Black Liberation*. Haymarket
Books.

——— (2019). *Race for Profit: How Banks and the Real Estate Industry Undermined
Black Homeownership*. University of North Carolina Press.

Taylor, R. B. (2001). *Breaking Away from Broken Windows: Baltimore Neighborhoods and the Nationwide Fight against Crime, Grime, Fear, and Decline*. U.S.
Department of Justice.

Teaford, J. C. (1990). *The Rough Road to Renaissance: Urban Revitalization in
America, 1940–1985*. Johns Hopkins University Press.

——— (2006). *The Metropolitan Revolution: The Rise of Post-Urban America*.
Columbia University Press.

Thomas, M. E., Moye, R., Henderson, L., & Horton, H. D. (2018). Separate and
Unequal: The Impact of Socioeconomic Status, Segregation, and the Great
Recession on Racial Disparities in Housing Values. *Sociology of Race and
Ethnicity*, 4(2), 229–44.

Thompson, D. (2017). An Exoneration of Black Rage. *South Atlantic Quarterly*,
116(3), 457–81.

Thompson, H. A. (2017). *Whose Detroit? Politics, Labor, and Race in a Modern
American City*. Cornell University Press.

Thompson, J. P. I. (2006). *Double Trouble: Black Mayors, Black Communities, and
the Call for a Deep Democracy*. Oxford University Press.

Thomson, D. E. (2021). Philanthropic Funding for Community and Economic
Development: Exploring Potential for Influencing Policy and Governance.
Urban Affairs Review, 57(6), 1483–523.

Till, K. E. (2012). Wounded Cities: Memory-Work and a Place-Based Ethics of
Care. *Political Geography*, 31(1), 3–14.

Tilly, C. (2003). *The Politics of Collective Violence*. Cambridge University Press.

Timberlake, J.M., and Johns-Wolfe, E. (2017). Neighborhood Ethnoracial
   Composition and Gentrification in Chicago and New York, 1980 to 2010.
   Urban Affairs Review, 53(2), 236–72.
Tissot, S. (2015). *Good Neighbors: Gentrifying Diversity in Boston's South End*. Verso.
Travis, J., and Western, B. (2017). Poverty, Violence, and Black Incarceration. In
   A.J. Davis (ed.), *Policing the Black Man: Arrest, Prosecution, and Imprisonment*,
   294–321. Pantheon.
Trounstine, J. (2018). *Segregation by Design: Local Politics and Inequality in
   American Cities*. Cambridge University Press.
Ture, K., and Hamilton, C.V. (1992). *Black Power: The Politics of Liberation*.
   Vintage.
Turner, M.A., Popkin, S.J., and Rawlings, L. (eds.) (2009). *Public Housing and
   the Legacy of Segregation*. Urban Institute Press.
Underhill, S.M. (2016). Urban Jungle, Ferguson: Rhetorical Homology and
   Institutional Critique. *Quarterly Journal of Speech*, 102(4), 396–417.
U.S. Department of Housing and Urban Development (1967). *HUD 3rd Annual
   Report*.
U.S. Department of Justice (2017). *Federal Reports on Police Killings: Ferguson,
   Cleveland, Baltimore, and Chicago / United States Department of Justice*.
   Melville House.
U.S. National Advisory Commission on Civil Disorders (1968). *The Kerner
   Report*. U.S. Government Printing Office.
Vale, L.J. (2013). *Purging the Poorest: Public Housing and the Design Politics of
   Twice-Cleared Communities*. University of Chicago Press.
—— (2019). *After the Projects: Public Housing Redevelopment and the Governance
   of the Poorest Americans*. Oxford University Press.
Vargas, R. (2016). *Wounded City: Violent Turf Wars in a Chicago Barrio*. Oxford
   University Press.
Venkatesh, S.A. (2000). *American Project: The Rise and Fall of a Modern Ghetto*.
   Harvard University Press.
—— (2006). *Off the Books: The Underground Economy of the Urban Poor*.
   Harvard University Press.
—— (2008). *Gang Leader for a Day: A Rogue Sociologist Takes to the Streets*.
   Penguin Press.
Vicino, T.J. (2008). *Transforming Race and Class in Suburbia: Decline in Metropol-
   itan Baltimore*. Palgrave Macmillan.
von Hoffman, A. (2003). *House by House, Block by Block: The Rebirth of America's
   Urban Neighborhoods*. Oxford University Press.

Wachter, S.M., and Smith, M.M. (2011). *The American Mortgage System: Crisis and Reform*. University of Pennsylvania Press.

Wacquant, L. (2008). *Urban Outcasts: A Comparative Sociology of Advanced Marginality*. Polity.

—— (2009). *Punishing the Poor: The Neoliberal Government of Social Insecurity*. Duke University Press.

Walter, J.C. (1988). *The Harlem Fox: J. Raymond Jones and Tammany, 1920–1970*. SUNY Press.

Walter, I., and Kramer, J.E. (1969). Political Autonomy and Economic Dependence in an All-Nego Municipality. *The American Journal of Economics and Sociology*, 28(3), 225–48.

Walters, S.J.K., and Miserendino, L. (2008). *Baltimore's Flawed Renaissance: The Failure of Plan-Control-Subsidize Redevelopment*. Institute for Justice.

Wang, J. (2018). *Carceral Capitalism*. Penguin Random House.

Watkins, D. (2016). *The Beast Side: Living and Dying While Black in America*. Hot Books.

—— (2017). *The Cook Up: A Crack Rock Memoir*. Grand Central Publishing.

—— (2019). *We Speak for Ourselves: A Word from Forgotten Black America*. Atria Books.

Websdale, N. (2001). *Policing the Poor: From Slave Plantation to Public Housing*. Northeastern University Press.

Welsh, B. C., Braga, A.A., and Bruinsma, G.J.N. (2015). Reimagining Broken Windows: From Theory to Policy. *Journal of Research in Crime and Delinquency*, 52(4), 447–63.

Wesenberg, R. (2004). City Neighborhoods: Housing Stability, Quality, and Affordability. In B. Baybeck and T. Jones (eds.), *St. Louis Metromorphosis: Past Trends and Future Directions*, 217–34. Missouri Historical Society Press.

West Baltimore Commission on Police Misconduct and the No Boundaries Coalition (2016). *Over-Policed, Yet Underserved: The People's Findings Regarding Police Misconduct in West Baltimore*.

Western, B. (2006). *Punishment and Inequality in America*. Russell Sage Foundation.

Wilkerson, I. (2011). *The Warmth of Other Suns: The Epic Story of America's Great Migration*. Vintage.

—— (2020). *Caste: The Origins of Our Discontents*. Random House.

Williams, B. (2016). Beyond Gentrification: Investment and Abandonment on the Waterfront. In D. Hyra and S. Prince (eds.), *Capital Dilemma: Growth and Inequality in Washington, DC*, 227–38. Routledge.

Williams, R. Y. (2004). *The Politics of Public Housing: Black Women's Struggles against Urban Inequality.* Oxford University Press.

Wills, S. (2018). *Black Fortunes: The Story of the First Six African Americans Who Escaped Slavery and Became Millionaires.* Amistad.

Wilson, W. J. (1996). *When Work Disappears: The World of the New Urban Poor.* Knopf.

Winch, J. (2011). *The Clamorgans: One Family's History of Race in America.* Hill and Wang.

—— (ed.) (2018). *The Colored Aristocracy of St. Louis.* University of Missouri Press.

Wolman, H., and Horak, M. (2015). Contexts for Neighborhood Revitalization: A Comparative Overview. In C. N. Stone and R. P. Stoker (eds.), *Urban Neighborhoods in a New Era: Revitalization Politics in the Postindustrial City,* 33-49. University of Chicago Press.

Woods, B, and Soderberg, B. (2020). *I Got a Monster: The Rise and Fall of America's Most Corrupt Police Squad.* St. Martin's Press.

Wright, J. A., Sr. (2000). *Kinloch: Missouri's First Black City.* Arcadia Publishing.

—— (2001). *The Ville: St. Louis.* Arcadia Publishing.

—— (2002). *Discovering African American St. Louis: A Guide to Historic Sites.* Missouri Historical Society Press.

—— (2004). *St. Louis: Disappearing Black Communities.* Arcadia Publishing.

Wright Austin, S. D. (2006). *The Transformation of Plantation Politics: Black Politics, Concentrated Poverty, and Social Capital in the Mississippi Delta.* SUNY Press.

Wyly, E. (2010). Things Pictures Don't Tell Us: In Search of Baltimore. *City,* 14(5), 497-528.

Wyly, E. K., Atia, M., and Hammel, D. J. (2004). Has Mortgage Capital Found an Inner-City Spatial Fix? *Housing Policy Debate,* 15(3), 623-85.

Yin, R. K. (2018). *Case Study Research and Applications: Design and Methods.* SAGE.

Zelizer, J. E. (2016). *The Kerner Report.* Princeton University Press.

Zipp, S. (2010). *Manhattan Projects: The Rise and Fall of Urban Renewal in Cold War New York.* Oxford University Press.

Index

Baltimore *(continued)*
decisions in, 165, 199; racial composition of, 135, 137, 138*fig.*, 231*table*, 269n24; segregation by class in, 188–89; segregation by race in, 137, 138*fig.*, 148, 171, 195; slavery in, 134–35; slow violence in, forms of, 164–65, 170–71; spatial inequality in, 10, 134, 151–52; TIFs in, 156, 160; tourism in, 151–53; as two cities, 164, 195, 197; vacant homes in, 152, 155, 162–63, 163*fig.*, 221, 273n97; vision in, lack of, 195–99; white business elites in, 189–91; white political coalition of, 147–48. *See also specific locations*

Baltimore, Black communities in, 132–99; achievements of, 135–36, 139–40; Black middle-class flight from, 140, 141–43; double disrespect for, 179, 198; highway construction through, 141, 143–44, 145*fig.*; hypersegregation in, 137, 138*fig.*, 148; intraracial class conflict in, 198–99; migration to, 134–37; new urban renewal in, 164–65; old urban renewal in, 143–45, 165; policing in, 150, 169, 171–74; population of, 135, 137, 231*table*, 269n24; poverty concentration in, 161–62, 195; redlining in, 140, 149; subprime and foreclosure crisis in, 142, 162–64. *See also specific locations*

Baltimore, Black politicians in: administrative fragmentation and, 192; vs. Ferguson, 14, 130–31, 132; limited effect on racial inequality, 14–15, 134, 197–98, 210–11; redevelopment priorities of, 152–53;

response to uprisings by, 221; rise in power of, 136, 269n24; at time of Gray's death, 134, 170. *See also specific politicians*

Baltimore, policing in, 167–99; in Black vs. white areas, 150, 169, 171–74; city vs. state control of, 192; culture of violence in, 173–74; displacement combined with aggressive, 178–79, 198; vs. Ferguson policing, 170; housing policies and, 171–72, 174–79; Justice Department report on, 169, 177–78, 275n20; misconduct cases in, 170, 174; under O'Malley, 170, 176–79, 198, 199; of pedestrians, 169, 172; political fragmentation and, 171, 192, 194; in "ring of blight," 169, 173–74, 199; under Schmoke, 175–76, 198; stop-and-frisk, 169, 170, 172–73, 194; street violence linked to, 170–71, 194; in uprisings of 2015, 38, 142, 178, 207–8

Baltimore, political fragmentation in, 183–96; administrative fragmentation and, 192, 194; in Democratic party, 183–89; lack of political machine in, 184–87; lack of vision in, 195–97; in origins of violence, 183–91; policing and, 171, 192, 194; street violence and, 171, 192–94, 196

Baltimore, public housing in: construction of, 144–46; locations of, 146; number of units of, 158; after uprisings of 2015, 221–22; waitlist for, 151, 269n9, 272n67; as walls of separation, 145–47, 159; white residents of, 267n108

Baltimore, public housing in, demolition of, 157–62; HOPE VI funding for, 159–62, 272n73; in

Black communities: as-is, making
investments in, 217; policy
recommendations for uplifting, 225.
See also specific locations
Black flight: in Baltimore, 140, 141–43;
in St. Louis, 76
Black Guerrilla Family, 193
Black insurgency, use of term, 24
Black Lives Matter (BLM) movement,
3, 79, 235n25
Black migration. *See* migration
Blackness: public housing associated
with, 158; in stereotypes of
ghettos, 111
Black Placemaking, 217
Black political representation. *See*
politicians
Black revolts, use of term, 24
"blighted" neighborhoods, 61, 64, 70,
123–24
BLM. *See* Black Lives Matter
Blumeyer, Arthur, 64
Blumeyer Homes (St. Louis),
89–90
Bosley, Freeman, Jr., 75, 93
Boston: drug trade in, 281n177; history
of riots in, 23; Operation Ceasefire
in, 194; redevelopment in, 152
Boston Massacre of 1770, 23
Boston Tea Party of 1773, 23
Boyles, Andrea, 2, 12, 19, 68–69, 130,
235n25
BPD. *See* Baltimore, policing in
Bratton, William, 176, 177
Brewer, Margaret, 139
Bridgeford, Erricka, 174, 179–80, 209,
223–24
broken windows policing, 167–99;
definition of, 167–68; harm caused
by, 168–69; in New York City,
176–77; origins of, 14, 167–68, 176;

unrest linked to, 169. *See also*
Baltimore, policing in
Bronzeville (Chicago), xxii, 40
Brooklyn Heights (New York), 82
Brown, Charles, 101
Brown, Gwen, 142, 188–89, 196
Brown, LaTasha, 7, 103–5, 112–13, 121,
129
Brown, Lawrence, xxiii, 10, 44, 150,
157, 194, 225
Brown, Michael, 1–3; body in street
after death of, 2, 126–27, 218, 219*fig.*;
events leading to killing of, 1–2, 38;
location of death, 1–2, 98, 114;
memorial to, 2, 127, 219–20; police
response after death of, 2–3, 3*fig.*;
redevelopment of sites associated
with, 218–21; slow violence as
context for death of, 10, 49–50,
126–27; TIFs and, 126. *See also*
Ferguson uprisings
Brown, Michael, Sr., 219–20
brownfield sites, 156
Brown v. Board of Education, 35
Bruce, Blanche K., 60
Buchanan v. Warley, 56
BUILD. *See* Baltimoreans United in
Leadership Development
Bullock, John, 182, 209, 282n190
bureaucratic fragmentation, in
Baltimore, 192, 194
Burns, Clarence H. "Du," 175, 189,
269n23, 277n72
Burns, Robert, 124, 125
Busch, August A., Jr., 64
Butler, Paul, 12

Calloway, Cab, 140
Calloway, Ernest, 68
Camden Yards Railway Station
(Baltimore), 139

Campbell, Tracy, 61–62, 63, 73
Canfield Green Apartments (Ferguson), 1–2, 98, 218, 220
capitalism, racialized, 108, 212
Carney, Thomas, 148
Carter, Jimmy, 190
casinos, in Baltimore, 270n38
caste system, 127
Castro, Julián, 127
Central Corridor (St. Louis), 78–94;
    Black communities in, 57;
    expansion of, 80, 84–90; gentrification in, 80, 81–83, 92; location and
    boundaries of, 81; public investments in, 76, 82–83; Rouse
    Company in, 269n17
Central Trades and Labor Union, 55
Century Electric Company, 83
Chabot, Robert, 19, 106–7, 118
Charles Center (Baltimore), 269n3
Charles Folwell Apartments (Kinloch), 97
Charlotte (North Carolina), xxii
Chauvin, Derek, 6
Cherry Hill (Baltimore), 267n104
Chicago: plantation politics in, 103;
    poverty concentration in, 32; public
    housing in, xxii, 33; riots in, xx, 32;
    street violence in, 275n29
Chicago Urban League, xx
children, poverty rates for, 28
chronic displacement trauma, 10–12;
    definition of, 10; need for policies
    on, 225; vs. PTSD, 10–11; in St.
    Louis, 51, 77, 95–96; in urban
    renewal unrest framework,
    209–10, 212
chronic ghetto, 10, 14, 111, 209–10, 212
Cisneros, Henry, 158
cities: back-to-the-city movement, 70,
    100; history of riots in, xx–xxi;

stereotypes of, 112; superstar, 79–80;
    wounded, 95. *See also specific cities*
citizenship, U.S., 136
Citizens Planning and Housing
    Association, 148, 187–88
City Foundry STL, 83
Civic Progress, Inc., 64
civil disorders, use of term, 24
Civil Rights Act of 1964, 35, 36
civil rights movement: cycle of
    progress and regress in, xxi; rising
    Black expectations in, 35–36
Clampet-Lundquist, Susan, 161
Clark, Joseph W. B., 68
Clark, Kenneth B., 1, 17, 19, 29, 36, 38,
    267n101
class: intersection with race, in slow
    violence, 210; vs. race, in Ferguson
    uprisings, 105–8, 128–30
class conflict, intraracial: in Baltimore, 198–99; in St. Louis, 66–68
class segregation, in Baltimore,
    188–89
Clinton-Peabody (St. Louis). *See*
    Peabodys
Clover, Joshua, 203
Coates, Ta-Nehisi, 157, 198, 207, 212
Cobbina, Jennifer, 7, 8, 12, 128
Cochran Gardens (St. Louis), 89–90
cognitive empathy, 228
collective violence, terminology of,
    23–26
Commission on the City Plan, 148
Committee for Downtown, 148
Committee on Segregation, 147
community development policies: as
    driver of uprisings, 8–12; gaps in
    scholarship on, 12; in racial
    inequality, 12–14; recommendations for, 216–17. *See also specific
    locations and policies*

community organizations, 217,
282n190
community policing, 175–76, 215
competition, intergroup, as driver of
unrest, 29–31, 205
concentration of poverty. *See* poverty
concentration
Connelly-Bowen, Jenny, 86–87
constitutional amendments, 135, 136
contact theory of unrest, 29–31, 205
containment, Black: in Ferguson,
112–13; in St. Louis, 70–77
Cook Up, The (Watkins), 192
Coppin State University, 136
CORE, Project, 221–22
Cornblatt, Theodore, 148
corruption, political, in Baltimore,
184
covenants, restrictive: in Baltimore,
140, 148; in St. Louis, 56–59, 65;
Supreme Court on, 35
COVID pandemic, 18, 227–29
crack epidemic, 109
Crenson, Matthew: on Black
achievements, 135; on Black
migration, 135–36; on drug gangs,
193–94; on extremes of Baltimore,
182; on political fragmentation,
183–85, 187; on racial discussions,
218
Creole village of St. Louis, 51–52,
63–64, 75
crews, 281n182
crime: impact of broken windows
policing on, 168; in stereotypes of
Blackness, 111
Crossings at Halls Ferry, The
(Ferguson), 124–26
Cummings, Elijah, 5
Cummings, Harry S., 136
cumulative dehumanization, 244n135

cycle of racial and spatial repression,
17, 44–45, 44*fig.,* 209

Dahl, Robert, 185
D'Alesandro, Thomas, Jr., 147, 189
Daley, Larry, 186
Daley, Richard J., 186
Dark Ghetto, The (Clark), 29
Darst, Joseph, 64
Darst Apartments (St. Louis), 85,
86*fig.*
*Davis et al. v. St. Louis Housing
Authority,* 71, 85
Deep Morgan (St. Louis), 60
dehumanization, cumulative, 244n135
deindustrialization: in Baltimore,
151–52; as driver of unrest, 31; in St.
Louis, 75–76. *See also* postindustrial
economy
Delmar Divide, 78–82
DeLuca, Stefanie, 156, 161
democracy, U.S.: racial inequality in
conflict with ideals of, xxi, 28, 214;
riots in formation of, 23
Democratic Bohemian Club, 189
Democratic party: in Baltimore,
fragmentation of, 183–89; and
street violence, 275n29
Denny, Reginald, xx
deprivation, as driver of unrest, 8, 30,
37, 205–7
DESCO Group, 123–24
design politics, 43
Desmond, Matthew, 42
Detroit riot of 1967, 31
Dikeç, Mustafa, 17, 28, 42, 44, 99
disinvestment (divestment): in cycle
of repression, 44*fig.,* 45, 209; in
Sandtown-Winchester (Baltimore),
143–44; slow violence in, 9–10; in
St. Louis, 71–72, 74–77

Disneyfication, 16, 152, 155, 238n111
displacement: in cycle of repression,
44–45, 44*fig.*, 209; as driver of
unrest, 32–35, 208–9, 213; from Great
Recession, 41–42; HOPE VI's role in,
41, 42, 168, 272n73; political effects
of, 99; root shock of, 10, 33–34, 95,
208; serial, definition of, 43; slow
violence in, 9–10, 44; trauma of (*See*
chronic displacement trauma). *See
also specific locations*
dispossession, in cycle of repression,
44, 44*fig.*, 209. *See also* displacement
disrespect: double, 179, 198; as driver
of unrest, 224
dissimilarity index, 56
divestment. *See* disinvestment
double disrespect, 179, 198
double gentrification, 43
Douglass Homes (Baltimore), 146
Downtown Partnership of Baltimore,
187–88, 190
drug trade: in Baltimore, 154, 158,
192–94, 196, 281n177; in St. Louis,
109; violent fallout of, 278n83
Dunbar Gardens (Kinloch), 97
Durr, Kenneth, 137

East Baltimore Development, Inc.
(EBDI), 272n73
East St. Louis, riot of 1917 in, xx,
55–56, 97
EBDI. *See* East Baltimore Development, Inc.
economic deprivation, as driver of
unrest, 8, 30, 37, 205–7
economic exploitation: in Ferguson,
118–27, 130; racialized capitalism as
form of, 108; in subprime crisis, 118;
through TIFs, 122–26

economic growth: in Baltimore, 137;
in St. Louis, 52–54; of superstar
cities, 79–80. *See also* postindustrial
economy
Economic Opportunity Act of 1964, 35
economic revitalization, 40
economics: vs. race, in Ferguson
uprisings, 105–8, 128–30; trickle-
down, 150, 166
economic slack, 194, 282n187
Edin, Kathryn, 161
education. *See* public schools
educational levels, in Baltimore, 154,
271n43
Ehrenhalt, Alan, 100
Ellearsville. *See* Ville
Embry, Robert, 184, 186, 190, 191
eminent domain, 65, 123, 143
empathy, cognitive, 228
Empowerment Zones (EZs), 40–41,
195
Enterprise Foundation, 153
Ervin, Keona, 66, 248n112
Esquire (magazine), 178
European immigrants, in Baltimore,
138–39
Eviction Lab, 42
Ewing, Eve, 95
Excel Academy, 180–81
expectations, rising, as driver of
unrest, 35–37, 205–7
EZs. *See* Empowerment Zones

fair market rate, 115
Faneuil Hall (Boston), 152
Farris, Charles, 64
Federal Hill (Baltimore), 155
Federal Housing Administration
(FHA), 13, 59
federal spending: on highway
construction, 266n82; on Inner

federal spending *(continued)*
Harbor, 151; on urban renewal, 32. *See also specific departments and programs*

Fells Point (Baltimore), 138–39

Ferguson, 101–31; Black migration to, 96–97, 108–12; explicit racism in 1970s, 109; foreclosure crisis in, 117–18; Great Recession in, 116–19; and Kinloch, relationship between, 96, 98–99; location of, 96; poverty concentration in, 80, 96, 107–8, 114–16; racial composition of, 96, 101–2, 255n4, 258n71; racial hierarchy of, 103; racial tension in, 98–99; racism vs. economic problems of, 105–8, 128–30; revenue sources in, 106, 118–22, 124–26; segregation in, 112–13; serial displacement in, 98–99, 118–19; slow violence in, forms of, 102, 126–27; Southeast, 110–16, 130, 220–21; spatial inequality in, 10, 112–16; as sundown town, 96, 129; systemic racism in, 107, 218; after uprisings, 218–21. *See also specific locations*

Ferguson, Karen, 197, 199

Ferguson, politics and policies of, 113–30; vs. Baltimore, 14, 130–31, 132; Black politicians in, 14, 129–30, 132; fees and fines in, 105, 106, 119–22, 125–26; LIHTCs in, 110, 112, 114–16; plantation style of, 103–5, 119–22; racial zoning in, 96; racist vs. economic motivations in, 105–8, 128–30; TIFs in, 124–26; after uprisings, 218–21; white control of, 99, 102–8, 130

Ferguson City Council, 129–30

Ferguson Market, 1, 220

Ferguson Municipal Court, 120

Ferguson Police Department: Black people targeted by, 101–3, 106, 120–21; cost of misconduct cases by, 170; economic motivations of, 102–3, 105–6, 125–26; fees and fines collected by, 105, 106, 120–21, 125–26; headquarters of, 113, 125, 261n161; racial composition of, 122

Ferguson uprisings of 2014: vs. Baltimore uprisings, 133, 170; Black Lives Matter and, 3, 235n25; events leading to, 1–2; multiple drivers of, 7, 204; as part of Great Rebellion, xxii, 203; police response to, 2–3, 3*fig.*; police role in, 38, 204; race vs. class in, 105–8, 128–30; redevelopment of sites associated with, 218–21; as riots vs. uprisings, 25; situational factors in, 38–39; slow violence as context for, 49–50. *See also* Brown, Michael

FHA. *See* Federal Housing Administration

Fifteenth Amendment, 136

Finnie, Duane, 3

Flag House Courts (Baltimore), 146, 161, 267n108

flashpoints theory of unrest, 39–40, 205, 208

Fleming, Arron, 181

Florida, Richard, 164

Floyd, George, murder of, 5–7; events leading to, 5–6; protests after, xxii–xxiii, 6–7, 228; slow violence as context for, 10

foreclosure crisis, 41; in Baltimore, 142, 162–64; in Ferguson, 117–19; in low-income communities, 243n119; in serial displacement, 118–19

Fourteenth Amendment, 136

Foxx, Redd, 60
France, riots of 2005 in, xxii, 99
Frayser (Memphis), 263n2
Freeman, Frankie Muse, 67, 68, 71
Freixas, Catalina, 56
Fullilove, Mindy, 10, 33–34, 43–44, 165

Gale, Dennis, 29
gambling, in Baltimore, 270nn37–38
gangs, in Baltimore, 192–94, 281n182
Gans, Herbert, 228
Gateway Arch (St. Louis), 61–64,
    62*fig.*, 77
General Motors, 151
gentrification: in 1990s vs. 2000s, 40;
    in cycle of repression, 44–45, 44*fig.*,
    209; definitions of, 80–82; double,
    43; as driver of unrest, 42, 213;
    homogenization in, 157; in
    middle-income areas, 82; and polic-
    ing, relationship between, 171;
    public abandonment before,
    266n91; in racially mixed vs.
    segregated neighborhoods, 80–81;
    slow violence in, 9–10, 14;
    state-led, 90–91. *See also specific
    locations*
ghetto(s): chronic, 10, 14, 111, 209–10,
    212; iconic, 111–12, 130; Kerner
    Report on unrest in (*See* Kerner
    Report); stereotypes of, 111–12;
    suburban, Southeast Ferguson as,
    111–12, 130; urban renewal in
    formation of, 33
ghetto revolts, use of term, 24
ghetto uprisings, use of term, 24
Gilje, Paul, 23
Gillespie, Andra, 197
Gillette, Howard, 221
Gilmor Homes (Baltimore), 146, 221
Gioielli, Robert, 42

Giuliani, Rudy, 176
Glaude, Eddie, 119
Goetz, Edward, 41, 42, 91
Goldseker, Morris, 147
Goldseker Foundation, 190
Gomez, Marisela, 144
good old boys system, 256n27
Gordon, Colin, 19, 66, 76, 81, 106, 127,
    248n112
Gordon, Daanika, 207–8
Gray, Freddie: arrest and rough ride
    leading to death of, 4, 38, 133, 222;
    funeral for, 5; memorial to, 222*fig.*;
    peaceful protests after death of, 133;
    redevelopment of sites associated
    with, 221–22; slow violence as
    context for death of, 10. *See also*
    Baltimore uprisings of 2015
Great Black Depression, 41, 119
Greater Baltimore Board of Realtors,
    188
Greater Baltimore Committee, 148,
    152, 187–88, 190, 268n3
Great Migrations, 36, 65, 137
Great Rebellion (2014–2020), xxii–xx-
    iii, 8, 11, 203–4
Great Recession: in Baltimore, 163;
    displacement from, 41–42; in
    Ferguson, 116–19; Obama policies
    during, 211, 284n39
Great Streets, 220–21
Great Uprising (1963–1972), xxi, 36,
    204
Green, Percy, 60
Gregory, Dick, 60
Griffin, Fran, 19, 107, 129–30, 218
Grills, Cheryle, 49
Grimshaw, Bill, 103
group competition, as driver of
    unrest, 29–31, 205
Gun Trace Task Force (GTTF), 174

HABC. *See* Housing Authority of
   Baltimore City
Haldipur, Jan, 168
Hands Up, Don't Shoot (Cobbina), 7
Harcourt, Bernard, 168
Hard Rock Café, 151
Hardy, David, 281n177
Harlem (New York), xix, 40, 139, 140
Harlem Park (Baltimore). *See*
   Sandtown-Winchester
Harlem Renaissance, 140
Harmon, Clarence, 75, 93
Harris, Frederick, 197
Harris, Fred R., 29
Harry and Jeanette Weinberg
   Foundation, 190
Harvey, David, 167, 196, 282n198
Hawkins, William Ashbie, 139
HCV. *See* Section 8 vouchers
Head, Louis, 2
Heathcott, Joseph, 61, 248nn111–12
Herman, Max, 30, 34
Hesse, Barnor, 102
Hickman, Donté, 5
Hicks, Helen, 132
highway construction: in Baltimore,
   141, 143–44, 145*fig.*; federal
   funding of, 266n82; number of
   people displaced by, 266n86; role
   in ghetto formation, 33; role in
   old urban renewal, 13, 143; in
   St. Louis, 66
Hill, Marc Lamont, 12, 26, 224
Hinton, Elizabeth, 24, 26, 237n56
Hirsch, Arnold, 147, 148, 266n99
Hogan, Larry, 221
HOLC. *See* Home Owners Loan
   Corporation
Holder, Eric, Jr., 127
Holiday, Billie, 140
Hollander Ridge (Baltimore), 161

Home Owners Loan Corporation
   (HOLC), 58–59, 79, 140
Homer G. Phillips Hospital, 75, 76
homes: values in Baltimore, 159;
   values in Ferguson, 110, 118–19;
   white vs. Black homeownership
   rates, 28, 119. *See also* foreclosure
   crisis; redlining; subprime loans;
   vacant homes
homogenization, in gentrification, 157
Hooker, Juliet, 102
hope, as driver of unrest, 35–36
HOPE VI program: in Baltimore,
   159–62, 272n73; impacts of, 40–42,
   168, 216, 272n73; as new urban
   renewal policy, 13, 40–41, 91; in St.
   Louis, 84–85, 89–92
Horseshoe Casino Baltimore, 270n38
Housing and Urban Development
   (HUD), U.S. Department of: and
   Ferguson uprising, 127; on Kinloch,
   97; on St. Louis, 84. *See also* HOPE
   VI; Section 8 vouchers
Housing Authority of Baltimore City
   (HABC), 146, 148, 158–59, 221–22.
   See also Baltimore, public housing
   in
Housing Choice Vouchers (HCV). *See*
   Section 8 vouchers
Housing Finance Agencies, 114
Housing Opportunities for People
   Everywhere. *See* HOPE VI
housing policies: as cause of upris-
   ings, 8–12; gaps in scholarship on,
   12; in racial inequality, 12–14;
   recommendations for, 216–17. *See
   also specific locations and policies*
HUD. *See* Housing and Urban
   Development
Hughes, Jim, 160
Hunter, Marcus, 217

hypersegregation: in Baltimore, 137, 138*fig.*, 148; in St. Louis, 56, 57*fig.*, 70–77

iconic ghetto, 111–12, 130
Igoe, William Leo, 249n43. *See also* Pruitt-Igoe
immigrants, European, in Baltimore, 138–39
income, median household: in Baltimore, 155; in Ferguson, 114, 257n69
inequality. *See* racial inequality
inner cities. *See* cities; *specific locations*
Inner Harbor (Baltimore), 150–57, 151*fig.*; expansion of, 154, 164, 270n38; gentrification around, 154–57; lack of vision after, 195; origins of plan for, 150–52; in postindustrial economy, 151, 154; public funding for, 151, 152, 155–56; in redevelopment priorities, 152–53; Sandlot at, 156, 156*fig.*; vacancy rate around, 155
institutional mourning, 95
insurgencies, use of term, 24
insurrections, use of term, 24
interest groups, in Baltimore, 187–88
intergroup competition, as driver of unrest, 29–31, 205
intersectional analysis, 210
Interstate Highway Act of 1956, 266n82

Jackson, Howard, 147
Jacobs, Jane, 33
Jacobs' Laws, 135
Jacobson, Joan, 158, 272n67
James, Sharpe, 184
Jennings (Missouri), 106, 129
Jim Crow, New, 12–14

Johns Hopkins Hospital, 190–91
Johns Hopkins University, 160, 191, 272n73
Johnson, F. Willis, 51, 105, 107, 126–31
Johnson, Lyndon B., 24
Johnson, Walter, 50–51, 119, 124–25, 249n142
Jones, Ella, 19, 109, 117–18, 129–30
Joplin, Scott, 60
Joseph M. Darst Apartments (St. Louis), 85, 86*fig.*
Justice, U.S. Department of: on Baltimore police, 169, 177–78, 275n20; on Ferguson police, 101, 120, 121, 127

Katz, Michael, xxii–xxiii, 7–8, 203
Kelling, George L., 167–68
Kelly, Raymond, 161, 171–74, 178, 194, 222
Kemper, Ellie, 246n33
Kennedy, David, 194
Kerner Report (1968): on complexity of unrest drivers, 27; on police role in unrest, 37–38; on rising Black expectations, 35, 36; on segregation, 8, 28–29, 148, 165; use of term "civil disorders" in, 24; on white racism, 28–29, 210
King, Martin Luther, Jr., uprisings after assassination of, xxi, 7, 96, 133, 141–42, 236n56
King, Rodney, xix–xx
King Louis Square (St. Louis), 85
kingpins, 192–93
Kinloch (Missouri): Black migration to, 55, 97; Black population of, 96, 97; expansion of airport in, 97–98; and Ferguson, relationship between, 96, 98–99; public housing in, 97–98, 249n137

McMillan, Michael, 105, 120–21
McSpadden, Lesley, 2
Meachum, John Berry, 60
Meachum Park, 122–24
Mele, Christopher, 130, 197
Memphis, xxii, 133, 262n2
messiah mayors, 153
Metzger, Molly, 78, 81–83, 99, 252n19
MICs. *See* mortgage investment
   companies
middle class, Black: in Baltimore, 136,
   140, 141–43; flight by, 76, 140,
   141–43; in St. Louis, 58, 74–76
middle-class communities: Ferguson
   as, 107, 110; gentrification in, 82
Midtown Cortex Innovation District
   (St. Louis), 83
migration, Black: to Baltimore,
   134–37; to Ferguson, 96–97, 108–12;
   to Kinloch, 55, 97; to North County,
   84–85, 94, 108–12; to Sandtown-
   Winchester, 139–40, 162; to St.
   Louis, 51–55, 65; to suburbs, as
   national trend, 110
Miles, Douglas, 144, 153, 165, 178, 193,
   195–96, 266n93
Mill Creek Valley (St. Louis), 57–58;
   Black achievements based in, 60;
   Black migration to, 55; Black
   relocation from, 71, 75, 249n142;
   demolition and redevelopment of,
   65–66, 248nn111–12; location of,
   58, 65
Minneapolis, 10. *See also* Floyd,
   George
misconduct, police, 170, 174
Mississippi Delta, 103
Missouri: eminent domain in, 65;
   slavery and statehood in, 52. *See
   also specific cities*
Missouri Compromise, 52

Missouri Housing Development
   Commission, 115
Mitchell, Clarence, Jr., 136
Mitchell, Parren J., 136
mixed-income communities: in
   Baltimore, 140, 158–59; in St. Louis,
   85, 90–92
Mohl, Raymond, 33
Mollenkopf, John, 105–6, 127
Moore, Ralph, Jr., 150, 162–63
Moore, Sandra, 103, 108, 110, 116,
   118
Moran, Matthew, 39, 240n27
Morgan State University, 136
mortgage investment companies
   (MICs), 117
mortgages. *See* foreclosure crisis;
   redlining; subprime loans
Mosby, Nick, 5, 18, 142
Moses, Robert, 140–41
Moskos, Peter, 172, 173
Muhammad, Khalil Gibran, 111
multifamily properties, in Ferguson,
   96, 98, 110, 116, 129
murder rates, in Baltimore, 169,
   175–76, 178–80, 194
Murphy, John H., Sr., 136
Murphy, Máire Agnes, 61, 248nn111–
   12
Murphy Homes (Baltimore), 146
Museum of Westward Expansion, 63
Mutual Chemical Company, 156
Myrdal, Gunnar, xxi, 214

NAACP, 68, 136, 188
Nassauer, Anne, 12, 38–39
National Advisory Commission on
   Civil Disorders, 8, 24. *See also*
   Kerner Report
National Civil Rights Museum
   (Memphis), 263n2

National Geospatial-Intelligence
    Agency (NGA), 223
neighborhood networks, vs. gangs,
    use of terms, 281n182
neighborhood racial inequality: as
    cause of unrest, 8–9; definition of,
    10; policies of slow violence in, 10,
    12. *See also specific locations*
New Jim Crow, The (Alexander), 12
New Urban Renewal, The (Hyra), 40
New York City: broken windows
    policing in, 176–77; gentrification
    in, 82; reactions to beating of
    Rodney King in, xix
NGA. *See* National Geospatial-Intelli-
    gence Agency
Nixon, Rob, 9
No Boundaries Coalition, 171–72
nonviolence. *See* peaceful protests
Norris, Ed, 177
North City (St. Louis): Black migra-
    tion to North County from,
    108–9; gentrification in, 81, 252n19;
    LIHTCs in, 115; public investments
    in, lack of, 83. *See also* Pruitt-Igoe
North County (Missouri): aggressive
    policing in, 106; Black migration to,
    84–85, 94, 108–12; poverty
    concentration in, 80. *See also*
    Ferguson
Northwinds Apartments (Ferguson),
    116
N.W.A. (rap group), 120

Obama, Barack: Great Recession
    policies of, 211, 284n39; racial
    inequality under, 206–7, 210–11;
    response to Brown's death, 127;
    rising expectations under, 206–7;
    silence on topic of race, 218; unrest
    after election of, 203

Oliveri, Rigel, 59, 98
Olson, Sherry, 144
Olzak, Susan, 29–31
O'Malley, Martin: election as mayor,
    176–77; policing under, 170,
    176–79, 198, 199
Operation Ceasefire (Boston), 194
opportunity neighborhoods, 216
Opus, 123
Origins of the Urban Crisis, The
    (Sugrue), 31
Orr, Marion, 147, 187
Osterberg, Eric, 219–20
Osterweil, Vicky, 26

Palmer, Mike, 130
pandemic, COVID, 18, 227–29
Park, Robert, xx–xxi, 23
Patapsco River, 155
Pattillo, Mary, 217
pay-to-play schemes, 184
Peabodys (St. Louis), 85, 94
peaceful protests, before start of
    unrest, 26–27, 37–39, 133
pedestrian stops: in Baltimore, 169,
    172; in Ferguson, 121
Perkins, Clarence, 147
Perkins Homes (Baltimore), 146,
    267n108
Perry, Ivory, 66
Perry, Ravi, 197
PHAs. *See* public housing authorities
Pigtown (Baltimore), 139
Pill, Madeleine, 185, 191
Pill City (Deutsch), 193
Pittsburgh, serial displacement in,
    43
Placemaking, Black, 217
plantation futures, 103–4, 122
plantation politics, in Ferguson,
    103–5, 119–22

Pleasant View Gardens (Ferguson), 218, 219*fig.*, 220
pluralism, in Baltimore, 185–86, 275n29
Poe Homes (Baltimore), 146
Police Power and Race Riots (Schneider), 37
police violence: as driver of unrest, scholarship on, 7–8, 37–38, 205, 207–8; as one of many causes of unrest, 7–9, 204; policy recommendations for ending, 215; sudden, slow violence as context for, 9–12, 209–10
policies: "race-neutral," 218; racialized, 15, 218; racist, as driver of uprisings, 8–12, 209; recommended, for breaking cycle of unrest, 214–26. *See also* slow violence; *specific policy areas*
policing: and gentrification, relationship between, 171; misconduct cases in, 170, 174; as one of many causes of unrest, 7–9, 204; policy recommendations for, 215; predatory, 120; race-based, 122, 128. *See also specific locations and tactics*
political economy of unrest, 39–40
political fragmentation, in Baltimore, 171, 183–94
political machine, in Baltimore, lack of, 184–87
Political Process and the Development of Black Insurgency (McAdam), 36
political slack, 194, 282n187
politicians, Black, 14–15; in Ferguson, 14, 129–30, 132; limited effects on racial inequality, 14–15, 197–99, 210–11; in new urban renewal, 92–93; silence on topic of race, 218; in St. Louis, 14, 67–68, 75, 92–93.

See also Baltimore, Black politicians in; *specific politicians*
politicians, white: in Baltimore, 147–48; in Ferguson, 99, 102–8, 130
Poro College, 75
postindustrial economy: of Baltimore, 151, 154; of St. Louis, 75–76, 79–80
postindustrial policing, 14. *See also* broken windows policing
post-traumatic stress disorder (PTSD), 10–11
poverty concentration: as driver of unrest, scholarship on, 28–35, 205–6; policy recommendations for, 215–16; rise in, 31–32. *See also specific locations*
poverty rates: in Baltimore, 154, 161; Black, 28, 30–32; in Ferguson, 119
Powell, Laurence, xx
predatory inclusion, 119
predatory loans, 117
predatory policing, 120
Preston, James H., 147
Priest, John G., 54
Primm, James, 63
Project CORE, 221–22
property damage: in Baltimore uprisings, 5, 133, 263n8; in George Floyd protests, 6–7
Pruitt-Igoe (St. Louis), 71–74; construction of, 71–72; demolition of, 49, 73–74, 74*fig.*; future redevelopment plans for, 222–23; location and size of, 71; poverty concentration in, 72–73; relocation of residents to, 70, 71, 249n142
pseudonyms, 229
PTSD. *See* post-traumatic stress disorder

Renaissance Place (St. Louis), 90–91
renewal, suburban, 69–70. *See also*
  urban renewal
Renwick, Edward R., 118
repression, cycle of racial and spatial,
  17, 44–45, 44*fig.*, 209
research methods, 17–19, 213, 227–30
residential displacement. *See*
  displacement
respect, need for, 223–25. *See also*
  disrespect
restrictive covenants. *See* covenants
Revels, Hiram H., 60
revolts, meaning and use of term,
  24–27, 233n1. *See also* unrest
Rhodes, Sharonda, 180–81
Rihanna, 120
Rios, Jodi: on Black Lives Matter,
  235n25; on fees and fines, 106, 120;
  on housing market, 110, 117; on
  political representation, 104; on
  racialized politics, 128; on suburban
  ghettos, 111
riot gear, 3
riots: meaning and use of term, 23–27,
  233n1; in origins of America, 23–24,
  225–26; overview of history of,
  xx–xxiii, 234n14. *See also* unrest;
  specific events and locations
road construction. *See* highway
  construction
Roberson, Helen, 73–74
Robinson, Bishop L., 269n24
Rogers, Jamala, 51
Roosevelt, Franklin D., 58
root shock, 10, 33–34, 95, 208
Rose, Kwame, 169
Rose, Mark, 33
Rothstein, Richard, 100, 116
rough rides, 4, 38, 133
Rouse, James, 147, 152–53, 268n3

Rouse Company, 152, 269n17
Rousification, 155
rubber bullets, 3
Russell, George, 186

Saarinen, Eero, 63
Saegert, Susan, 42, 118–19
sales tax revenue, 124–25
Sandlot at Inner Harbor (Baltimore),
  156, 156*fig.*
Sandtown-Winchester (Baltimore),
  139–44; Black migration to, 139–40,
  162; boundaries of, 236n45, 265n57,
  271n45; economic decline of,
  140–41, 155; highway construction
  in, 141, 143–44; policing in, 171–73,
  178; poverty concentration in, 134,
  141–42, 162, 195; public housing in,
  146, 221–22, 273n89; racial
  composition of, 139–40, 142, 163;
  redevelopment plans for, 153,
  221–22; redlining in, 140; subprime
  and foreclosure crisis in, 142,
  163–64; uprisings of 1968 in,
  141–42; after uprisings of 2015,
  221–22; vacant homes in, 155, 221.
  See also Baltimore uprisings of 2015;
  Gray, Freddie
Sassen, Saskia, 41
Schaefer, William Donald: Black
  politicians and, 175, 189, 269n24;
  election as governor, 152; machine-
  like structure under, 186–87;
  redevelopment priorities of, 152,
  153; in white political coalition, 147;
  years as mayor, 152
Schmoke, Kurt, 174–76; education and
  career of, 175, 189; election as
  mayor, 152, 174–75, 189–90; Inner
  Harbor under, 153; legacy of,
  197–98; limited effect on racial

ethnic diversity in, 51–52; founding and early history of, 51–55, 245n13; Gateway Arch in, 61–64, 76–77; key locations in, 69*fig.*; LIHTCs in, 90, 114–15; postindustrial economy of, 75–76, 79–80; progrowth coalition of, 64–65; public schools of, 59–60, 109; racial composition of, 53, 54, 231*table*; racial hierarchy of, 53–54, 59; slavery in, 52; slow violence in, forms of, 92–95; TIFs in, 82–83, 122, 124–25; ward consolidation attempts in, 67–68. *See also specific locations*

St. Louis, Black communities in, 49–77; achievements of, 59–60; containment of, 70–77; current status of, 51, 60; hypersegregation in, 56, 57*fig.*, 70–77; intraracial class conflict in, 66–68; location of, 57–58, 69*fig.*; migration to, 51–55, 65; new urban renewal in, 89, 91–94; old urban renewal in, 60–70, 89, 91–94; population of, 53, 54, 231*table*; poverty concentration in, 72–73; redlining in, 58–59; restrictive covenants in, 56–59, 65; riot of 1917 in, xx, 55–56; Section 8 vouchers in, 115–16. *See also specific locations*

St. Louis, gentrification in, 78–100; in Central Corridor, 80, 81–83; debate over existence of, 81–82; demolition of public housing in, 84–92; on north side, 81, 89–93, 252n19; on south side, 84–89, 87*fig.*, 252n19

St. Louis, public housing in: construction of, 71–72; demolition of, in gentrification, 84–92; financial problems with, 84; HOPE VI and, 84–85, 89–92; locations of, 70–71,

85; in mixed-income developments, 90; number of units of, 84, 85; relocation of suburban residents to, 70; segregation in, 67, 71, 85; as walls of separation, 84, 91–92; white residents of, 71, 85. *See also specific locations*

St. Louis, serial displacement in: in Ferguson uprising, 49–51; for Gateway Arch, 61–64, 62*fig.*, 77; HOPE VI in, 91; political effects of, 99; in Pruitt-Igoe, 73; in south side, 87–89, 88*fig.*; in suburbs, 69–70, 97–100

St. Louis, suburbs of: expansion of airport in, 80, 97–98; relocation to public housing from, 70, 71; segregation in, 79; serial displacement in, 97–100; suburban renewal in, 69–70. *See also* Ferguson

St. Louis Airport Authority, 98

St. Louis County: LIHTCs in, 115; racial composition of, 231*table*; redlining in, 59; Section 8 vouchers in, 115–16; suburban renewal in, 69–70. *See also* North County

St. Louis Housing Authority (SLHA), 67, 70–71, 84–85. *See also* St. Louis, public housing in

St. Louis–Post Dispatch (newspaper), 115–16

Stokes, Carol, 175

Stone, Clarence, 197

stop-and-frisk policing, in Baltimore, 169, 170, 172–73, 194

street-level violence: in Baltimore, 170–71, 192–94, 196; Democratic party and, 275n29

stress: of displacement, 10–11, 33–34; post-traumatic stress disorder, 10–11

strikes, by railroad workers, 53
Strode, Blake, 105, 108–9, 130, 211,
     214–15
structural violence, serial displace-
     ment as, 43
subprime loans, 117–19; in Baltimore,
     162–64; definition of, 117; in
     Ferguson, 117–18; held by Black
     homeowners, 41, 117–18
suburban ghettos, Southeast Ferguson
     as, 111–12, 130
suburban renewal, in St. Louis,
     69–70
suburbs, national trend of Black
     migration to, 110
sudden violence: definition of, 9;
     linkage between slow violence and,
     9–12, 205, 209–10
Sugrue, Thomas, 25, 31–32, 33, 35
Suiter, Sean, 174
Sumner High School, 75, 76
sundown towns, 96, 129
super gentrification, 82
superstar cities, 79–80
Supreme Court, U.S., 35, 52, 56, 137
Swanstrom, Todd: on Central
     Corridor, 81–82; on economic
     drivers of unrest, 105–6, 127; on
     gentrification in St. Louis, 81–82, 87,
     251n15, 252n19; role in research, 19;
     on south side of St. Louis, 87–88, 89
systemic racism, in Ferguson, 107, 218

Tager, Jack, 33
tax credits. See Low Income Housing
     Tax Credit
Tax Increment Financing (TIFs): in
     Baltimore, 156, 160; definition of,
     82–83; in Ferguson, 124–26; in
     gentrification, 83; in Kirkwood,
     122–24; as new urban renewal

policy, 13, 40–41; in St. Louis, 82–83,
     122, 124–25
tax revenue: in Baltimore, 270n37; in
     Ferguson, 106, 118–22, 124–25
Taylor, Keeanga-Yamahtta, 8, 119
Teaford, Jon, 34
tear gas, 3
term slavery, 135
Thirteenth Amendment, 135
Thompson, Philip, 197
Thompson v. HUD, 273n89
Thornton, Charles, 123–24
TIFs. See Tax Increment Financing
Till, Karen, 95
tourism, in Baltimore, 151–53. See also
     Inner Harbor
Townes, Lillian, 73–74
Transportation, U.S. Department of,
     129
trauma, in Baltimore, 179–80, 196. See
     also chronic displacement trauma
Treasury, U.S. Department of, 127
trickle-down economics, 150, 166
Trump, Donald, 211
Tucker, Raymond, 64
Tulsa Massacre of 1921, xx
Turner, Tina, 60
twice-cleared communities, 43, 91,
     159, 208

Understanding Urban Unrest (Gale), 29
University of Baltimore, 160
University of Chicago, xxii
University of Maryland at Baltimore,
     160
unrest (uprisings): alternative terms
     for, 23–27, 233n1; meaning and use
     of terms, 24–27, 233n1; overview of
     history of, xx–xxiii, 234n14, 236n56;
     peaceful gatherings before start of,
     26–27, 37–39, 133; policy recommen-

dations for breaking cycle of, 214–26. *See also specific events and locations*

unrest, causes and drivers of, 27–40; multiplicity of, 7–9; other than police brutality, 7–9, 204; policies of slow violence in, 9–12; theories of, 27–40, 205–8. *See also specific factors and theories*

uprisings. *See* unrest

Urban Affairs Review (journal), 239n120

urban areas. *See* cities

urban development policies. *See* community development policies

Urban History Association, 25

Urban Institute, 160–61

Urban Rage (Dikeç), 42

Urban Redevelopment Act of 1945 (Missouri), 65

urban renewal: Black removal equated with, 208; definition of, 32; as driver of unrest, scholarship on, 32–35. *See also* displacement; *specific locations and policies*

urban renewal, new, 41–43; Black politicians' role in, 92–93; contemporary unrest associated with, 42, 204–5; definition of, 13, 41; as form of violence, 14; vs. old urban renewal, 13, 41–43; types of policies of, 13–14, 41, 204–5. *See also specific locations and policies*

urban renewal, old, 41–43; dates of, 60–61; definition of, 13, 14; as form of violence, 14; highway construction in, 13, 143; vs. new urban renewal, 13, 41–43; types of policies of, 13; unrest of 1960s associated with, 42, 204. *See also specific locations and policies*

urban renewal unrest framework, 40–45, 208–14; cycle of racial and spatial repression in, 44–45, 44*fig.*, 209; elements of, 40–45, 208–11; shortcomings and strengths of, 212–14

vacant homes: in Baltimore, 152, 155, 162–63, 163*fig.*, 221, 273n97; in Ferguson, 117–18; in St. Louis, 72, 76, 83

Vale, Lawrence, 34, 43–44, 91, 165

Vargas, Robert, 275n29

Vaughn Homes (St. Louis), 72

Veiled Prophet parade and ball, 53–54, 246n33

victim blaming, 240n21

Ville, the (Ellearsville, St. Louis), 74–77; Black achievements based in, 60, 75; divestment in, 74–77; economic diversity of, 75–76; history of, 74–75; location of, 58

violence. *See specific locations and types*

violent crime, impact of broken windows policing on, 168

voting rights, 35, 36, 136

Voting Rights Act of 1965, 35, 36

Waddington, David, 39, 240n27

"walking while Black," 121

Wallace, Rodrick, 43

Washington, DC, xx, 266n91

Washington, Walter, 175

Watkins, Bip, 192

Watkins, D.: on Baltimore uprisings, 196; on drug trade, 192–93; on gentrification, 157; on Obama, 207; on policing, 173, 178; on political fragmentation, 188; on public housing demolition, 159; on violence, 180, 182

wealth gap, racial, 28, 41
wealth loss, in Great Recession, 119
Webbe Apartments (St. Louis), 85,
86*fig.*
Webber, Brandon, 263n2
weight of violence, in Baltimore,
179–81
Wells Fargo, 162
West Florissant Avenue (Ferguson), 3,
3*fig.*, 10, 113, 221
white Americans: homeownership
rates of, 28, 119; in public housing,
71, 85, 267n108. *See also* politicians,
white
white maneuvering, 68–69, 130
white racism. *See* racism
Why Don't American Cities Burn?
(Katz), xxii, 203
Wilkins, Roy, 60, 65
Williams, Brett, 266n91

Williams, Damian, xx
Williams, Homer, 97–98
Williams, Rhonda, 146–47
Williams, Rosalind, 115
Wilson, Darren, 1–2, 38
Wilson, James Q., 167–68
Wind, Timothy, xx
Wire, The (television series), 157–58,
192
Wolman, Harold, 154
wounded cities, 95
Wright, John A., Sr., 51
Wright Austin, Sharon, 103

Yeary, Todd, 11, 191, 192
Young, Coleman, 175

zero tolerance, 168. *See also* broken
windows policing
zoning, racialized, 56, 96

Founded in 1893,
UNIVERSITY OF CALIFORNIA PRESS
publishes bold, progressive books and journals
on topics in the arts, humanities, social sciences,
and natural sciences—with a focus on social
justice issues—that inspire thought and action
among readers worldwide.

The UC PRESS FOUNDATION
raises funds to uphold the press's vital role
as an independent, nonprofit publisher, and
receives philanthropic support from a wide
range of individuals and institutions—and from
committed readers like you. To learn more, visit
ucpress.edu/supportus.

www.ingramcontent.com/pod-product-compliance
Lightning Source LLC
Chambersburg PA
CBHW020821270326
41928CB00006B/398